NEAR EASTERN CULTURE
AND SOCIETY

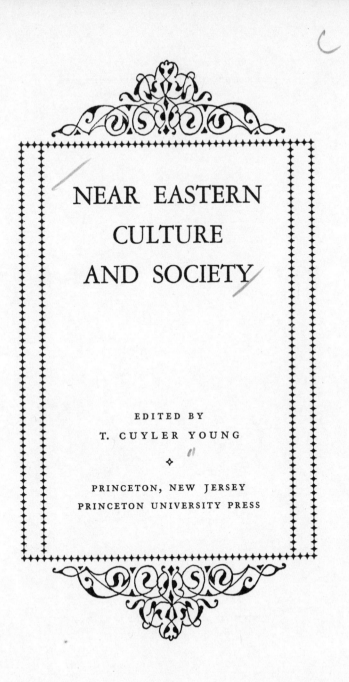

NEAR EASTERN CULTURE AND SOCIETY

EDITED BY
T. CUYLER YOUNG

PRINCETON, NEW JERSEY
PRINCETON UNIVERSITY PRESS

FOREWORD

THE increased responsibilities thrust upon the United States as a result of the last World War, and the postwar developments—political, economic, and military—have served to accentuate the importance of understanding the peoples of the Near East and the significance of appreciating the varied aspects of their culture. More than ever before are we beginning to realize that the Arabs and Muslims are neighbors of ours with common interests and common problems.

Princeton, which was the first American university to recognize the importance of the study of the Arabic-Islamic field and to accord it its rightful place in its curriculum, included in the celebration of its bicentennial a conference on Near Eastern culture and society held in March 1947. It was a three-day conference in which participated, besides professors and diplomats from America, educators from Lebanon and Syria, scientists from Turkey and Egypt, and scholars from 'Iraq and Iran. The principal papers read were subjected to critical comment from the audience, later revised by their authors, addressed to the reading public and edited by my colleague Professor Young. The result is this book which, we trust, will contribute in its small way to the achievement of a relationship of mutual understanding and respect between the West and the Near East.

PHILIP K. HITTI

Department of Oriental Languages
Princeton University

CONTENTS

vii

ILLUSTRATIONS

The illustrations (which relate to Mr. Ettinghausen's chapter, "Islamic Art and Archeology") follow p. 22

1. Royal Muslim Fabric Used as Church Vestment. Cope of Mamlūk Brocade Inscribed with "al-Sulṭān al-'ālim" (the learned Sultan). Early 14th Century. Danzig, St. Mary's Church.

2. Fabric Made for a Caliph as Object of Christian Veneration. Section of "the Veil of St. Anne." Silk Tapestry Made in Damietta, Egypt, in 1096 (or 1097) for the Fāṭimid Caliph al-Musta'lī bi'llāh and his Vizier al-Afḍal. Apt (France), Church of St. Anne.

3. A Fāṭimid Decoration Re-used in a Late Gothic Vessel for the Consecrated Host. Carved Rock Crystal Ring of the Calif al-Ẓāhir li-i'zāz dīn Allāh (1021-36) Set into a Gilded Silver Monstrance of the 15th-16th Century. Nuremberg, Germanisches National-museum.

4. Muslim Fabric with Iranian Motif Serving as Wrapping for "the Veil of Our Lady." Detail of the Fabric. 7th-8th Century. Chartres, Cathedral.

5. Fāṭimid Rock Crystal Vessel Used as Container of the Miraculous Blood. Late 10th Century Carving in an Italian Mounting of the Late 14th Century. Venice, Saint Mark's.

6. Simulated Arabic Writing on a Cathedral Door. Section of the Door of the Cathedral of Notre Dame du Puy.

7. Simulated Arabic Writing in the Halo of the Madonna. Detail of "Madonna and Child" by Gentile da Fabriano (ca. 1360-1427). Washington, National Gallery of Art, Kress Collection.

8. An Early Muslim Rug with Geometric Patterns on a Flemish Painting of the 15th Century. "Madonna and Child with Angels" by Hans Memling (ca. 1430/35-1494) Showing an Oriental Carpet Under the Throne. Washington, National Gallery of Art, Mellon Collection.

9. An Early Muslim Rug with an Animal Design on an Italian Painting of the 15th Century. "The Adoration of the Child" by Sano di Pietro (1406-1481) Showing an Oriental Rug with a Pattern of Two Addorsed Birds on Either Side of a Tree. Washington, National Gallery of Art, Kress Collection.

10. A Muslim Art Object Executed in Europe. Tray with Inlaid and Engraved Design Made by a Muslim Craftsman in Venice. Baltimore, Walters Art Gallery.

INTRODUCTION

1

NEAR EAST PERSPECTIVE: THE PAST
AND THE PRESENT

BY T. CUYLER YOUNG

THE MEETING OF EAST AND WEST discussed in this volume involves primarily the last century and a half since the Napoleonic era, secondarily the whole of the modern period encompassing roughly the last five centuries, yet also in certain instances the complete Islamic era of the last thirteen centuries. Contributors to the symposium draw in varying degrees upon this history for the illumination of the problems of the present. But they know, and the reader should know, that these spans of time are but a small part of the total history of man in the Near East affecting the present encounter of East and West in this area. It may contribute to an appreciation and understanding of the symposium if we begin by sketching something of the deeper background that contributes to any true Near East perspective.

No reader needs to be reminded that Western Asia was the cradle of civilization, that considerably more of recorded history's time span lies before Muhammad and Jesus than has elapsed since their days, and that the civilization of the Near East is several times older than that of the West, especially of western Europe. What perhaps is less appreciated by many is the full depth of the perspective involved in the long story of the meeting and interaction of East and West and especially the fact that we are presently perhaps near the crest of the fourth major period in such East-West relationships.

The urban civilization developed in the Nile and Tigris-Euphrates valleys spread eastward and westward until at its climax in the Late Bronze Age (1600-1200 B.C.) there was a remarkable degree of cultural interchange between this ancient Near Eastern civilization and the Minoan-Mycenaean civilization of Crete and

3

the Aegean, with the western of these cultures largely in debt to the eastern. This dominant trend of influence moving westward was enhanced in the subsequent centuries when the Aegean was overrun by northern invaders in need of civilizing and when the Near East, though shaken and disrupted, was able to expand its ancient imperialism in new configurations. During most of this period, building on the Semitic-Hamitic and Sumerian foundations in the great river valleys and continually fructified by infusions from the mountain and steppe peoples to the north and east, the dominant people of the area were Semites. Originally differentiated as a distinctive cultural entity in prehistoric times somewhere in the Arabian peninsula, they moved from thence into the Fertile Crescent continuously and in waves from the fifth millennium onwards—as Akkadians, Babylonians, Assyrians, Canaanites, Arameans, Hebrews, and Arabs, to mention but the major groups. For all the important contributions of diverse peoples and cultures during the Bronze Age, it was the Semites who stamped the Near East with its distinctive pattern of life—aesthetic, reflective, and active. Moreover, during this Semitic ascendancy the flow of cultural influence was still for the most part steadily from East to West.

This ancient Near East of competing urbanized imperialisms reached a new climax in the vast Persian Empire stretching from the Aegean to the Indus, the Nile to the Jaxartes. It was essentially a "Syriac" civilization—to use Professor Toynbee's expressive but not wholly accurate phrase—but was ruled by an eastern Indo-European people. In spite of its apparent climactic fulfilment of ancient Near Eastern civilization, its ecumenicity and genius for political and economic organization allowing for the toleration of diversity in unity, the Persian Empire was truly of a transitional character in the development of civilization in the Near East and therefore comparatively short-lived (550-530 B.C.).

It was transitional because around the Aegean Sea there had come to the threshold of maturity a superior culture which, heir to all the riches of the mythopoetic East, had wrought an intellectual revolution and laid new foundations for science and philosophy. Science and philosophy were not lacking in the Near East and in many instances were superior to some of the second-rate varieties in the West, but unquestionably the Greek genius freed man from many of the intellectual shackles of his own devising and set his mind to work in literally a new world of ideas. Stimulated into maturity by the pressures of the Persian Empire's universality, Greek culture flowered and produced a dynamic that awaited only the appearance of an Alexander to go crusading to the ends of the East. Although its military conquest of the hinterland of the Near East was short-lived, the West's Hellenistic cultural influence became profound and continued even after the resurgence of the East under the Parthians, although with diminishing effect under the Persian Sasanians. More lasting was the cultural influence of the West on the Near East's perimeter ·of the Mediterranean when it developed the military, governmental, and social genius of the Latins to give structure and stability to Greek civilization. Here there was real and vital acculturation, yet for almost a thousand years after Alexander the flood of influence in the East-West cultural interchange moved steadily eastward.

With Muhammad and the emergence of Islam the tide again turned suddenly, although the historian can trace the undercurrents as they built up for this dramatic reversal in the cultural flow. Out of Arabia came a resurgence of the Semitic peoples who carried their religion and language east to the borders of China and west across the Pyrenees. In the Golden Age of Islam under the 'Abbāsids the Muslims laid under tribute their heritage of Greek, Persian, and Hindu civilizations and themselves created a dynamic culture that dominated the Middle Ages positively and influenced more backward Europe, which was engaged in the slow process of civilizing the barbarian hordes that had brought the downfall of classical Rome. Up to the climax of medieval civilization in the thirteenth century the tide of cultural influence was largely set from East to West; indeed the West did not feel itself wholly free from the pressure of Eastern Islam until the Ottomans were turned back from the gates of Vienna in 1683.

Yet the intervening centuries had been that period of transition when the Renaissance and Reformation had effected the rebirth of Western civilization and unleashed dynamic forces that have

5

not yet spent themselves as they have since circled the globe. From roughly 1500 onwards the tide of cultural influence has moved steadily and continuously from West to East. Varied may be opinions as to just where we stand in relation to the surge of this cultural tide. Certainly the mid-twentieth century marks a critical juncture in the determination of future East-West relationships. This symposium aims to be a modest contribution to the delineation and understanding of this critical juncture in history.

II

Against this background of the long story of the meeting of East and West, this volume addresses itself primarily to the contemporary scene of these relationships as they focus upon Near Eastern society and culture. The book is in two distinct but closely related parts. The first half, summarizing and evaluating the past progress and present prospect of Islamic studies in Europe and America, attempts to give the reader appreciation of how the West has met the East and has been enriched in its culture—actually and potentially—by the encounter. The second half, analyzing the complex current problems involved in the relations of Islamic peoples and states with those of the West, centers attention upon the effects of this cultural contact upon the older, but presently less dynamic, societies of the Near East.

By the very nature of the case, the discovery of the East by Western scholarship and research calls for more historical treatment and criticism, howbeit the contributors to this half of the symposium have tried to focus their material on the present and its demands for accelerated improvement of the means whereby Western thought can truly penetrate, and thereby understand and appreciate, Near Eastern culture. The volume tries to accomplish this by exploring four major highways over which the material and spiritual goods of acculturation travel: art and archeology, literature, science, and religion.

On the first of these highways Dr. Ettinghausen of the Freer Gallery of Art in Washington explores all the contributing byways—the trade in handicraft materials from medieval times onward, appreciation of painting and the decorative arts from the seventeenth century, the whole gamut of archeological concerns (coins, epigraphy and paleography, architectural antiquities), and the variety of minor arts. He posts the turnings of the road effected by developments, new approaches, and specializations, recording the names and exploits of the major contributors and showing that Islamic art and archeology have been stimulated primarily by two disciplines—general Islamic studies and the history of art, which in cooperation have done the best work in the field and hold the best promise of the future. Only when individual phenomena are related to their total cultural matrix and context can the interpreter be reasonably sure that he has understood them and that they, in turn, are able to articulate freely and accurately the spirit of the age and culture to which they witness. The essay concludes with some indications as to how the interpreters of Islamic art and archeology can better approximate this ideal.

Literature, another form of cultural expression, in the Near East stands in a class by itself. The genius of the Semite, who has dominated the Near East during most of its history, finds its peculiar and significant articulation in the art and in the science of the Word. To attain determinative and lasting influence in the Near East men have always had to have something substantial to say, but equally if not more important has been the demand that they be masters of the wizardry of words and able to clothe their thought in garments of beauty and light.

In any meeting of the Near East by the West it is therefore of paramount importance to explore the literature of Islamic peoples. The fascinating story of the West's discovery of the two major literary traditions of the Islamic Near East—Arabic and Persian—is here traced by Professors von Grunebaum of Chicago and Arberry of Cambridge. Starting from meager beginnings, proceeding gradually but with increasing acceleration, this story of literary appreciation and criticism gains breadth and depth and the authors conclude with valuable and stimulating indications of the next steps to be taken by Western scholars for more adequate understanding and appropriation of the rich values inherent in this great cultural tradition.

The illumination of Muslim science, its stewardship of the ancient and classical heritage and its contribution to the beginnings of Western science, owes more probably to Professor Sarton of

Harvard than to any other single person. Most of this is enshrined in his monumental *Introduction to the History of Science* and the issues of the periodical *Isis*. In his contribution[1] to this volume he reviews the highlights of the passage of ancient Eastern science to the modern West by way of the Muslims of medieval times, with some estimate of the significance of this to human culture. Of very practical value to the student who may wish to contribute a share to the enhancement of the West's appreciation of Muslim science and its place in the human story is the methodological advice with which Professor Sarton concludes his chapter.

The inner soul of a people or culture is mirrored most clearly in religion, the eyes of the corporate personality as it looks outward upon Reality objective to itself. It is difficult, however, for the Westerner to understand Islam, the dominant faith of the Near East and in many respects a totalitarian, religio-social system far removed from him in space and time. Yet for the Westerner who himself has "eyes to see" there is no surer way to the understanding of Near Eastern society and culture than a profound comprehension of Islam, one of the great and noble ethnic faiths of mankind.

To revert to the original figure, it is tragic to observe that without doubt the most frequented yet roughest road along which Westerners have traveled to meet the Muslim Near East has been that of religion. Here the entail of the heritage of suspicion, misunderstanding, hostility, and even hatred has been so large that in comparatively recent times only has this highway of cultural intercommunication afforded the man of the West any true or profound understanding and appreciation of Islam as the religion of his counterpart in the Near East. Professor Calverley of the Hartford Seminary Foundation describes the steps by which this misunderstanding has arisen and how its pitifully slow dissipation is being accomplished, concluding with some basic, stimulating suggestions for more fruitful interaction between East and West at the more profound levels of faith and religion.

Against this background of the attempts of Western scholarship and thought to understand the Muslim Near East, the contributors to the second half of this symposium offer their interpre-

[1] Previously published in *Ignace Goldziher Memorial Volume*, part i, Budapest, 1948.

8

tations of the reaction of the area to the dynamic impact of Western civilization upon it. They are concerned primarily with contemporary social and cultural phenomena, but for their illumination lay under tribute the whole span of the centuries during which this Western impact has been gathering force, to deliver its critical blows in the current century and on the threshold of the Atomic Age. To give depth to the discussion of the various national and international relations the first section of this second half of our symposium endeavors to analyze and evaluate the major factors involved in the interaction in modern times between Islamic and Western thought. For convenience, yet rather arbitrarily, the area has been subdivided into the Turkish, Iranian, and Arab subspecies of Near Eastern civilization.

For Turkey, Dr. Adnan[2] of Istanbul points out that this interaction in the modern era began only in the eighteenth century, coinciding with the decline of Ottoman military power, and did not become significant until after the French Revolution, reaching noticeable proportions in 1839 in the "Tanẓīmāt" or period of "Organization and Reform." During the remainder of the nineteenth century Western ideas continued to penetrate, but generally were recognized only to be refuted by Muslim thinkers. With the new period of ferment accompanying the Young Turk Revolution of 1908 came a conscious but unavailing effort to reconcile the old and the new, but this was interrupted by the military struggles of the decade following 1912. In the more recent period of the Turkish Republic the tables of authority have been completely turned, with Western thought in the form of scientific positivism as dogmatically ruling affairs as did the old Islam. Dr. Adnan is forced to the conclusion that free interchange and interaction between Islamic and Western thought still awaits the future.

As for Iran, the editor asserts that, for all the promising contacts with the West in Ṣafavi times, there was no real penetration of Western thought into Iran until the nineteenth century, and then only in recognizable force at its close, when Iran awoke suddenly from its slumbers and began to grapple with the new ferment

[2] With the exception of the opening paragraphs, Dr. Adnan's chapter, substantially as delivered at the Princeton Bicentennial Conference, appeared in the *Middle East Journal*, vol. 1, July 1947, pp. 270-280.

imported from the West. This ferment has found expression, and here receives analysis, in Western imperialism, nationalism, and secularization which have deeply affected Iranian thought and action. But the conclusion is reached that "for all the interaction that forms material for its prolegomena, there has been no real, creative interaction of Western and Islamic thought at the deeper levels of faith and philosophy."[3]

Professor Kurani of Beirut, for the Arabs, gives more space in his account of interaction to the more distant points in time: the birth of Islam and its rise to world power and the medieval Arab-Latin contacts. The modern story begins with the Napoleonic era when Western ideas penetrate the Arab world over four bridge-heads: Constantinople and the Ottomans, Basrah and the British, Cairo and Muhammad 'Ali's use of the French, and Lebanon with its flourishing French and American missionary activities. The major Western influence is traced in connection with nationalism and the Arab struggle for independence, with varying manifestations of Arab reaction to Western culture. Reviewing the problems faced by educational leaders in the Arab world, a conclusion similar to that of the preceding investigators is reached: that interaction between Islam and the West at the more profound levels of thought and culture has yet to take place; and to that urgent task seven penetrating queries are addressed which are equally valid for the other sections of the Muslim Near East.

In the light of all this it is not surprising to find that in the second section of Part II, dealing with national and international relations, the common theme in all these three areas of the Near East is how to establish the newly emergent nationalisms on a solid and secure foundation.

Professor Thomas of Princeton devotes the major portion of his chapter to delineating the historical and sociological process whereby the present leaders of Turkey have achieved the demonstrable reality of "Turkey for the Turks," now assumed by most other nations. There follows an analysis of the present attainments and future potentialities of Turkish leaders in developing "enough *new* Turks to enable *New* Turkey to survive in the twentieth cen-

[3] Substantial portions of this chapter appeared in *The Middle East Journal*, vol. II, January 1948, pp. 47-59, under the title "The Problem of Westernization in Modern Iran."

tury." With these two propositions adequately elaborated, it requires little space to indicate their implications for the understanding of Turkey's policy in international relations, which can be realistically summarized as the determination "(1) to survive, and (2) with survival assured, to prosper and develop internally."

For Iran the editor begins by contrasting the nature and course of the international relations of Iran and the West in the Ṣafavi and Pahlavi periods, then concentrates attention on the basic pattern that obtains in the three successive phases of mutual interaction of the last sixty years: "the so-called 'constitutional phase,' continuing to 1911 or 1914 and the outbreak of World War I; the Rezā Shāh period between the World Wars; and the present period, almost a decade old since the accession of Muhammad Rezā in 1941. This historical analysis helps to throw light upon contemporary Iran and its major problem of attaining true integrity and unity if its modern nationhood is to be established firmly and is to survive; and the subsidiary problems of religion, language, and social organization—especially the tribal, political, and economic—are examined for their possible contribution to a satisfactory answer to this paramount question of national unity and integrity.

President Zurayk of Damascus traces the rise of Arab nationalism in the nineteenth century and the vicissitudes of its development in the twentieth. He then considers the fundamental national and international problems of the various Arab states: achieving and maintaining independence and unity, modernism and the development of resources, and the acquisition of a distinct national unity. "They have now reached a crisis in their spiritual evolution and are wondering what is to be their peculiar contribution to modern civilization: whether they are destined . . . to represent something individual and positive in the modern world, or whether they will lose their essential identity and be completely assimilated by the West." It is doubtless fitting that this section of the symposium should end on the emphatic statement of a leading Near Easterner that the final answer to the primary query regarding the future depends much upon a new attitude toward the Near East on the part of the West, "based on principle and justice rather than interest and power politics."

There will undoubtedly be readers who, at this point, will be critical of this symposium on two counts: the lack of any treatment of Israel and the vigor of President Zurayk's description and analysis of the current situation facing the Arabs. Regarding the first, the reader is reminded that the Princeton bicentennial conference which originated the volume occurred before the Arab-Zionist war and the establishment of Israel as an independent state and that the conference was affected by the limitations of time, as is this volume in respect to space. Moreover, the thoughtful reader will readily observe that the discussions of current problems among Turks, Iranians, and Arabs attempt, for the most part, to dig among the roots of several centuries of inter-relationships to effect more understanding of the present growth and development of the *Islamic* peoples. The problem posed by Israel as a nation and culture, howsoever important as a major aspect of East-West relationships in this century, lacks this depth in Islamic history. It is hoped that this volume may contribute valuable background to the proper appreciation and evaluation of this significant new development in the relations of the West and the Near East. As for the foregoing essay on the Arab position and problem, brought in some respects relatively up-to-date, it may be stated that, despite some disagreement between its author and the editor, this chapter constitutes an invaluable contribution to any estimate of the present situation by a distinguished educator, trained in the best traditions of Western scholarship yet standing as an active participant in the situation he describes and analyzes. Without such a vigorous presentation this symposium would scarcely be faithful to the current psychological and spiritual climate of the Arab Near East.

In the concluding chapter Professor Gibb of Oxford guides the reader to a high vantage point of perspective and reflection from which the significance of these studies for the true mutuality of East and West may be viewed. The present status and future prospects of this momentous global colloquy are assessed with penetration and insight. "The overall picture today is full of deep shadows, and fills many an observer with despair. Only by standing a little further back can we perceive and try to estimate the significance of the lighter strokes that relieve the general somberness of tone." Significant as was the progress in East-West understanding during the nineteenth century, Professor Gibb affirms that the twentieth has been complicated by a growing resistance, if not revulsion, to the West on the part of the East, precipitated by the demands of Eastern nationalisms and aggravated by the political and economic injustices and ineptitudes of the West. He believes that several generations of Muslim thinkers, concentrating on the complicated problem of understanding the true nature of Western culture and its relation to their own as well as grappling "with the task of integrating technological advances with their national cultures," will be necessary before any results in true mutuality may be apparent; and that desired mutuality will be contingent as much upon the success of the Western nations in solving their own crisis in civilization as upon a like success of the nations of the Near East in respect to their peculiar, yet not essentially dissimilar, crisis.

In conclusion, the editor would like to record his gratitude to all the scholars who have made this symposium possible and who, by their cordial cooperation, lightened the task of compilation, making his editorship more a pleasure than a duty. Particular thanks are due the editors of *The Goldziher Memorial Volume* and *The Middle East Journal* for permission to reproduce contributions to the Princeton bicentennial which have already appeared under their auspices. Similar appreciation is also expressed to the members of the staff of Princeton University Press whose cooperation and skills have been unfailing and a substantial contribution to the finished product. The reward of each of us concerned in the creation of the volume will be ample if the reader, whether he be of the East or the West, finds here an appreciable and appreciated contribution to the understanding of Near Eastern society and culture.

PART I

The West Meets the East:
Progress and Prospect in Islamic Studies

•

2

ISLAMIC ART AND ARCHEOLOGY

BY RICHARD ETTINGHAUSEN

IT HAS BEEN STATED that the language of the artist "is the only effective universal language that has ever been invented."[1] Without the help of a translator the thoughts of the philosophers and poets of other lands are barred to us because of their foreign tongues, and even when translated they need extensive explanatory comment. The creations of the architect, painter, potter, weaver, and other craftsmen, on the other hand, are readily available for our aesthetic enjoyment, although they, too, need some further interpretations by the expert to be fully grasped.

This truism applies to the arts of all civilizations and so also to the arts of Islam. Indeed, as soon as Islamic art became known in the West it was greatly appreciated and those objects which reached Europe, and later America, were often given a place of honor. It was, however, more than twelve hundred years after the rise of Islam before the arts of the Muslim world were *critically* studied. Actually, even today this study is only in its infancy. Yet for the European and American student it is a source of great satisfaction that in this field of research the West did pioneering work for the East, and tried, for the first time, not only to collect all available historical and archeological data, but also to evolve criteria with which to judge the works of the Muslim artists.

During the Middle Ages, when Islam and Christendom were arrayed against each other as opposing camps with but little communication between them, the acquaintance of the West with the arts of the Muslim East was naturally limited. But we have only to remember the way in which Muslim crafts were received in the Christian world to see how much they were appreciated. At

[1] Charles Rufus Morey, "The Fine Arts in Higher Education," *College Art Journal*, III, 1943, p. 4.

a time when Muhammed was called "a voluptuary, defiled to the very core, a brigand, profligate, murderer and robber,"[2] the handiwork of believers in his heretic message was, nevertheless, deemed worthy enough to be associated with the most venerated forms of the Christian cult. In the greatest cathedrals of Christendom textiles from various Muslim weaving centers provided the precious fabrics with which to wrap the relics of saints (Fig. 4), or to serve as priestly vestments (Fig. 1). Sometimes they were even the very object of veneration (Fig. 2). In many instances these textiles had Arabic inscriptions, some even praising Allah, but this indication of their origin did not interfere with their appreciation. Indeed, when at the end of the Middle Ages and during the early Renaissance painters wanted to represent the Madonna in a worthy garment, they very often adorned her robes with border designs in which Arabic writing was imitated.[3]

No less significant is the medieval use of carved rock crystal vessels and implements which, in the tenth and eleventh centuries, were made in Ikhshīdid and Fāṭimid Egypt. On reaching Europe they were inserted like precious stones and enamels in processional crosses, monstrances, and ecclesiastical lighting fixtures. It was in this manner that a crescent-shaped ring, carved with the name of the Sultan al-Ẓāhir li-I'zāz-dīn-Allāh (1021-1036), made the metamorphosis from an ornament probably once worn by the Sultan's horse to the crowning element of a late Gothic monstrance (Fig. 3.)[4]

Even more frequently crystal vessels became reliquaries in cathedrals and churches. A characteristic example of this group is the "Reliquiario de Sangue Miraculoso" in Saint Mark's in

[2] Bartholomew of Edessa (thirteenth century). The attitude of the Latin West was not much different from this Eastern writer; i.e. in the first half of the twelfth century Guibert of Nogent speaks in a derogatory way of Muhammad, who is said to have been "devoured by pigs while unconscious in one of his epileptic fits." This disgraceful end is thus no match for Christ's passion, death and resurrection. (The two quotations are from G. E. von Grunebaum, *Medieval Islam. A Study in Cultural Orientation*, Chicago, 1946, pp. 45, 47, which reproduces a number of other medieval invectives against "Mahomet.")

[3] Although there is no doubt that the artists simulated Arabic writing, they may at times have taken these characters to be Hebrew.

[4] It is also possible that the crystal ring was originally used as the finial of a ceremonial staff or scepter (C. J. Lamm, *Mittelalterliche Gläser und Steinschnittarbeiten aus dem Nahen Osten*, Berlin, 1929-1930, vol. I, p. 213, no. 21).

Venice. Its cylindrical body shows an arabesque decoration and, in addition, a Kufic inscription demonstrating its original dedication to Allah, which, however, did not prevent its later use as a receptacle for the Holy Blood (Fig. 5). There are many such reliquaries, i.e. bottles with relics of the Holy Virgin, John the Baptist, Mary Magdalen, and so on. These Muslim objects served not only the function of precious containers for venerated relics, but, because of their transparency, they represented to the medieval mind a symbol of the Saviour's virgin birth. For, had not Christ said to St. Bridget: "I have assumed the flesh without sin and lust, entering the womb of the virgin just as the sun passes through a precious stone."[5]

We could go on citing objects made of other materials, such as ivory and metal, to show how the Muslim influence worked in these media. There is also no need to discuss at length the very common use of debased Arabic writing in all kinds of ecclesiastical works of art (Figs. 6-7), especially since this form of medieval decoration has been studied for more than a hundred years.[6] Perhaps only one other medium should be singled out for a short reference, since it exercised a fascination on the West that has persisted from the waning centuries of the Middle Ages until the present day. As early as the 14th century we find Oriental rugs in Italian paintings, and rather simple ones at the beginning, under the throne of the Madonna, under the feet of the saints, as floor coverings in rooms and courtyards, and as table covers— in short, nearly always in a place of honor (Figs. 8-9). In many instances these representations are very precious to us, since they alone have preserved carpet designs of which no originals have come down to us.

[5] In her first revelation (M. Meiss, "Light as Form and Symbol in Some Fifteenth-Century Paintings," *Art Bulletin*, XXVII, 1945, p. 177).

[6] In our Fig. 7, which is taken from A. de Longpérier, "L'Emploi des caractères arabes dans l'ornementation chez les peuples chrétiens de l'occident," *Revue archéologique*, II, 1845-1846, p. 700, the debased Arabic is stressed by hatching. Later literature on this subject is listed in S. Reich, "Une Inscription mamlouke sur un dessin italien du quinzième siècle," *Bulletin de l'Institut d'Egypte*, XXII, 1940, p. 127. It is worth pointing out that Reich discusses in this article (pp. 123-131) the much rarer (if not unique) case of an actual copy of an Arabic inscription by a European artist, i.e. the copy of the dedicatory inscription on a Syro-Egyptian enameled glass lamp of Sultan al-Malik al-Mu'ayyad Shaykh (1412-1421) by a Venetian master of the fifteenth century, now in the Musée du Louvre.

Although the minds of the Renaissance were focused on the art of classical antiquity, the artistic world of Islam was not a closed book. Western artists were fascinated by Muslim ornamentation, especially by the arabesque. When, in Venice in the first half of the 16th century, Near Eastern metal workers created vessels and platters with rich and yet well-balanced arabesque decorations, Western artists were not slow to imitate this kind of design (Figs. 10-11). The arabesque, with all its intricacy, became a favorite subject of the Renaissance artist and even a master like Hans Holbein the Younger did not think it below his station to paraphrase patterns in this vein (Figs. 12-13).[7]

The fact that no less a figure than the great Rembrandt was one of the first to be captivated by the artistic quality of figural painting from a Muslim country speaks for itself. He owned a collection of twenty-five Mughal miniatures which he liked so much that he copied them when, about 1656, adverse conditions forced him to part with them.[8] The Musée du Louvre owns one of these copies, which, like the others, was obviously done with speed but also with extraordinary grasp of the essential details. It shows part of the illustrious lineage of the Mughal emperors: Tīmūr seated in right center under a parasol (chatr), the symbol of royalty; the emperors Akbar and Jahāngīr kneeling in the foreground, and finally, three other rulers at left rear, probably 'Umar Shaykh, Bābur, and Humāyūn (Fig. 14). That it was not an unusual caprice of Rembrandt to have such miniatures in his possession is shown by the fact that these same paintings were later owned by several leading English painters of the 17th, 18th, and early 19th centuries. The president of the Royal Academy, Sir Joshua

[7] About the use of the arabesque in ornamental etchings and in other graphic arts of the Renaissance see P. Jessen, *Der Ornamentstich. Geschichte der Vorlagen des Kunsthandwerks seit dem Mittelalter*, Berlin, 1920, pp. 63, 103, 105, 373, and figs. 41, 42, 72 (which is the model of E. Kühnel, *Die Arabeske*, Wiesbaden, 1949, fig. 24, after which our Fig. 12 has been made), and 73. The decoration on the outside of this volume is another instance of the interest in the arabesque during the Renaissance, since it is taken from Peter Floetner's *Maureskenbuch*, published in Zürich in 1549 (about this book see P. Jessen, *op. cit.*, p. 105). The design is reproduced by courtesy of the National Gallery of Art (Rosenwald Collection).

[8] F. Sarre, "Rembrandts Zeichnungen nach indisch-islamischen Miniaturen," *Jahrb. d. Königl. Preuss. Kunstsamml.*, xxv, 1904, pp. 143 ff.; *idem*, "Ein neues Blatt von Rembrandts indischen Zeichnungen," *loc. cit.*, xxx, 1909, pp. 283 ff.

Reynolds, greatly admired another fine set, now one of the treasures of the British Museum.

With the 18th century we finally reach the point where a scholarly interest in Muslim archeology begins. Among the first Muslim antiquities to enter European collections were Kufic coins dating from the 8th to the early 11th century. These had been highly coveted in Northeastern Europe in the early Middle Ages and appeared now in large numbers in many places around the shores of the Baltic Sea, in the Scandinavian countries, in Northern Germany, and in Russia. They instigated serious research in numismatics and created a fairly large literature. In 1724 there appeared in Leipzig a monograph by George Jacob Kehr[9] which, because of its correct readings of the inscriptions and full comments, has been called the first scholarly book on Muslim numismatics[10] and so also of Muslim archeology in the widest sense.

By the end of the century we already find catalogues of coin collections in various parts of Europe, such as those of the Museum Cuficum Borgianum in Rome, the Museo Naniano in Padua, the Royal Library in Göttingen, and the Stockholm collection. This early era culminates in the work by C. M. Fraehn, who, at the beginning of the nineteenth century, "prepared a systematic classification of Muslim coins which though corrected in minor detail has not only not been superseded, but no serious attempt has been made to replace it by another."[11]

This head start of numismatics, which put it in advance of all other branches of Muslim art and archeology, still prevails. In the years 1875-1890, Stanley Lane-Poole brought out his eleven-vol-

[9] G. J. Kehr, *Monarchiae Asiatice-Saracenicae Status qualis VIII et IX . . . seculo fuit, ex nummis argenteis prisca Arabum scriptura kufica . . . cusis, et nuper . . . effossis, illustratus.* The same author published also another monograph on a memorial medal of the Mughal Emperor Awrangzēb from the collection of Frederic II, Duke of Saxe-Gotha: *Monarchae mogolo-indici, vel Mogolis Magni Aurenk Szeb numisma indo-persicum argenteum quinquelibrale rarissimum in solennen renovationem et confirmationem clientelarum urbis ac sedis imperatoriae Dehli, nunc dictae Dschihanabad signatum. . . .* A copy of this rare booklet, published in Leipzig in 1725 and now nearly forgotten, is in the Library of Congress.

[10] Leo A. Mayer, *The Rise and Progress of Moslem Archaeology* (in Hebrew), Jerusalem, 1935, p. 6. Professor Mayer was kind enough to provide the writer with an English translation of this paper, his inaugural lecture as professor of Near Eastern art and archeology at the Hebrew University, Jerusalem. This earlier publication has been very valuable in the preparation of this survey.

[11] Leo A. Mayer, *op. cit.*, pp. 6-7.

ume catalogue of the Oriental coins in the British Museum, which was followed by similar though less voluminous volumes of the collections in St. Petersburg (1881), the Bibliothèque Nationale in Paris (1887-1896), the Imperial Ottoman Museum in Istanbul (1894-1903), and the Royal Museum in Berlin (1898-1902). All during the nineteenth and twentieth centuries many outstanding orientalists and numismatists have worked in the field. To mention the names of even the leading scholars is not necessary, especially since L. A. Mayer published a *Bibliography of Muslim Numismatics* (London, 1939) which covers the literature up to 1934. More recently, this field has found devotees in the United States. Indeed, the *Numismatic History of Rayy,* by G. C. Miles (New York, 1938), has shown new approaches in its systematic survey of coinage in one of the main centers of medieval Islam and its correlation with the reports of Muslim historians.

It is hardly necessary to state here that Islamic coins, important as they are from an archeological point of view, cannot be regarded as works of art. The overwhelming majority of them carry only inscriptions, and a coin with figural representations is an exception. Nevertheless, it is an auxiliary branch of research in this field, providing the historical data for its investigations.

After numismatics other archeological branches with a predominantly historical flavor opened up. The most important of these were epigraphy and paleography. Carsten Niebuhr, in his *Beschreibung von Arabien* (Copenhagen, 1772), illustrated a Kufic Koran, but it was some fifty more years before a more systematic development of this field was started. It was only in 1828 that inscriptions form an important part in J. T. Reinaud's *Description des monumens musulmans du cabinet de M. le duc de Blacas,* which is also the first important book dealing with a whole collection of Muslim minor arts. The prolific orientalist, Joseph von Hammer-Purgstall, dealt with a Kufic inscription in the al-Ḥākim Mosque in Cairo (1838) and in 1848 gave an academy lecture on seals which was later published. In 1840 Michelangelo Lanci wrote a book on Arabic tombstones and followed it up in 1845-1846 with his three-volume *Trattato delle simboliche rappresentanze arabiche e della varia generazione de' musulmani caratteri sopra differenti materie operati,* which deals not only with various types of in-

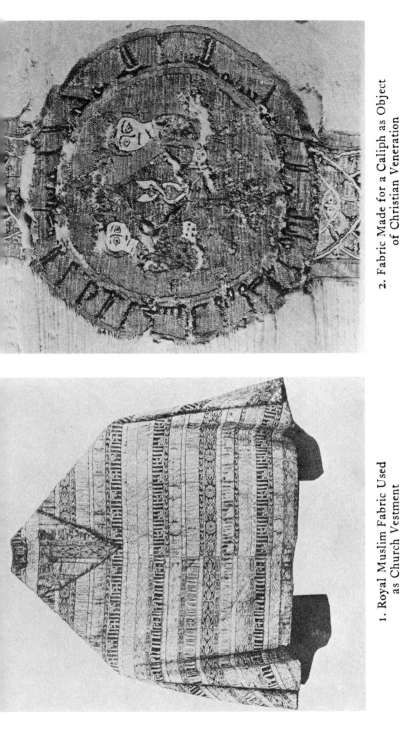

1. Royal Muslim Fabric Used as Church Vestment

2. Fabric Made for a Caliph as Object of Christian Veneration

3 A Fátimid Decoration Re-

4 Muslim Fabric with Iranian

5 Fátimid Rock Crystal

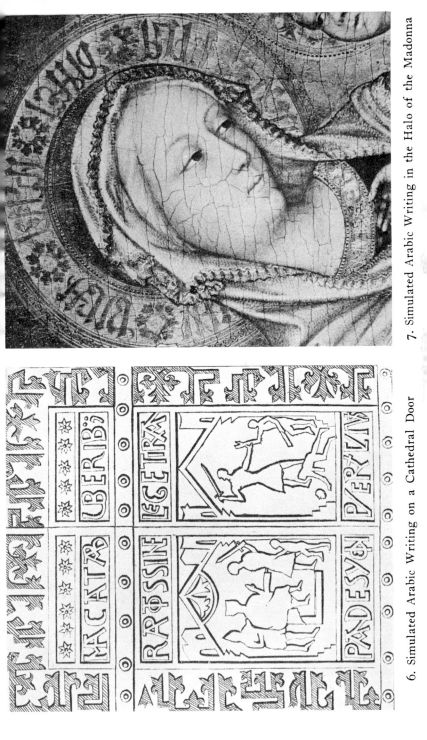

6. Simulated Arabic Writing on a Cathedral Door

7. Simulated Arabic Writing in the Halo of the Madonna

8. An Early Muslim Rug with Geometric Patterns on a Flemish Painting of the Fifteenth Century

9. An Early Muslim Rug with an Animal Design on an Italian Painting of the Fifteenth Century

11. An Early European Paraphrase of Muslim Metalwork

10. A Muslim Art Object Executed in Europe

13 A Turkish Parallel to Holbein's Tankard Design

12 Arabesques of Muslim Derivation Used by Holbein

14. Rembrandt as One of the Earliest Admirers of Mughal Painting

15. A "Turquerie" in Eighteenth Century English Art

16. The Awakening of Scholarly Interest in Muslim Architecture

17. A Romantic View of a Moorish Architectural Masterpiece

18. Egypt's Monuments Surveyed on Napoleon's Command

10. A Western View of an Egyptian Café at Rosetta, with barber

20. A Mid-Nineteenth Century View of Persian Palaces and Gardens

21. Aerial View of an Eighth-Century Muslim Town in the
Form of a Horseshoe

22. Aerial View of a Ninth-Century Cloverleaf Racetrack
with the Grandstand in the Center

23. Aerial View of an Iranian Mosque Showing Basic Structure and Additions

24 and 25. Finds from Saräi Berke, a Near-Forgotten Excavation Site

scriptions on objects, but also with representations of planets in the minor arts, talismans, weapons, flags, and garments.

Early in the nineteenth century we finally witness an awakening of interest in the artistic monuments of Islam, especially its buildings. The first country to arouse such interest and instigate a sizable literature of many folio volumes was Spain. The pioneer was James Cavanah Murphy, with his *Arabian Antiquities of Spain,* a book which expresses enthusiasm for everything Islamic, not only in its handsome illustrations of Moorish buildings, their decoration and inscriptions, but even in its title page, which proudly displays the Hijrah year, 1228, next to the A.D. date, 1813 (Fig. 16). Many other writers were active in Spain in the first half of the nineteenth century and published the results of their investigations. Among these were A. de Laborde, Girault de Prangey, J. Goury, Owen Jones, and so on (Fig. 17).[12] About the same time there were also other writers who in their discussion of Sicilian monuments included the Muslim remnants.

One wonders, of course, what caused this new appreciation of Muslim art. There is little doubt that it was due to the Romantic movement with its enthusiasm for early and distant civilizations. The period which admired the noble Greek and pious medieval knight, which relished Greek and Gothic revivals, was naturally drawn to an art that had produced a structure like the Alhambra, "a palace gilded by the spirits like a dream and filled with harmony."[13]

The new research was but a part of a rising trend in European scholarship, which, beginning in 1762 (when the first volume of Stuart and Revett's *Antiquities of Athens* appeared), set out to discover the true architectural forms of the past. It should be remembered, however, that even before this, in the eighteenth century, an interest in exotic buildings had existed, but the aim of

[12] A. de Laborde, *Voyage pittoresque et historique de l'Espagne*, Paris, 1806-1820; Girault de Prangey, *Monuments arabes et moresques de Cordoue, Séville et Grenade, dessinés et mesurés en 1832 et 1833*, Paris, 1836-1839; *idem, Essai sur l'architecture des Arabes et des Mores en Espagne, en Sicilie et en Barbarie*, Paris, 1841; [J. Goury and O. Jones], *Plans, Elevations, Sections and Details of the Alhambra from Drawings taken on the spot in 1834 by the late M. Jules Goury and in 1834 and 1839 by Owen Jones, Archt.*, London, 1842-1845.

[13] This is the motto of the folio publication by Goury and Jones listed in the preceding footnote; it is printed in large gold letters in the center of the richly decorated frontispiece of volume I.

the Rococo age was to stimulate moods and associations by means of quasi-Oriental buildings and to create picturesque views, especially in gardens. Thus it seems symptomatic that when, about 1761, Sir William Chambers designed the gardens and buildings of Kew in Surrey he built a whole group of architectural extravaganzas such as a Temple of Pan, a Theater of Augusta, a Gothic Cathedral, a House of Confucius, a Chinese Pagoda, and so on, a group which also included "a Moresque building commonly called the Alhambra" (which, however, had nothing of a Moorish structure), and a mosque in Turkish style, the first such building erected in the Western world (Fig. 15).[14] Though Sir William asked the learned Dr. Moreton to provide suitable Arabic inscriptions for the mosque, the lack of a miḥrāb in its interior reveals how little this age knew of the actual character of a house of Muslim divine worship. But the architect's aim was to achieve the picturesque forms of a "Turquerie," and in designing it he created something of a fashion in Europe.[15]

There was yet another impetus to studies of the Near Eastern world, and this is sometimes forgotten. We are referring to imperialism and modern power politics in the Near East. When Napoleon invaded Egypt in 1798, he brought scholars along to

[14] W. Chambers, *Plans, Elevations, Sections and Perspective Views of the Gardens and Buildings at Kew in Surrey*, London, 1763, pp. 5-6, pls. 20, 21, 27, and 28. Both the "Alhambra" and the Mosque were demolished before 1824.

[15] One of the monuments inspired by the Kew Garden Mosque, the mosque in the gardens of the palace of the Electors of the Palatinate at Schwetzingen in Baden (near Mannheim), built by Nicholas de Pigage in 1778 and the following years, is still standing. Its style is, on the whole, French classicistic and only its two minarets and Arabic inscriptions provide the Oriental associations which the age demanded. The Muslim character of the rather complex Schwetzingen building is even more misunderstood than in its English prototype, yet these early buildings are important as the first indication of a new general sentiment in favor of Muslim art forms. (K. Martin, *Die Kunstdenkmäler des Amtsbezirks Mannheim. Stadt Schwetzingen [Die Kunstdenkmäler Badens, x, 2]*, Karlsruhe, 1933, pp. 289-312.)

Another turquerie influenced by the mosque in Kew Garden is the Turkish Kiosk in Haga Park north of Stockholm. It was built in 1786 for the Swedish King Gustaf III, after various designs submitted to him by F. M. Piper, and is still standing. (O. Sirén, *China and Gardens of Europe in the Eighteenth Century*, New York, 1950, p. 192, color plate preceding p. 191 and pls. 164-166; see also pl. 31.) The eighteenth-century architectural books on garden pavilions "à la mode" contain not only designs for the more popular structures in Chinese style, but occasionally also Turkish mosques and kiosks (see, e.g. G. L. Le Rouge, *Détail des nouveaux jardins à la mode*, Paris, 1776-1787). Muslim forms in American architecture have recently been discussed by Clay Lancaster in "Oriental Forms in American Architecture, 1800-1870," *Art Bulletin*, XXIX, 1947, pp. 185-90.

survey the country in an exhaustive and systematic fashion. These men prepared plans of towns and buildings, drew architectural views of streets, mosques, houses and gates, copied inscriptions and coins, included illustrations of the various crafts at work, of tools, garments, musical instruments, and so on, the result being incorporated in the monumental *Description de l'Égypte* published in 1809-1828 in nine volumes of text, ten volumes of plates, and an atlas, a work which "forms the real basis of our knowledge of Muslim archeology" (Figs. 18-19). Later on, when the French armies conquered Algeria in 1830, this event led indirectly not only to Eugène Delacroix's trip to Morocco in 1832 and his famous sketches of Muslim life,[16] but also to the publishing in 1846 of Ravoisié's *Exploration scientifique de l'Algérie pendant les années 1840, 41, 42*. This combination of domination of a Near Eastern country by a Western power and her active support of archeological work therein continued until our own times, e.g. the organization in 1920 of the Department of Antiquities of Palestine by the British, after they had taken over the mandatory power, and the issuance of a very valuable archeological *Quarterly* since 1931. Whatever one may think of the advantages or disadvantages of European rule in the East, this particular activity has borne rich fruit.

Toward the middle of the nineteenth century there ensued more detailed studies of Muslim buildings and objects found in the eastern part of the Islamic world, investigations which were usually carried out by architects and draftsmen. Pascal Coste's *Architecture arabe*, in which he reproduced measured drawings of the monuments of Cairo (published in 1839, but already surveyed from 1818 to 1825), is one of the first. This was followed by a series of works on Persian architecture by the same author, partly in collaboration with the painter E. Flandin, which came out between 1851 and 1867. The art of Egypt received further treatment

[16] Three of these sketchbooks are now in the Musée du Louvre (Paris, *Musée national du Louvre. Exposition Eugène Delacroix . . . juin-juillet 1930*, Paris, 1930, nos. 773-775), a fourth is in the Musée Condé at Chantilly (*Le Voyage de Eugène Delacroix au Maroc; facsimilé de l'album du Château de Chantilly . . .* ed., J. Guiffrey, Paris, 1913, and a fifth, with unpublished drawings, was acquired by The Pierpont Morgan Library in New York a few years ago (*New York, The Pierpont Morgan Library, Review of the Activities and Acquisitions of the Library from 1936 through 1940*, New York, 1941, pp. 62-64 and pl. XII).

by J. Bourgoin (1873-92) and A.C.T.E. Prisse d'Avennes (1877) in works which include not only architecture but also the various minor arts and, in the case of Bourgoin, also a minute study of the geometrical designs in Saracenic decoration. The plates of these works are valuable and meritorious, even though they are, at times, somewhat too imaginative. The text sections can, however, in no way be regarded as scholarly. The authors were not familiar with the inscriptions on the buildings or objects and they likewise lacked knowledge about their historical setting. Even considering their aims as being purely aesthetic, they still lacked the understanding of the essential, often preferring the later and more showy monuments and objects. Thus, Coste reproduces mostly Ṣafavī buildings of the seventeenth century in his book on Persian architecture, and when he gives the ground plan of the Great Mosque of Isfahan he overlooks the small dome chamber of A.D. 1088, a structure now regarded as one of the crowning achievements of medieval Persian architecture.[17] And, beautiful though the plates are in the folio atlas of 1859 accompanying Hommaire de Hell's *Voyage en Turquie et en Perse* (Fig. 20), they please one more as a mid-nineteenth century artist's impression of Persia (in a vein similar to that of Italian views by contemporary artists) than as precise archeological documents. In this respect they follow the tradition of the older folio volumes, with their views of Spanish monuments all charmingly enlivened by groups of natives. However, one contribution of these early writers on the art of the Near East must not be forgotten, namely that they provided most valuable if not the only information on buildings which have since disappeared.

The turning point toward a more scholarly approach to Islamic art was the result of the life work of two men who were preoccupied with the archeological aspect of the history of Muslim art. The older of the two, the Austrian Joseph von Karabacek (1845-1918) not only was a numismatist and epigraphist, but also opened new fields of research. He was the founder of Arabic papyrology and the one who inaugurated the work in Islamic heraldry. By dealing with the Arabic inscriptions on the liturgical vestments

[17] P. Coste, *Monuments modernes de la Perse, mésurés, dessinés et décrits*, Paris, 1867, pl. IV.

of the Marienkirche in Danzig (1870), he initiated the important exploration of inscriptions on Muslim textiles, just as in his *Persische Nadelmalerei Susandschird* (Leipzig, 1881) he was the first to give historical data from Arabic and Persian sources for the understanding of Oriental carpet weaving. Altogether he was a pioneer in placing Muslim archeology in a wide historical perspective, since he clearly realized the importance of epigraphy and of Oriental sources for the interpretation of an art object. Unfortunately, the results of von Karabacek's investigations were often inadequate, if not downright erroneous, because he was guided too much by an unbridled imagination. Thus, oddly enough, one of his chief, though indirect, contributions to progress in Islamic research resulted from the criticisms of his work, and in particular, from the investigations which he provoked from his shocked contemporaries and successors. Von Karabacek is also noteworthy from another point of view. Through him for the first time Muslim archeology became, so to speak, professionally and socially acceptable, since in recognition of his work he was knighted, appointed director of the Hofbibliotek in Vienna, and made secretary of the Vienna Academy.[18]

An entirely different personality was the Swiss Max van Berchem (1863-1921), who became the unsurpassed master of Arabic epigraphy. Thoroughly trained as an orientalist, especially as historian, and likewise possessed by a love for Islamic art, he was naturally led to Muslim archeology, in which he primarily saw a means to further historical studies. He thus defines (in 1891) the various branches of Arab archeology (architecture, decorative arts, inscriptions, numismatics, seals) as "all the documents with the exception of manuscripts which supply some historical data, be it through their own forms, or through the texts which they provide." As to the significance of this new field he has this to say after his first stay in Cairo: "I was struck by the importance of this branch of historical studies and the precious help which this science, though still young and poorly established, can give to the history of customs and ideas of Muslim civilization." He saw a double task before the students of Muslim archeology: "to collect the inscriptions of Egypt and Syria so that they can constitute the

---

[18] Carl Heinrich Becker, *Islamstudien*, Leipzig, 1924-32, vol. II, pp. 491-498.

basis of a *Corpus inscriptionum arabicarum* and to deduce from the study of monuments a kind of *Manual of Arab Archaeology*."[19] For himself he chose the first task. He presented the inscriptions, however, in the form of a book entitled *Matériaux pour un corpus inscriptionum arabicarum* (Cairo, 1909 ff.) since he did not wish to restrict himself to the corpus form, which contains merely the inscriptions, while he intended the *Matériaux* as a clearing-house for epigraphic, historical, and archeological data. The mass of material forced him later on to restrict the work to epigraphic-historical investigations, for which he built up a scholarly organization to carry the task through. He himself did volumes on Egypt and Jerusalem and collaborated with Halil Edhem on the first fascicle of the volume on Asia Minor, while M. Sobernheim and E. Herzfeld handled Northern Syria and Aleppo, and G. Wiet brought out the second volume on Egypt. Besides the organization of the gigantic work, he published many epigraphic studies ranging all the way from the Merinids in Morocco to Muslim antiquities in Ch'üan Chou in China, though his main interest was always concentrated on Egypt and Syria.[20] The work on the *Matériaux* was slowed down by van Berchem's death, but G. Wiet and J. Sauvaget are now preparing additional volumes on Mecca, Medina, and Damascus, and possibly on Brussa and Istanbul.[21]

Owing to the vast amount of epigraphic material in Muslim areas, research in this field continues unabated. It becomes more and more complex as whole new countries are opened up for study. We have only to remember, for instance, that very few non-Muslims had been able to enter Persian mosques before the late 1920's and only from that time on could inscriptions in the interiors be extensively photographed.[22] Besides the many books

[19] The quotations are from M. van Berchem, "Notes d'archéologie arabe. Monuments et inscriptions fatimites," *Journal asiatique*, 8ᵉ série, vol. 17, 1891, pp. 411, 412, and 424.

[20] E. Herzfeld, "Max van Berchem," *Der Islam*, XII, 1922, pp. 206-13. A. Boissier, "In memoriam Max Van Berchem," with "Bibliographie des publications de Max Van Berchem (1886-1922)," *Revue archéologique*, Vᵉ série, t. XVII, Jan.—av.1923, pp. 148-54.

[21] J. Sauvaget, "L'Archéologie musulmane en France de 1939 à 1945," *Ars Islamica*, XIII-XIV, 1948, p. 157. Sauvaget's sudden death in March 1950 (after this survey had been written) will prove to be a great blow to these plans. The completion of the project, if ever accomplished, seems now to be a task for a future generation.

[22] The mosques in Morocco and some in Tunisia are still not accessible to non-Muslims, which makes the fine publications of G. Marçais, H. Terrasse, and of other French scholars even more valuable.

and articles dealing with the great centers of Islam there are others, hardly less significant, which treat of the marginal countries, e.g. the *Epigraphia Indo-Moslemica* brought out by J. Horovitz (1909-12) and Ghulām Yazdāni (since 1913), the *Inscriptions arabes d'Espagne* by E. Lévi-Provençal (Leyden-Paris, 1931), and the publications on Arab inscriptions in Russian territory and collections by Mme. Vera A. Kratchkovskaya. In recent years Gaston Wiet has created a new and most useful tool for the whole field by organizing (with E. Combe and J. Sauvaget) the *Répertoire chronologique d'épigraphie arabe* of which thirteen volumes, with all the known Arabic inscriptions (i.e. 5200) until the year 705 H. (A.D. 1305), have so far been published (Cairo, 1931-1944). The latest development is a new serial publication exclusively devoted to Oriental epigraphy edited by Mme. Kratchkovskaya, of which so far only the first number (dated 1947) containing mostly Muslim material has reached the Western world. Although its language and poor illustrations (unfortunately so characteristic of many recent Russian publications) make it less effective than might be assumed, especially since the usual French résumés are omitted, its continued existence will nevertheless prove to be a boon to epigraphical studies.

While epigraphy seems to be well established as a scholarly pursuit, research in the related field of paleography has been hardly started. If we disregard the specialized study of the papyri (of which A. Grohmann is the outstanding expert) about all we can point to at this time are the collections of characteristic specimens of writing compiled by W. Wright, B. Moritz, C. Huart, E. Tisserant, A. J. Arberry, E. Kühnel, G. Levi della Vida, and others. With the exception of the investigations of the early forms of Kufic writing by Miss Abbott, notably her *Rise of the North Arabic Script* (Chicago, 1939), there has been very little critical research, especially for the periods after the third Islamic century. This is all the more regrettable since the high regard for accomplished writing in the Muslim world would actually command sustained studies in this important field.

One particular branch of historical studies within the large field of Muslim archeology, namely heraldry, deserves to be singled out in this short survey because it is the one that is now more or

less fully mapped. After Yacoub Artin Pacha had done preliminary work from 1887 to 1910, Leo A. Mayer in 1933 brought out
his model publication *Saracenic Heraldry*, which gives a thorough
survey of this Ayyūbid and Mamlūk institution, basing it on contemporary historical sources and on all the blazoned monuments
and objects discovered up to that time. In subsequent articles Mayer
has supplemented this material with a view to giving new interpretations of difficult coats of arms and of listing newly found
objects with heraldic symbols.

A different approach to Islamic art and archeology was taken
by a number of other scholars who approached the material mainly
from the artistic point of view. They needed such facts as names
of royal donors, dates, and artists as the historical skeleton of their
research, but the categories with the help of which they now interpreted the material were style, iconography, and technique.

The outstanding figure in this group is Friedrich Sarre (1865-
1945), who, from 1896 on, in about 200 books and articles, ranged
over the whole Muslim world from Spain to India, covering not
only architecture, painting, and the minor arts, but also the forerunners of Muslim art and its relationship with European and Far
Eastern arts and crafts. In many careful monographs, and often
in collaboration with distinguished epigraphists, he fixed the
exact historical and geographical place of whole groups of objects
and monuments, sometimes even against initial opposition which
later proved to be unwarranted. Owing to the significance of his
work, it was in a way only natural that he was the first scholar in
the field of whose manifold writings an annotated bibliography in
book form was published.[23]

Two other significant figures were H. Saladin and Gaston
Migeon, who, following the more restricted pioneer work of the
numismatist, Stanley Lane-Poole (*The Art of the Saracens in
Egypt,* London, 1886) published a two-volume *Manuel d'art
musulman* (Paris, 1907) dealing with the whole range of architecture, painting, and the minor arts. Though these volumes were
actually premature, owing to the limited amount of knowledge
then available, they were courageous undertakings; indeed, Saladin's work on architecture has never been superseded by a later

[23] J. H. Schmidt, *Friedrich Sarre. Schriften,* Berlin, 1935.

work treating the whole subject; it is, therefore, still of a certain importance. The *Manuel* was brought out in a second edition in 1927, but although each section was twice the original size, it could not cope with all the material. The architectural volumes written by G. Marçais, excellent as they are, deal only with the Maghreb, Spain, and Sicily, while the two volumes of Migeon are not always exact. The *Manuel* became the prototype for several handbooks on Islamic art (or at least on the minor arts and painting) by E. Diez (1917), E. Kühnel (1925), H. Glück and E. Diez (1925), and finally M. S. Dimand, whose handbook on painting and the minor arts was the first in English and also the first to be based exclusively on a single collection, that of the Metropolitan Museum of Art (1930, second edition 1944).[24] In the Arab world, too, the same approach has been followed by Zaky M. Hassan, whose well-illustrated survey of the arts in Muslim Iran, *Al-Funūn al-Īrānīyah fī al-'Aṣr al-Islāmi* has recently been published in Cairo in a second edition (1946).[25] In all of these books architecture (if it was included) was treated separately from painting and the minor arts, which again were split into the various media to be discussed one after the other. Even A. U. Pope's monumental *A Survey of Persian Art* (1938-39), in whose six folio volumes sixty-nine authors deal with the various aspects of Iranian art from the Stone Age to the nineteenth century, follows this general scheme. While this method (which is related to the nineteenth century style of arranging museums) makes it fairly easy to follow the development of the various types, it is impossible to get a true historical perspective and achieve a proper understanding of the *Zeitgeist* of each period which expresses itself in the style of all the media. E. Kühnel, in his contribution to A. Springer's *Handbuch der Kunstgeschichte* (1929), was the first to go beyond

[24] E. Diez, *Die Kunst der islamischen Völker* (*Handbuch der Kunstwissenschaft*), Berlin, 1917; E. Kühnel, *Islamische Kleinkunst*, Berlin, 1925; H. Glück and E. Diez, *Die Kunst des Islam* (*Propyläen-Kunstgeschichte*, vol. v), Berlin, 1925; M. S. Dimand, *A Handbook of Mohammedan Decorative Arts,* New York, 1930; the second edition was published under the title: *A Handbook of Muhammadan Art*.

[25] The first edition had been published in 1940. In 1935 the same author had already brought out the first volume of a history of Islamic art in Egypt, *Al-Fann al-Islāmi fī Miṣr*. These publications by Zaky M. Hassan appeared as publications of the Musée Arabe in Cairo. The same author has recently also published a handbook on the arts of all Islamic countries entitled *Funūn al-Islām* (Cairo, 1948) which, however, was not available to the present writer.

Saladin and Migeon and to treat all the arts of each period together. This enabled him to show the connecting links between
the various art centers and also between the various media. Recently, G. Marçais published the first separate handbook of this
type, which is short, precise, and a most useful introduction to
the subject (*L'Art de l'Islam*, Paris, 1946).

The first major figure to combine the methods of historical
research and style analysis was Ernst Herzfeld (1879-1948).
Trained as an architect, art historian, and orientalist, he was pre-
eminently qualified to combine the strict methods of historical
research based on an interpretation of the literary sources, inscriptions, and coins, with the more subjective evaluation of artistic
content. In many trips to the Near East and with the help of important excavations and archeological reconnaissance he explored
the arts of Iran, Iraq, and Syria, particularly their architecture,
ornamentation, iconography, and epigraphy, and his numerous
and many-sided publications are thus indispensable to every student in the field.[26]

The tendency for specialization, which has become more and
more evident as the twentieth century progresses, is also noticeable
in the field of Islamic art and archeology. We thus find scholars
who restrict themselves to a region or to certain media. Although
such a development has its drawbacks, owing to the possibility
of overlooking certain cultural links among the various Muslim
centers and the interchange of artistic ideas among the different
craftsmen, a limitation in certain major fields such as architecture,
painting, or the textile arts is unavoidable, and in view of the ever-
rising number of published monuments and objects, it is perhaps
to a certain degree even advantageous. One of the leading figures
among such specialists is K. A. C. Creswell, historian of Muslim
architecture, the main results of whose research are contained in
the two volumes of his monumental *Early Muslim Architecture*
(Oxford, 1932-40) and in his volumes on *Muslim Architecture of
Egypt,* still in progress. Another architectural historian to whom
we owe a great deal is Albert Gabriel who, in several volumes,
has dealt with the architectural monuments of Turkey (*Monu-*

---

[26] George C. Miles, "The Writings of Ernst Herzfeld," *Ars Islamica*, VII, 1940, pp.
82-92; a Supplementary Bibliography will be published in *Ars Islamica* XV-XVI, 1951.

ments turcs d'Anatolie, 2 vols., Paris, 1931-34; *Voyages archéo-logiques dans la Turquie*, 2 vols., Paris, 1940; *Châteaux turcs de Bosphore*, Paris, 1943). Distinguished service in this field has also been rendered by Gertrude Bell, C. Gurlitt, E. Diez, O. Reuther, E. Cohn-Wiener, H. Terrasse, A. Godard, J. Sauvaget, M. B. Smith, D. N. Wilber, and others. Unfortunately, it is impossible to enumerate in this short survey the many excellent investigations made by various scholars in each and every medium and we have to restrict ourselves to a mere mention of only a few names. In the vast field of decorative arts we can point to the pioneer work of H. Wallis, A. Riegl, and W. Bode, to the model publications of F. Sarre and E. Kühnel, and finally to the valuable studies of F. R. Martin, R. Koechlin, G. Marçais, O. von Falke, R. M. Rief-stahl, M. S. Dimand, M. Aga-Oglu, C. J. Lamm, K. Erdmann, F. E. Day, A. Lane, D. S. Rice, M. Bahrami, and many others. Painting, too, has attracted the minds of many scholars and connoisseurs—men like E. Blochet, P. W. Schultz, G. Marteau, H. Vever, Sir Thomas Arnold, A. Sakisian, I. Stchoukine, E. de Lorey, U. Monneret de Villard, M. M. Diakonov, E. Schroeder, H. Buchtal, and especially L. Binyon, J. V. S. Wilkinson and B. Gray, whose *Persian Miniature Painting* (London, 1933) represents the best book on the subject. Other specialists have set out to elucidate the archeological past of a specific region. To this category belong M. Gómez-Moreno, L. Torres Balbás, and J. Ferrandis, whose interests center around Hispano-Moresque art, and A. K. Coomaraswamy, P. Brown, and H. Goetz, who explored the Muslim arts of India. The modern stress on "digging up the past" has, finally, produced yet another group of specialists, that of the excavators. E. Herzfeld is their unexcelled master, while J. M. Upton, W. Hauser, and C. K. Wilkinson are their best exponents in the United States. In recent years D. Schlumberger has perhaps been the most successful representative of this group.

The development of such specialized fields of research is in itself an indication of the rising interest in Islamic art and the continued success in unearthing and interpreting new material. When, in 1877, J. von Lessing published his portfolio of oriental carpets represented in European pictures of the fifteenth and sixteenth centuries, he assumed that no originals had been preserved. A publication brought out five years later already contained six old pieces.[27] Now we have to express the number of carpets made before 1800 in four figures and we even have fragments that go back to the early Middle Ages. The publications in this field are now so numerous that one needs a bibliography for one's guidance, though the work of proper analysis and interpretation is only in its infancy. This refers not only to the designs, but also to the poetic inscriptions in Persian.

A similar rise of interest can be shown in the study of paintings. When, in 1891, van Berchem listed the different sections of a prospective *Manual of Arab Archaeology*, he did not mention painting, because practically nothing was known about it at that time. It was only in 1898 that A. Musil discovered the eighth-century wall paintings in the Umayyad castle of Quṣayr 'Amra. When they were brought to the attention of the somewhat amazed and puzzled European orientalists this led, in view of the traditionally anti-iconic attitude of Muslim theological literature, to a long, drawn-out discussion of the theoretical position of painting in Islam. Later on, in 1911, Herzfeld's discoveries of wall paintings in Sāmarra definitely established this art form as another facet of Muslim civilization, and when excavators more recently found large-scale paintings at Qaṣr al-Ḥayr al-Gharbi (1936) and in Nīshāpūr (1939), the fact that these paintings existed was in itself no longer regarded as surprising and scholars were interested only in their date, style, and iconography. How this extension of our knowledge progressed can be shown also by a bibliographical index. For instance, the first inventory and description of a miniature collection (i.e. that of the Bibliothèque Nationale) in book form was brought out in 1900 by E. Blochet.[27] The first book on Muslim painting dealing with all known schools in the main collections was published in 1912 by F. R. Martin;[28] the same year saw also the first book on a single illuminated manuscript,[29] al-

[27] K. Erdmann, "Orientalische Tierteppiche auf Bildern des XIV. and XV. Jahrhunderts," *Jahrb. d. Preuss. Kunstsamml.*, L, 1929, pp. 261-98.

[27] *Inventaire et description des miniatures des manuscrits orientaux conservés à la Bibliothèque Nationale*, Paris, 1900.

[28] *The Miniature Painting and Painters of Persia, India and Turkey from the Eighth to the Eighteenth Century*, London, 1912.

[29] *Idem, Les Miniatures de Behzad dans un manuscrit persan daté de 1485*, Munich, 1912.

though additional volumes on single manuscripts came out with greater frequency only from 1925 on.[30] It was not until 1948, however, that the first book devoted to a single painting appeared.[31] While all the earlier "first publications" were brought out in Europe by Europeans, the last-mentioned book appeared in a Near Eastern country, Egypt, and was written by an Arab scholar.

The ever-growing awareness of the importance of Islamic art in due time necessitated the making of systematic inventories, i.e. lists of buildings and catalogues of objects. The first surveys, those undertaken by the scholars attached to Napoleon's army in Egypt, have already been mentioned. It took more than half a century for this type of work to be resumed. The pioneer among those to examine a whole country was Victor Guérin, who in 1868-1880 brought out his investigations of many buildings and sites in Palestine, and prepared the ground for the Surveys of the Palestine Exploration Fund.[32] Another important milestone was reached in 1881 when, on the order of the Khedive Muhammad Tawfîq, Julius Franz Bey and Rogers Bey created the Comité de Conservation des Monuments de l'Art Arabe to function under the ministry of Awqâf. In its first meeting, on February 1, 1882, the tasks of this Committee were thus described:

1. To prepare an inventory of Arab buildings of architectural and historical importance;

2. To watch over the maintenance and conservation of these buildings by advising the minister of Awqâf about the work to be undertaken and to indicate to him the most urgent cases;

3. To examine repair projects of these buildings, approve them and see to it that they are carried out exactly;

4. To be responsible for the safe custody in the archives of the

---

[30] H. Glück, *Die indischen Miniaturen des Haemzae-Romanes*, Wien, 1925; Sir T. W. Arnold, *The Miniatures in Hilālī's Mystical Poem, The King and the Dervish*, Vienna, 1926; F. R. Martin, *Miniatures from the Period of Timur*, Vienna, 1926; F. R. Martin and Sir T. W. Arnold, *The Nizami MS, Illuminated by Bihzad, Miraḳ and Qasim Ali* . . . British Museum (Or. 6810), Vienna, 1926 and so on. Monographs in book form on album collections of Islamic miniatures had been published at an earlier date: F. Sarre and E. Mittwoch, *Zeichnungen von Riza Abbasi*, München, 1914; E. Kühnel and H. Goetz, *Indische Buchmalereien aus dem Jahāngīr-Album der Staatsbibliothek zu Berlin*, Berlin, 1924, and so on.

[31] Bishr Farès, "Une Miniature religieuse de l'école arabe de Bagdad," *Mem. de l'Institut d'Egypte*, vol. 51, Le Caire, 1948.

[32] Leo A. Mayer, *op. cit.*, p. 12.

minister of Awqāf of all plans carried out, and to indicate to the ministry which architectural remains should be transferred to the National Museum for safekeeping.[33]

Thus not only were the important buildings of Egypt to be listed, but they were also to be protected. The work of this committee continues down to the present day, and the thirty-eight issues of its transactions (the last published in 1944) are important sources of information.

The example of Egypt was followed by other countries: in Iran, for instance, by the Anjuman-i-Āthār-i-Milli. In recent years the Departments of Antiquities of the various Muslim nations have continued making surveys of their national monuments and seeing to it that the most important ones in want of repair are restored and taken care of.

During the last decades a few scholars have, in addition, brought out check-lists of important buildings, which are most useful tools for the student of architecture and the historian. Examples are Creswell's *Brief Chronology of the Muhammadan Monuments of Egypt to A.D. 1517* (1919), Sauvaget's inventory of 121 Muslim buildings in Aleppo (1931),[34] and Godard's survey of the monuments of Isfahan (1937).

The systematic cataloguing of collections has proved a more formidable task than that of buildings; the mass of material was overwhelming and spread over several continents, so that a proper classification and confrontation of analogous material was most difficult. However, F. Sarre (in collaboration with E. Mittwoch) published a catalogue of his collection of metalwork as early as 1906 and it is still an important reference book. The only public institution which has so far brought out an extensive series of catalogues is the Musée Arabe in Cairo where, under the leadership and with the active participation of Gaston Wiet, sixteen large, well-illustrated, and richly-annotated volumes have been published to date.[35] They have greatly enriched our knowledge

[33] *Comité de Conservation des Monuments de l'Art Arabe, I, Procès verbaux des Séances. Rapports,* Le Caire, 1884.

[34] J. Sauvaget, *Inventaire des monuments musulmans de la ville d'Alep,* Paris, 1931; this inventory was originally published in *Revue des Études Islamiques,* 1931, pp. 59-114.

[35] M. Wiet himself published *Lampes et bouteilles en verre émaillé,* 1929; *Les objets en cuivre,* 1932, and *Stèles funéraires,* vols. II, IV, 1936, and vols. V-X, 1937-1942; vols.

of the minor arts, especially by giving us the historical and epi-graphic data pertaining to each object.

Archeological reconnaissance in the Near East had its precursors in the famous travelers from the Middle Ages to the eighteenth century in men like Marco Polo, Chardin, Tavernier, Thévenot, de Bruin, Pocoke, and many others. In modern times their chance observations have been superseded by the careful investigations of such well-trained explorers and archeologists as the Dieulafoys, Musil, Jaussen, Savignac, Brünnow, von Domaszewski, Gertrude Bell, Sarre, Herzfeld, and Riefstahl. Inconspicuous as are many of the inscriptions or objects which they recorded and analyzed, nevertheless they have proved of great historical significance; the same applies to buildings, which often were in ruins. During the last few decades a new form of reconnaissance has been added to the old established ones, that of aerial surveying, which enables us to find and examine archeological sites and to study with ease the various forms of city planning and the complex combinations of urban structures (Figs. 21-23).[36]

To have a real insight into the life and civilization of Islam in its cultural heyday it was necessary to excavate some of the old famous centers. Perhaps the first digging at a purely Muslim site was that at the ancient Qal'at Bani Ḥammād, the capital of Ḥammādids in the eleventh and twelfth centuries (in Algeria), which was started in 1898 by P. Blanchet and in 1908 was continued by General de Beylié. About the year 1910, R. Velásquez Bosco began to explore and excavate the ruins of another capital, that of Madīnat al-Zahrā', the residence of the Umayyad caliphs of Córdoba. More important were the excavations at Sāmarra on the Tigris, under Sarre and Herzfeld in 1911-1913, which yielded not only important information about the arts of this ephemeral capital of the 'Abbāsids in the ninth century, but served also (thanks to the exact date of its finds) as a guide for other sites and objects

---

i and iii of the last named series were brought out by Hassan Hawary and Hussein Rached, 1932, 1938; other catalogue volumes are: J. David-Weill, Les Bois à épigraphes jusqu' à l'époque mamlouke, 1931, and Les Bois à épigraphes dépuis l'époque mamlouke, 1936; E. Pauty, Les Bois sculptés jusqu' à l'époque ayyoubide, 1931, and P. Olmer, Filtres des gargoulettes, 1932.

[36] E. F. Schmidt, Flights over Ancient Cities of Iran (Chicago, 1940), is particularly rich in material of great interest to the Muslim archeologist.

not as readily datable. There were excavations also at al-Fusṭāṭ, the first Muslim capital of Egypt; at Sarai Berke on the Volga, the capital of the Golden Horde; at the site of several other old Muslim centers, such as Nīshāpūr, Isṭakhr, Rayy, Tirmidh, Bālis, Tahert, etc., and also at the site of ancient castles, such as the Umayyad Khirbat al-Munyah, Qaṣr al-Ḥayr al-Gharbi, Khirbat al-Mafjar, etc. In addition, there were other places which were excavated mainly for the sake of older civilizations, but where the Muslim layer at the top found, at times, a friendly recorder (e.g. Susa, Miletus, Baalbek, Ḥamāh, Antioch, Alishar Hüyük, etc.). Considering the complexity and wide geographical distribution of Muslim civilization, the number of sites so far excavated is insufficient; the result of these undertakings for further research is unfortunately even less adequate, since in many cases the finds were barely announced or were published in fragmentary fashion. It is strongly hoped that this situation will be remedied, though in some cases the death of the explorers, alas, makes this no longer possible. Archeological efficiency in scholarly excavations is the more necessary since many key cities, such as Baghdad, provide no possibility of successful excavation, while other important centers, like al-Raqqah or al-Rayy, have been ransacked by commercial diggers who have destroyed most, if not all, of the historical data.

The growing awareness of Muslim art led naturally to an increase of Muslim objects in public museums and libraries, and hence there rose a group of specialized curators, such as E. Kühnel, R. L. Hobson, J. V. S. Wilkinson, M. S. Dimand, B. Gray, and others, who sifted, analyzed, and published the objects under their care. The public collections in Europe have been formed from Near Eastern objects found among the nationalized or otherwise dispersed ecclesiastical or princely treasures, from the purchases of travelers and residents in the East, and, since the late nineteenth century, from the pioneering work of private collectors and connoisseurs. The growth of departments of Islamic art in the American museums has been quite spectacular. The interest in Eastern arts found first expression in the collections of very wealthy businessmen who were attracted by the refined sumptuousness of this branch of art, which easily lent itself as decoration for their palatial homes. Several of them, such as Henry Walters and Charles L. Freer, later gave their collections to the public;[37] while the collections of others, such as John Pierpont Morgan and George Hewitt Myers, constituted semi-public museums of their own.[38]

In Europe we find large public collections of Islamic art usually only in the capitals, while in the United States museums throughout the country have an extensive number of Muslim objects. This is conditioned not only by the national wealth and general interest, but also by the fact that when these museums started to build up their collections it was comparatively easier to buy good examples of Asiatic art, which had just recently come on the market, than European paintings and sculptures which, by this time, had already found their permanent homes in public institutions. Our picture of collections would not be complete without mentioning the museums and libraries in the Near Eastern capitals of Istanbul, Cairo, Jerusalem, Damascus, and Tehran, some of which are old and housed in ancient palaces, while others have been built up only during recent decades and occupy specially constructed buildings. To their number may now be added provincial museums, which will be a better guarantee for the care of local treasures and prevent their disappearance into the limbo of the antique trade.

Owing to the wide dispersal of Muslim art objects, no museum is rich enough to give a complete picture of the development of all the arts. Therefore, from a rather early period exhibitions of Islamic art were arranged at some central point. This fashion was started in 1885 with an exhibition of Persian and Arab art at the Burlington Fine Arts Club in London and has continued ever since in most countries of Europe, in the United States, and also in the Near East, where the first such show was arranged in Alexandria in 1926.

The first exhibition of real significance was held in Munich in 1910. It led to a large publication to which all the outstanding experts of the time contributed, a fact which explains the tremendous impetus it gave to Islamic art studies. The same can be said

[37] To form the Walters Art Gallery in Baltimore and the Freer Gallery of Art, Washington, respectively.

[38] To form the Pierpont Morgan Library in New York and the Textile Museum in Washington, respectively.

about the exhibition of Persian art in London in 1931, which produced a whole series of important publications directly or indirectly connected with it. At a comparatively early date, more specialized exhibitions were fostered by collectors and connoisseurs. One of these, the great exhibition of Near Eastern carpets in the Handelsmuseum in Vienna in 1891, started research in this medium, while the first exhibition of Persian, Indian, and Turkish miniatures in the Musée des Arts Décoratifs in 1912 was one of the first public expressions of the new interest in this field of collecting. Of late, progressive specialization has brought about exhibitions of only one branch within a medium, such as the shows of the so-called Polonaise carpets in the Metropolitan Museum (1930) or of dragon rugs in the Textile Museum of Washington, D.C. (1948).

In the early period, the result of archeological investigations, if not brought out in book form, were published in the principal journals of oriental studies. With the rise of public collections a great deal, such as the research of Sarre and Künnel, was published in museum yearbooks and bulletins. The publications of the European archeological institutions in the Near East likewise began to show an increasing number of articles devoted to the Muslim period, while the official organs of the newly-founded departments of antiquities (such as A. Godard's excellent *Āthār-é Īrān,* and *Sumer*)[39] announced new finds or archeological investigations in their respective countries. A special impetus to research was given by *Ars Islamica,* the first journal specially devoted to the study of Muslim art and archeology; it was founded in 1934 by Mehmet Aga-Oglu and is brought out under the auspices of the University of Michigan. Lately, the Oriental Department of the Hermitage Museum in Leningrad has started a new type of publication which avoids the all-too-mixed character of European and American museum bulletins. Between 1939 and 1947 it has published four volumes of "Travaux du Départment Oriental" which deal with the arts of the ancient Near East and Asia. In these publications the arts and crafts of Islam and of the preceding periods play a dominant role, and since this museum and the

[39] Published by the Archeological Service of Iran and the Directorate General of Antiquities of Iraq, respectively.

provincial collections of the U.S.S.R. contain a great deal of important but unknown material, it is hoped that this series will continue to appear. Finally, two important publication media for the study of Hispano-Moresque art should be mentioned: the journal *Al-Andalus,* brought out by the Schools of Arabic Studies in Madrid and Granada, and *Notes Hispanic,* published by the Hispanic Society of America between 1941 and 1945 but unfortunately now discontinued.

The great diversity of publications, coupled with the wide geographical dispersion of scholars writing anywhere between the United States and India, made proper bibliographical reference works a necessity. After various sporadic trials the proper solution to this problem seemed to have been found when L. A. Mayer brought out his *Annual Bibliography of Islamic Art and Archaeology* in 1935; after three volumes, the Second World War put an unfortunate end to this cooperative enterprise, which we hope will eventually be resurrected. Another desideratum would be a bibliography of past publications, since it is otherwise feared that many investigations, especially those undertaken in countries like Russia, Spain, and India, will soon be forgotten. A further similar reference work will be necessary to survey the archives of photographic negatives, prints, transcripts of inscriptions, and sketches by deceased scholars which are now kept in various public institutions, such as those of van Berchem in Geneva, Riefstahl in New York, and Herzfeld in Washington, and likewise, if possible, those of scholars still living. Until this work has been done, a great deal of research will be unnecessarily time-consuming and dependent upon chance finds; it may even try to duplicate earlier and better efforts.

Finally, some words should be devoted to the question of teaching. Although nearly all scholars who have made a name in the field of Islamic art and archeology are "autodidacts," it has always been the aim to create a new generation of students who would receive an early training in the special requirements and new methods. The University of Vienna was probably the first to have a chair which, in view of the interests of the first incumbent, von Karabacek, was devoted to the study of the "Auxiliary Historical Sciences of the East." Many leading figures have since been nominated to chairs at various universities in four continents, men like van Berchem, Gómez-Moreno, Marçais, Creswell, Riefstahl, Kühnel, Aga-Oglu, Mayer, Sauvaget, Zaky Hassan, and so on, while others, such as Herzfeld and Sir Thomas Arnold, dealt with Islamic art and archeology as only one of their subjects. So far, Islamic art and archeology, with their broad requirements, have proved to be rather elusive subjects, since only a few students thus trained have reached the level of their masters.

This fact brings us to the special problems to be discussed if we are looking into the future and want to gauge our needs and prospects.

This survey has shown that the study of Islamic art and archeology has two roots: general Islamic studies, and history of art. Especially in the earlier periods we find numismatists, epigraphists, and historians who had an excellent background for their work, particularly in languages, literature, and history, but who had no training in the discernment of art forms. Later, there arose another group which was well versed in style analysis, but which brought with them far greater enthusiasm for objects and monuments and their own interpretations of them, than familiarity with religious thought, literary documents, and historical data. It was inevitable that the men of the second group would commit errors in historical details which would be objectionable to the men of the first group, even though their main trend of thought was often acceptable. Such criticism applied especially to the publications on Oriental (including Islamic) art by Joseph Strzygowski, who, in the formative years of the new field (the first two decades of this century), developed a number of provocative theories without being too particular about geographical and historical data. On the other hand, the archeologists and epigraphists, too, could not always base their conclusions on definite facts; they, too, had to rely at times on their personal feeling and use style analyses just as the art historian, when they dealt with undated artifacts or inscriptions. Furthermore, the methods of orientalists writing on Islamic art, in spite of their more factual and "scientific" character, have not always shown themselves to be beyond criticism. To give an example: works were attributed to certain masters after signatures had been deciphered without realization that these "signatures" were later added to pictures painted in a style quite different from the authentic work of the painters, a fact which to an art historian would have been evident after a short examination.

A clear perception of the situation, it might be thought, would have led at an early stage to an amalgamation of the two methods, as has been done with such great success in the field of Western art. Although we have seen the two possible alternatives, either collaboration by two or more scholars or the special training of a single person, in a number of very successful cases (e.g. the joint works by Sarre-Mittwoch, and Sarre-van Berchem, or the individual publications of Herzfeld, Kühnel, or Sauvaget), the disparity of the two approaches often led to a mutual disregard and distrust between the two camps, which brought about a kind of split personality in the whole field.[40] Actually, the two approaches should not be separated, for they are supplementary to each other. We are preoccupied with Islamic civilization not just because it happened to exist, but because of its accomplishments and its special contributions to mankind. Thus we have to deal with both the typical and the special achievements. There is a vast body of material of "archeological" significance only; that is to say, it throws light on past ages without gratifying our aesthetic feelings. But there are also many pieces that show a decided effort to go beyond the common pattern and which reveal a definite intention and ability to create an "artistic" work. The objects in this second group are just as much historical documents, but, because they are the creations of great masters, they deserve special consideration and must be treated with different methods if we are to grasp their full significance. Hence, in the treatment of the material side of a civilization, we cannot be restricted to the methods of either an archeologist or an art historian, nor is this separation possible in the work of a museum. Our aim should be to develop the proper methods for every type of analysis and interpretation and to get beyond the stage that relies too much on uncontrollable subjective feeling.

If we now, in conclusion, try to look ahead to view future de-

[40] J. Sauvaget, *Introduction à l'histoire de l'orient musulman, éléments de bibliographie*, Paris, 1943, pp. 51-53.

velopments, it might be best to describe them in the most general terms, so as to follow the broad strokes in which we have painted the history of Islamic art and archeology in the preceding pages. Such a procedure seems to be all the more appropriate since E. Kühnel has recently listed the specific tasks of the immediate future and, in particular, the various archeological sites which it would be rewarding to excavate;[41] similar suggestions have also been made by K. A. C. Creswell.[42]

The further exploration of the field, through excavation and reconnaissance, survey of monuments, and intensive study of objects, remains, of course, the major task ahead of us. Nobody knows what the still-hidden monuments and objects will be able to tell us and how they will change our present understanding of the material civilization of Islam. To quote an illuminating example from the recent past: The excavations of Umayyad castles in Syria and Palestine have not only given us further information about the genesis of Islamic architecture, stucco decoration and painting, but they have also materially helped to destroy the long-held myth of the non-existing Muslim sculpture. Thus the more material we have at our disposal the sounder the picture of the past will be. Certain regions like Arabia and Afghanistan are, archeologically speaking, hardly touched. In Istanbul alone there are about 124,000 manuscripts, most of which have not yet been properly studied and some of which probably contain miniatures of great and vital interest; and in the same city there are great treasures of textiles, arms and armor, and so on.[43] Even in the easily accessible collections of the West, great surprises still await us. Finally, in the marginal countries of Islam, such as Russian Turkistan, the Caucasus, Pakistan, India, and Spain, our task, to judge from past experiences, will often have to be two-fold: there will be, first, the initial work of native investigators, and second, the dissemination of the results of their search, without which it

[41] E. Kühnel, "Ergebnisse und Aufgaben der islamischen Archäologie," in *Der Orient in deutscher Forschung*, Leipzig, 1944, pp. 255-59; also in *Beiträge zur Arabistik, Semitistik und Islamwissenschaft*, Leipzig, 1944, pp. 254-63.

[42] An article based on Mr. Creswell's Princeton Bicentennial paper is to appear in a forthcoming issue of the *Art Bulletin*.

[43] Tahsin Öz, *Türk Kumaş ve Kadifeleri*, no. 1, Istanbul, 1946; H. Stöcklein, "Die Waffenschätze im Topkapu Sarayı Müzesi zu Istanbul. Ein vorläufiger Bericht," *Ars Islamica*, 1, 1934, pp. 200-18.

is feared this important work might otherwise remain practically unknown in the Western world, as happened in the case of Sarai Berke (Figs. 24-25), Khwārizm, and many others.

Since it has always proved to be advantageous to view the world of Islam in a wider context, because of its historical and geographical position, its art cannot be exempt from this approach. Hence, for a full understanding of Muslim art, its forms alone cannot give all the necessary clues for its historical interpretation, and we will have to continue to consider pre-Islamic civilizations and those civilizations which are contemporary with Islam and which exerted an influence on it, i.e. the arts of Coptic Egypt and Sasanian Iran, the late classical arts of Syria, the arts of the Steppe countries, of Byzantium, Armenia, the Caucasus, India, and China. An archeological discovery in any of these fields can have important repercussions in our interpretation of Islamic art. Therefore future studies in Islamic art and archeology cannot remain insular; they must coordinate their own findings with those of related fields.

If we are also trying to visualize the future *trend* in research it can be assumed that it will be one which increasingly recognizes the fact that it is not enough to analyze the style of a monument (or painting, or object), its techniques and inscriptions—in other words, that it is not enough to look at it as a practically isolated phenomenon, more or less divested of the conditions and ideas under which it was created. After all, these buildings and objects were made for special use and enjoyment, created under specific conditions, and with definite ideas associated with them. Thus we have to study the monument's function or the object's use, the conditions of life, work, and trade under which it was made and all the associations that helped to create the work, whether they were derived from religious, magical, astrological, literary, or folkloristic concepts. Pleasing as may be the general impression and the artful decorations of a building, painting, or implement, we should still go on to consider its wider aspects and cultural context if we want to know the true meaning and significance of an object of the past.

The approach just now sketched is not something here proposed for the first time. Indeed, there have been a fair number of investigations which demonstrate the growing trend. To give a few examples: a study of the growth of a great Muslim city for which archeology and historical texts formed the source material;[44] a discussion of certain metal objects which deals not with their form and decoration alone, but also with their place in Muslim society;[45] and finally an examination of the background and development of an astronomical symbol[46]—all these use basically the same approach, though their applications are varied to solve the different problems. We have no doubt that the rapprochement of the history of Muslim art and of Muslim archeology will produce many more such integrated investigations. As van Berchem foresaw, they will contribute a great deal to our understanding of the whole Muslim civilization, of which art is one of the finest expressions.

It will be obvious that this approach will immeasurably increase our understanding and enjoyment of buildings and objects. It will in addition open up and develop new fields of research which have been little explored. One of these will be iconology, that is, investigations which coordinate imagery and peculiar forms with contemporary ideas expressed in literature. Another field will be terminology, of which we have had only sporadic attempts in the past, but of which more inclusive works are still missing. Here the nature of the work will make it clear that pure philological training in the languages is not enough. It has to be supplemented by a thorough understanding of the materials and technical processes. Finally, there will be investigations of the ideal beauty as prevalent in literature and mirrored in the fine arts. In this instance it may also be most revealing to contrast the Muslim categories of beauty—in case they can be established—with those postulated by the West, which, because of the dissimilar mentalities and the distances of time and space, are likely to be of a different nature.

A final question is still to be raised: Does such study represent just a fringe of the ever-growing quest for knowledge, a special

---

[44] J. Sauvaget, *Alep. Essai sur le développement d'une grande ville syrienne des origines au milieu du XIXᵉ siècle,* Paris, 1941.

[45] M. Aga-Oglu, "About a Type of Islamic Incense Burner," *Art Bulletin,* XXVII, 1945, pp. 28-45.

[46] W. Hartner, "The Pseudoplanetary Nodes of the Moon's Orbit in Hindu and Islamic Iconographies," *Ars Islamica,* v, 1938, pp. 113-154.

form of curiosity for the past, or is there any further significance in it?

In the Middle Ages Muslim scientists and philosophers exerted a powerful influence on the Western mind through the work of men like Rhazes, Avicenna, Averroes, and many others. In the eighteenth and nineteenth centuries Muslim literature and sentiment was widely admired, *vide* the many translations of the *Arabian Nights* since Galland's time, Goethe's *Westöstlicher Diwan,* Matthew Arnold's *Sohrab and Rustam,* and Fitzgerald's *Rubaiyat.* In our own time there is little doubt that Muslim art has by far the strongest appeal to the West and is indeed exercising it in many ways. It is the task of the historian of Muslim art to deepen this aesthetic appeal to an understanding of the whole civilization of a sizable part of mankind.

Muslim art can also have a special significance for the Muslim world of today. Since this is its one cultural achievement widely accepted and admired by the West, a rededication to it can compensate the East to a certain degree for its scientific and technological retardation, something which neither the oil fields nor strategic location can achieve. Be that as it may, there has been and still is no better ambassador of good will than art. If these considerations are more widely understood, Muslim art and its study will have an important role to play in the future.

3

ISLAMIC LITERATURE: ARABIC

BY GUSTAVE E. VON GRUNEBAUM

ROMANTICISM through its belief in a universal poetry manifest in each national literature, and the neo-humanism of the inter-war period with its realization of the conceptual autonomy of the individual civilization, have proved the principal intellectual stimuli toward the investigation of Arabic belles-lettres. The ideal goal of this investigation, as envisaged at this particular phase of our intellectual history—namely, the presentation of the artistic development of Arabic belles-lettres against its cultural background, interpreted in its own terms and for its own sake but correlated with setting and values of kindred literatures (including our own)—is still unattained. In fact, no systematic effort toward its achievement has been undertaken, although the trend of our studies over the last hundred years, and more intensively during the past two decades, has been to evolve those approaches to the ever-growing material whose elaboration must needs precede any synthesis that is to be in keeping with the scientific aspirations of this age.[1]

The beginning of Western study of Arabic literature is marked by the grandiose failure of Joseph von Hammer-Purgstall's (1774-1856) *Literaturgeschichte der Araber*, 7 vols., Vienna, 1850-1856. Paralleling his earlier works on Persian[2] and Turkish[3] literature, the 9,915 biographies with their bewildering specimen translations constitute an attempt, almost as irresponsible as it is imposing, to portray the whole of Arabic poetry, the significant along with the insignificant, undertaken on the basis of inadequate material in-

---

[1] This chapter is not planned as a bibliographical survey. Reference will be made to such publications that influenced our approach to Arabic belles-lettres. Neither the history of editorship nor that of the controversy regarding the genuineness of pre-Islamic poetry come within the scope of this study.

[2] *Geschichte der schönen Redekünste Persiens*, Vienna, 1818.

[3] *Geschichte der osmanischen Dichtkunst*, 4 vols., Vienna, 1836-1838.

adequately understood—perhaps the most deterrent example of premature boldness modern scholarship has to offer.

The immediate reaction was the introduction of the strictest philological method in research into Arabic poetry and a slowly broadening stream of competent editions and annotated translations; a more remote consequence was the abandonment of the concept of a history of poetry as a catalogue of poets. W. Ahlwardt (1828-1909), von Hammer's keenest critic (and, one may add, his finest interpreter),[4] who was perhaps both the most typical and the most outstanding representative of this early generation of philological students of poetry, shares with his predecessor the romantic outlook on literature.[5]

Accurate understanding of the poems required their interpretation as historical and cultural documents. Conversely, the properly interpreted verse was recognized as an important source for history[6] and, somewhat later, culture history.[7] The promise of these studies all but stopped investigation on more specifically literary lines.

The poetical universalism of the romantic mood proved a poor heuristic principle as soon as philology uncovered the foreignness and somewhat prosy technicality of pre-Islamic literature. Where self-identification was possible for the student steeped in playful nostalgia for medieval pomp and chivalry, the aesthetics of Arabic song remained accessible. Linguistic skill and an enthusiastic taste for the decorative enabled A. F. von Schack (1815-1894) to contrive an attractive picture of Arabic poetry in Spain and Sicily.[8]

[4] cf. the striking appreciation of von Hammer's scientific motivation in his *Chalef elahmar's Qasside*, Greifswald, 1859, pp. 6-8, introducing a monograph which is devoted to the demolition of von Hammer's scholarly reputation.

[5] cf. his *Ueber Poesie und Poetik der Araber*, Gotha, 1856, p. 68: the ideas of the Arab critics may show "dass, recht verstanden, bei aller Fremdartigkeit der Sprachbildung und der Sachbilder, dennoch in allen Zungen immerdar nur Eine Poesie erklungen sei."

[6] Pioneers of this approach were A. P. Caussin de Perceval (1795-1871), whose *Essai sur l'histoire des Arabes avant l'Islamisme, pendant l'époque de Mahomet, et jusqu'à la réduction de toutes les tribus sous la loi musulmane*, 3 vols., Paris, 1847-1848, labors from a misunderstanding of the evidentiary character of the poems and the prose account within which they appear, and Theodor Nöldeke (1836-1930).

[7] Characteristically represented by J. Wellhausen (1844-1918), *Reste altarabischen Heidentums*, Berlin, 1887, 2nd ed., 1897, and G. Jacob (1862-1937), *Altarabisches Beduinenleben*, 2nd ed., Berlin, 1897, much improved over 1st ed., 1895.

[8] *Poesie und Kunst der Araber in Spanien und Sizilien*, Berlin, 1865.

Schack tells his tale for the sake of both the beauty of this poetry and its historical significance as a mirror of Western-Arab mentality.[9] A prisoner of his universalism and of his lack of emotional immediacy, he was aware of change but hardly of development. Drawing mostly on the reflection of Spanish-Arab civilization in the work of al-Maqqari (d. 1632) that had been composed after the expulsion of the Moors from Spain as a repository of past glories, Schack's glowing descriptions of life in Cordoba and Granada sometimes appear at two removes from reality.

Philological conscientiousness enabled Ahlwardt,[10] and intuition enabled A. von Kremer (1828-1889),[11] to limn the first valid sketches of the total development of Arabic poetry. But neither Ahlwardt's experience nor Kremer's vision could fill in the gaps of information that still existed particularly with regard to the 'Abbāsid period (750-1258). Unfortunately, neither Ahlwardt nor Kremer followed up their sketches. Indeed, Ahlwardt's later concentration on the cataloguing of the Berlin Arabic manuscripts curiously parallels Th. Nöldeke's change of heart concerning the artistic value of ancient Arabic poetry: where, in 1864, Nöldeke had been impressed with its finesse and richness of expression, in 1899 he had come to wonder if it would *ever* repay the labors of investigation in terms of aesthetic pleasure. He had gradually come to view it as a means of penetrating into the character of the Arabs rather than as a source of enjoyment.[12]

It was only at the end of the century that C. Brockelmann (1868—) laid the foundation for a new and fully scientific start in literary research by publishing his *Geschichte der arabischen Litteratur* (Weimar, 1898-1902)—a well-organized *catalogus catalogorum* of extant literature. Brockelmann did not wish to go beyond the "äussere Geschichte,"[13] as the state of research did not as yet allow a tracing of the internal development except for some limited areas. In 1937, upon the appearance of his *Supplement*

[9] cf. 3rd ed., Stuttgart, 1877, I, vii-viii.

[10] *Poesie, passim.*

[11] *Culturgeschichte des Orients unter den Chalifen,* Vienna, 1875, II, 341-95.

[12] Contrast *Beiträge zur Kenntnis der Poesie der alten Araber* (Hanover, 1864), Introduction, esp. pp. xxiii-xxiv, with *Sitzungsberichte der Akademie der Wissenschaften,* (*SBAW*), phil.-hist. Cl., cxl, 1899, Abh. 7, p. 1.

[13] Preface of vol. I, p. iii.

(Leiden, 1937-42),[14] Brockelmann reiterated his position and declared that his book was meant solely to provide the biographical and bibliographical material for a study of Arabic literature in the modern sense—whatever interpretation a future generation might place on the nature of such a task.[15] Seen in a larger context, Brockelmann did for Arabic literature what H. Ethé (1844-1917) did for Persian[16] and K. Krumbacher (1856-1909) for Byzantine literature.[17]

On the basis of the immense information which Brockelmann himself had made accessible, a number of scholars including Brockelmann himself undertook to present the history of Arabic literature in readable form, perhaps the most successful being R. A. Nicholson (1868-1945).[18] In the preface to his work, which is distinguished by the author's taste for verbal beauty and his accurate but unostentatious erudition, Nicholson well describes the outlook on our studies of his time. "To write a critical account of Arabic literature was out of the question. Brockelmann's invaluable work is confined to biography and bibliography, and does not deal with the historical development of ideas. This, however, seems to me the really vital aspect of literary history. It has been my chief aim to sketch in broad outlines what the Arabs thought, and to indicate as far as possible the influences which molded their thought."[19] Actually Nicholson devotes as much attention to the cultural setting as to literature proper, and it is but the charm and ease of his presentation that makes one forget the peripheral position among his interests of aesthetic inquiry.

[14] G. Graf (1875-   ) has supplemented Brockelmann's work with his *Geschichte der christlichen arabischen Literatur*, 2 vols.; Città del Vaticano, 1944-1947.

[15] *Supplement*, 1, Preface, pp. 2-3.

[16] Neupersische Literatur; in *Grundriss der iranischen Philologie*, Strassburg, 1896-1904, II, 212-368.

[17] *Geschichte der byzantinischen Literatur*, Munich, 1891. The impulse for this type of work had come from classical philology with the publication of I. von Müller's (1830-1917) *Handbuch der klassischen Altertumswissenschaft*, Nördlingen and Munich, 1855 ff., which contained as two of its sections W. Christ (1831-1906), *Geschichte der griechischen Literatur bis auf die Zeit Justinians*, Munich, 1888, and M. Schanz (1842-1914), *Römische Literaturgeschichte*, Munich, 1890-1904. F. Susemihl (1826-1901), *Geschichte der griechischen Literatur in der Alexandrinerzeit*, Leipzig, 1891-1892, too, typifies this stage of research.

[18] *A Literary History of the Arabs*, London, 1907.

[19] Preface, p. ix. Brockelmann himself offered a rather attractive presentation of the material for the general reader in his *Geschichte der arabischen Litteratur*, Leipzig, 1901, published as vol. 6 of the series, *Die Litteraturen des Ostens in Einzeldarstellungen*.

Somewhat removed from the main line of development, the study of the formal means at the disposal of the Arabic poet had begun rather early with G. W. Freytag's (1788-1861) *Darstellung der arabischen Verskunst* (Bonn, 1830) and A. F. von Mehren's (1822-1907) excellent book on *Die Rhetorik der Araber*, Copenhagen and Vienna, 1853. It is characteristic for the source material known to the period that Mehren as well as Garcin de Tassy (1794-1878)[20] and, in the Persian field, F. Rückert (1788-1866)[21] and W. Pertsch (1832-1899)[22] had to base their presentation on relatively late authorities; it is equally characteristic for the prevailing outlook on the "Muslim" literatures that the picture drawn was completely static, any development of literary theory not being seriously investigated. It is true that the earlier Arab theorists are difficult to approach and that much of their doctrine has come to us in a disjointed fashion, but Ahlwardt had already realized, from al-Suyūṭi's (d. 1505) philological encyclopedia, *Al-Muzhir fī 'Ulūm al-Lughah*, the fact and the general direction of the evolution that had taken place in Arabic thought on literature. Speculations on the origin of the Arabic meters were indulged in, and it is from the study of post-classical prosodical developments that M. Hartmann (1851-1918) first came to shed light on the sequence of poetical forms.[23] The considerable heuristic value of prosodical investigation was to be demonstrated later, especially by J. Ribera (1858-1934), A. R. Nykl (1885—), and R. Menéndez Pidal (1869—) in their analyses of Spanish-Arabic forms and their influence on the songs of the Provençal troubadours.[24] But the empirical history of Arabic (and Persian) prosody remains to be written.[25]

---

[20] *Rhétorique et prosodie des langues de l'Orient musulman*, Paris, 1873.

[21] In *Wiener Jahrbücher*, XL-XLIV, 1827-28.

[22] Rückert-Pertsch, *Grammatik, Poetik und Rhetorik der Perser*, Gotha, 1874. E. J. W. Gibb's (1857-1901) introductory chapters to his *History of Ottoman Poetry*, London, 1900-1909, should be compared.

[23] *Das arabische Strophengedicht I. Das Muwaššaḥ*, Weimar, 1897.

[24] J. Ribera, *El cancionero de Abencuzmán*, 1912, now in *Disertaciones y opúsculos*, Madrid, 1928, 1, 3-92; A. R. Nykl, *El cancionero del šeih . . . Aben Guzman (Ibn Quzmān)*, Madrid, 1933; R. Menéndez Pidal, "Poesía araba y poesía europea," *Bulletin Hispanique*, XL, 1938, 387-423, and enlarged as a book under the same title, Madrid, 1941. (See also O. J. Tallgren-Tuulio, 1878-1941, *Ibn Quzman. Edition critique partielle et provisoire*, Helsinki, 1941.)

[25] Recently, R. Brunschvig, *La versification arabe classique* (Algiers, 1937; reprinted from *Revue Africaine*, 1937), restated, and A. Bloch, *Vers und Sprache im Altarabischen*, Basel, 1946, attempted to reinterpret the principles of Arabic prosody.

Arabic like classical poetry is highly kind-conscious, each kind being developed in accord with its own conventions of form and content. It would seem that I. Goldziher (1850-1921) was the first to realize that investigation of the individual kinds would have to precede any comprehensive presentation. In his studies on the *hijā'*, lampoon,[26] and the elegy[27] he provided models of approach and method. N. Rhodokanakis (1876-1945), using Goldziher's conclusions, subtilized his method so as to separate out the poet's individual contribution from traditional requirement. His work on al-Khansā' (fl. ca. 620) was probably the first analytical study of the individuality of an Arabic poet.[28] Ilse Lichtenstadter transferred Goldziher's and Rhodokanakis' method from the kinds to the stereotyped parts of the ode when she discussed its amatory prelude.[29]

Even before the methodological advance which Rhodokanakis' study represents, the contribution of the individual poet had come to be the object of monographic research with biography generally the center of attention. Thus, after von Kremer's abu-al-'Alā' al-Ma'arri (973-1058),[30] H. Lammens (1862-1937) had depicted al-Akhṭal's (d. 710) life and times.[31] P. Schwarz (1867-1939) followed suit with his work on 'Umar ibn-abi Rabī 'ah (d. 719)—an especially well-balanced presentation that considers language and style of the poet (and his contemporaries) no less than his biography and the circumstances of his period.[32] I. Kratchkovsky (1883—) in his al-Wa'wā' al-Dimashqi (d. 970-980), published in

---

[26] *Abhandlungen zur arabischen Philologie*, Leiden, 1896-1899, I, 1-105.

[27] *Wiener Zeitschrift für die Kunde der Morgenlandes*, XVI, 1902, 307-339.

A new impulse was given to these studies by the researches of A. Denomy, especially "An Enquiry into the origins of Courtly Love," *Mediaeval Studies*, VI, 1944, 175-260, and "*Fin amors*: the pure love of the troubadours, its amorality and possible source," *ibid.*, VII, 1945, 139-207, in which the author studies the significance of Avicenna's (d. 1037) *Treatise on Love* (trans. E. L. Fackenheim, *Mediaeval Studies*, VII, 208-28) for the formation of the concept of Courtly Love. Th. Silverstein, *Modern Philology*, XLVII, 1949, 117-26, has contributed a suggestive *mise au point*. In *Mediaeval Studies*, XI, 1949, 1-22, A. Denomy connects the troubadour notion of *jovens*, youth, with *futuwwah*.

[28] "Al-Ḥansā' und ihre Trauerlieder," *SBAW*, phil.-hist. Cl., CXVII (1907), Abh. 4.

[29] "Das Nasīb der altarabischen Qaṣīde," *Islamica*, v, 1932, 17-96.

[30] "Ueber die philosophischen Gedichte des Abul'alā Ma'arry. Eine culturgeschichtliche Studie," *SBAW*, phil.-hist. Cl., CXVII, 1889, Abh. 6 (originally presented in 1888).

[31] "Le chantre des Omiades," *Journal Asiatique*, 9th ser., vol. 4, 1894, 94-176, 193-241, 381-459.

[32] *Der Diwan des 'Umar b. ar-Rebi'a*, Leipzig, 1902-1909, pt. IV, 1909.

Recently A. Bloch has reexamined the problem of the *qaṣīdah* in *Asiatische Studien*, II, 1949, 106-32.

Petrograd in 1914, first put to use systematically a poet's choice of meter as a criterion of his school affiliation. The biographical study, usually joined to the reconstitution of the poet's work, has been continued and perfected by F. Gabrieli (1904—),[33] M. Nallino,[34] R. Blachère (1900—),[35] et al.

In the selection of subject matter, scholarly interest has been shifting from the classical to the post-classical periods in a more or less conscious effort to remedy that lack of familiarity with the poetry of the Islamic epoch that marred even M. J. de Goeje's (1836-1909) *Die arabische Literatur*.[36] Now A. Mez (1869-1917) devoted a scintillating chapter of his *Die Renaissance des Islams* to ninth and tenth century poetry,[37] and O. Rescher (1883—),[38] and most recently J. M. Abd-al-Jalil (1904—)[39] have been able to give special attention to that erstwhile neglected period.[40]

What the neo-humanism of the 1920's and 1930's added to the approach of scholars like Goldziher or Rhodokanakis was primarily a more self-conscious concern with the study of Arabic literature as an autonomous entity, autonomous that is, in the sense that its essence and growth, its aspirations and failings were to be understood from its function within the pre-Islamic and Islamic civilizations, and approached above all for the sake of reaching out to its *Eigenbegrifflichkeit*.[41] Research during the

[33] "Al-Walīd ibn Yazīd, il califfo e il poeta," *Rivista degli Studi Orientali* (*RSO*), xv, 1935, 1-64; Gamīl al-'Uḏri, studio critico e raccolta dei frammenti, *RSO*, xvii, 1938, 40-71, 133-172.

[34] "An-Nābijah al-Ġa'dī e le sue poesie," *RSO*, xiv, 1934, 135-190, 380-432.

[35] *Un poète arabe du IVe siècle . . . Abou 't-Tayyib al-Motanabbi essai d'histoire littéraire*, Paris, 1936. Blachère and M. Canard have been particularly successful in extracting historical information from topical verse. Nicholson's studies on ibn-al-Fāriḍ (d. 1240), *Studies in Islamic Mysticism*, Cambridge, 1921, pp. 162-226, and abu-al-'Alā' al-Ma'arri, *Studies in Islamic Poetry*, Cambridge, 1921, pp. 49-289, must be mentioned although, strictly speaking, they do not offer biographies.

[36] In *Die Kultur der Gegenwart*, ed. P. Hinneberg, Teil I, Abt. vii: Die orientalischen Literaturen, Berlin-Leipzig, 1906, pp. 132-159. It is, however, de Goeje's great merit to have indicated the importance of sociological considerations in his discussion of abu-Nuwās (d. 810) and abu-al-'Atāhiyah (d. 828), *op. cit.*, pp. 138-39.

[37] Heidelberg, 1922, pp. 244-64, English edition, London, 1937, pp. 254-74.

[38] *Abriss der arabischen Litteraturgeschichte*, Stuttgart, 1925-33.

[39] *Brève historie de la littérature arabe*, Paris, 1943.

[40] cf. Abd-al-Jalil's "plan général" as outlined on p. 8. The excellent presentation of Arabic belles-lettres in the *Enciclopedia Italiana*, iii, 1929, 842-65, by M. Guidi (1886-1946) also assigns commensurate space to post-classical poetry as does H. A. R. Gibb's (1895-) brief but penetrating *Arabic Literature: an Introduction*, London, 1926.

[41] To use B. Landsberger's apt term, *Islamica*, ii, 1927, 355.

past twenty-five years has been marked by increased methodological variety—economic and social factors having at long last
begun to be taken into consideration.[42]

But of much greater significance was the final abandonment
of the static conception of classical poetry. Subtler techniques of
analysis and a fuller realization of the selective conventions of pre-
Islamic literature[43] led to the establishment of schools[44] and the
tracing of generation-by-generation progress in certain sections of
the preserved material.[45] More important still, it became possible
to investigate the Arab (and Persian) outlook on poetry in its
evolution over the centuries. Goldziher had taken the first step.[46]
Now Kratchkovsky's studies on poetics[47] were followed by H.
Ritter's (1892—) masterpiece, *Ueber die Bildersprache Niẓāmīs*
(Berlin and Leipzig, 1927) where Arabic and Persian *Kunstwollen*
are convincingly contrasted. H. Pérès pictured the different attitudes toward poetry obtaining in Arab Spain as against the Arab
East and the literary relations between the two parts of the Arab
world on the basis of a thorough knowledge of native theory and
critical opinion.[48] Finally, the rationale of Arabic criticism was
recognized as a problem.[49]

[42] e.g. in H. A. R. Gibb's "Studies in Contemporary Arabic Literature," *London
University Bulletin of School of Oriental Studies*, IV, 1926-1928, 745-760; V, 1928-1930,
311-22, 445-466; VII, 1933-1935, 1-22.

[43] G. E. von Grunebaum, *Die Wirklichkeitweite der früharabischen Dichtung*, Vienna,
1937.

[44] Von Grunebaum, "Zur Chronologie der früharabischen Dichtung," *Orientalia*, n.s.
VIII, 1939, 328-345.

It is to be regretted that C. A. Nallino (1872-1938) never developed his Cairo lectures of 1910-1911 into a complete history of Arabic literature. These lectures, with
their magisterial chapter on the history of the term *adab*, were translated from the
original Arabic into Italian by Maria Nallino and published in the *Raccolta di Scritti
editi e inediti*, Rome, 1939-1948, VI, 1-174, under the title "La letteratura araba dagli
inizi all'epoca della dinastia umayyade."

[45] E. Bräunlich (1892-1945), "Versuch einer literaturgeschichtlichen Betrachtungs-
weise altarabischer Poesien," *Islam*, XXIV, 1937, 201-69.

E. García Gómez (1905-   ), "Convencionalismo e insinceridad de la poesía árabe,"
Al-Andalus, V, 1940, 31-43, marks an important step in this direction.

[46] "Alte und neue Poesie im Urtheile der arabischen Kritiker," *Abh. z. arab. Philologie*,
I, 122-74.

[47] From 1910. Not in Russian are notably "Die arabische Poetik im 9. Jahrhundert,"
MO, XXIII, 1929, 23-39, and the edition of ibn-al-Mu'tazz (d. 908), *Kitāb ab-badī'*, London, 1935, with an important introduction.

[48] *La poésie andalouse en arabe classique au XIe siècle* (Paris, 1927).

[49] Von Grunebaum, "Arabic Literary Criticism in the 10th Century A.D.," *JAOS*, LXI
(1941), 51-57.

The advance in factual information about, and comprehension of, Arabic thought concerning literature is brought home by M. Gaudefroy-Demombynes' (1862—) commentary on Ibn Qutaybah's (d. 889) *Book of Poets*.[50] The quest for *Eigenbegrifflichkeit* assisted by the new familiarity with Arabic theory led to the study of fundamental value judgments such as those underlying the universal conflict of plagiarism and originality.[51]

But beyond its comprehension as an autonomous phenomenon the integrating force of Arabic literature had to be assessed; in other words, the cultural influences that went into its making compelled investigation. Beginnings have been made to analyze the Greek and the Persian contributions,[52] but almost everything remains to be done. The companion enquiry into the influence exercised by Arabic poetry on that of other peoples has been less neglected—the problem of troubadour lyrics stimulating a great deal of effort. At first not infrequently paralyzed by insufficient equipment these endeavors have lately yielded valuable results.[53] U. M. Daudpota's *The Influence of Arabic Poetry on the Development of Persian Poetry* (Bombay, 1934) has not been followed up.

However divergent the immediate scope of the preliminary steps inaugurated by the neo-humanistic attitude—preliminary that is to the goal of an adequate history of Arab belles-lettres—the pri-

[50] *Ibn Qotaiba, Introduction au Livre de la poésie et des poètes*, Paris, 1947. Cf. also the recent translation by Von Grunebaum of the sections on poetry of al-Bāqillāni's (d. 1013) *I'jāz al-Qur'ān* under the title *A Tenth Century Document of Arabic Literary Theory and Criticism*, Chicago, 1950.

[51] Von Grunebaum, "The Concept of Plagiarism in Arabic Theory," *Journal of Near Eastern Studies*, III, 1944, 234-253.

[52] cf. J. Tkatsch (1871-1927), *Die arabische Uebersetzung der Poetik des Aristoteles*, ed. by Th. Seif (1894-1939), Vienna-Leipzig, 1928-1932; F. Gabrieli, "Estetica e poesia araba nell' interpretazione della *Poetica* Aristotelica presso Avicenna e Averroè," *RSO*, XII, 1929-1930, 291-331; Von Grunebaum, "Greek Form Elements in the Arabian Nights," *JAOS*, LXII, 1924, 277-92; "Observations on City Panegyrics," *ibid.*, LXIV, 1944, 61-65; *Medieval Islam*, Chicago, 1946, esp. chs. 9, 10. For the Persian element cf. e.g. F. Gabrieli's study on ibn-al-Muqaffa' (d. 757), *RSO*, XIII, 1931-1932, 197-247, and G. Richter, *Studien zur Geschichte der älteren arabischen Fürstenspiegel*, Leipzig, 1932.

[53] cf. A. R. Nykl's translation of ibn-Ḥazm (d. 1064), *The Dove's Neck-Ring*, Paris, 1931, Introduction, pp. lxi-cxx; the same author's *Hispano-Arabic Poetry and Its Relation with the Old Provençal Troubadours*, Baltimore, 1946; H. A. R. Gibb in *The Legacy of Islam*, ed. Sir Th. W. Arnold and A. Guillaume, Oxford, 1921, pp. 180-209; J. Hell (1875-1950), *Die arabische Dichtung im Rahmen der Weltliteratur*, Erlangen, 1927; F. Gabrieli, *La poesia araba e la poesia occidentale*, Rome, 1943, reprinted in *Storia e civiltà musulmana*, Rome, 1947, pp. 64-82.

macy of the aesthetic interest in the literary material appears as their common denominator. We have learned to use poetical documents effectively as evidence in historical, geographical, and similar disquisitions, but we no longer confuse studies of this kind with the history of literature. None of the approaches achieved by the labors of a century has as yet been brought to full fruition and our published material is still regrettably defective, but already we are forced by the logic of our work at least to envisage one further step: the systematic coordination of literary phenomena and intellectual history. It is important to note that it was the Mu'tazila that through Bishr ibn-al-Mu'tamir (d. 825) produced the philosophical poem, a form not taken up by other coteries; or that the allegorical fable was cultivated by the Ikhwān al-Ṣafā' (10th and 11th centuries) but abandoned when they left the scene. Yet stray observations of this type are necessarily of limited value, and it must finally be realized how unfamiliar we still are with the literary ideas and attitudes of sectarian circles.

II

All of the studies that have been considered need to be continued. None can be dispensed with if ever we are to attain our aim. But before their results can be meaningfully coordinated it will be necessary to explore the fundamental concepts which the bearers of Muslim civilization formed of the nature of literary creation and of his own literary creativeness. It is these concepts which, in the last analysis, will be seen to inform the theory of literature and, be it through this theory or more immediately, its practice as well.

These basic concepts, then, which direct and confine Arab literary endeavor in the Middle Ages, can be most conveniently described in the form of two hypotheses, the one concerned with the role of imagination, the other with the relation of content and form.

Generally speaking, medieval Muslim thought never abandoned Aristotelian psychology, which assigns imagination a comparatively low place, ranking it with the animal faculties. Theological considerations confirmed this low estimate of man's creative abilities. Aristotle's appreciation of reason, which the Muslims shared not without some uneasiness, while stimulating the intellectual effort of subsequent ages, was likely to result in profound distrust of the irresponsible outpourings of the poet;[54] ages of reason have never been times of superb artistic accomplishment as witness the low of European poetry after Descartes's ideas had taken effect in the early half of the Era of Enlightenment. Conversely, it may be added, the more encouraging view taken by mysticism of man's ability to rise above himself and to articulate his supreme emotion in his own symbols and images may be in part responsible for the continuance of mystical poetry as a growing form of self-expression when the creative impulse in the other branches of Arabic literature had long been fading.

With worthwhile insights vouchsafed by revelation or, within limits, worked out by ratiocination on the basis of objective data, and with that pessimistic view of human creativeness reinforced by restriction of divine inspiration to the prophetic office and the denial of authority to Nature, invention as such, as well as ever widening self-expression, is ruled out as the purpose of literature. Beyond its role as the archive (*dīwān*) of the community, it is allotted the twin functions of instruction and delight or, as the Prophet is supposed to have put it in two variants of the same saying, enchantment (*siḥr*) and (the conveying of) wisdom (*ḥikmah*). And it would appear that, in the minds of the theorists at least, the pleasurable function gradually came to outweigh the instructional.

In Islam, as in the West, poetry had to be defended against moral objections. Sir Philip Sidney unwittingly refutes the same charges —that poetry is nothing but lies and that it is the mother of abuse— with which its Arab champions contend rather successfully. Distrust of invention had its corollary in faith in tradition. Tradition is crystallized in rules governing scope and means of expression. For the most part the critic would like to see originality, which is prized, confined to elaboration and modification of prefigured patterns, with the poet's vocabulary as neatly delimited by authority as his motives and the prosodical forms at his disposal. It is significant to find *ikhtirāʿ*, invention, listed among *Sinnfiguren*

---

[54] The incompatibility of reason and poetry was neatly stated by Saint-Evremond (d. 1703); cf. R. Bray, *La formation de la doctrine classique en France*, Lausanne, etc., 1927, p. 121.

by ibn-Qayyim al-Jawzīyah (d. 1350), where it is assigned but an undistinguished thirty-first place (out of eighty-four).[55]

The minor part conceded to personal creativeness or superhuman inspiration in the genesis of the literary work of art leads to elaborate provisions for the training of the poet, who is expected to be a learned man in control of the whole fund of contemporary knowledge. It is not enough that he should be familiar with the traditional rules and conventions of his craft, ṣinā'ah, techne, ars, which the public is fond of calling a science; his is to be a comprehensive and highly bookish sort of erudition, for his work will be judged on its factual as well as its formal correctness. This emphasis on the writer's learning the Arabs share with the Alexandrians, the humanists of the Renaissance and their heirs, the classicists of the sixteenth and seventeenth centuries. It is extremely significant that this emphasis weakens in Europe and even comes to be combatted as pedantic in proportion as the role of imagination in literary production is realized, faith in human creativeness grows, and writing is valued for its psychological expressiveness.

The kind of beauty which is loved and enjoyed is determined by the second hypothesis, again Aristotelian in the basic approach it embodies. This is the view that form is an entity by itself which is somewhat arbitrarily joined to the content and that the element of beauty which lends more pleasure to one and whose absence detracts pleasure from another passage consists in "something additional superimposed upon the canvas of ordinary speech like an embroidery."[56] In other words, beauty is an ornament added at will to the treatment of a given motif. Practically all Arabic literary theory is predicated on this conviction. The subject matter, the individual ma'āni, severely limited per se, may be presented in different ways; al-Qazwīni (d. 1338), for instance, defines the 'ilm al-balāgha as the science teaching those several methods which are primarily distinguished according as they do or do not employ figures of speech, tropes, and the like.

This outlook on the basic relation of form and content, this mechanistic idea of beauty added from the outside by the applica-

---

[55] Fawā'id, Cairo, 1327/1909, pp. 156-157.
[56] B. Croce, Aesthetic, trans. D. Ainslie, 2nd ed., London, 1929, p. 427. Cf. the Arabic idea of the taḥbir; e.g. Goldziher, Abh. z. arab. Philologie, I, 129-132.

tion of a certain number of technical devices, leads to the defining of originality as the improved rendition of traditional motifs and of literary progress as the sequence of such improved renditions. The obvious consequence is a steady rise of both subtleness and ornateness of presentation. The latecomer discovers hidden relations between the elements of the motif, he notes unused possibilities for pointing it up, and he tends to evoke in the hearer or reader that pleasure which we derive from the dispelling of obscurity and the apprehension of unsuspected conceptual affinities—a pleasure noted by Aristotle and Arab theorists[57] in their discussion of the metaphor, which both to Aristotle and to the Arabs is "the queen of ornaments."[58]

Thus the author will aim at surprise, 'ajab, the extraordinary, nādir, and the unusual and strange, gharīb.[59] When some authorities go so far as to explain the Koran's uniqueness by its gharābah and so put the stamp of the highest approval on it, while others voice their disapprobation of the gharīb as unconventional and forced, the ambivalence of the term well reflects the conflict of some of the implications of the two hypotheses that otherwise supplement and reinforce each other effectively. This conflict arises when the first imposes adherence to the traditional treatment of traditional matter, while the other makes the unusual treatment of the traditional the only outlet of the poet's originality and almost the only justification of his efforts.

The same development is encountered in European secentismo, so well described by Toffanin as a "perfezionamento dell'Aristotelismo,"[60] whose instrument (acutezza) and whose result (concettismo), used and evolved in the service of the same fundamental hypothesis regarding form and content, are devoted to evincing that same feeling of wonderment and surprise (maraviglia) which the Arab author of the later periods strives to provoke. And once more it is an Aristotelian precept, the protophilosopher's call for

[57] Aristotle, Rhetoric III: 10; Fawā'id, p. 80.

[58] In Croce's phrase, op. cit., p. 427.

[59] Seventeenth century writers, like the Arabs, consider as "marvelous" anything which evokes admiration through surprise, including, to quote Chapelain, Préface à l'Adonis (1623), "la richesse du langage" (quoted by Bray, op. cit., p. 231).

[60] cf. G. Toffanin, La Fine dell'umanesimo, Turin, 1921, and A. Belloni, Il Seicento, Milan, 1929, p. 594. F. Gabrieli, La poesia araba e la letterature occidentale, p. 6, says of 'Abbāsid poetry: "È il secentismo avanti lettera, che lentamente ammorba e disfà quest' arte preziosa."

an element of the marvelous in tragic and even more so in epic production,[61] which is stretched to yield the theoretical justification.[62]

Wherever—East or West—the second hypothesis was accepted, the same effects are noticeable throughout the period of its dominion.[63] Not only does *secentismo* appear in Christian writers of the fifth and sixth centuries, to reappear again and again in the Middle Ages, but the very conceits at which Arabic and Persian writers arrive are not infrequently duplicated or near-duplicated by European authors of the seventeenth century. It is instructive to compare, for instance, the imagery resorted to by Niẓāmi (d. 1202-3) and by G. B. Basile (d. 1625) in his *Pentamerone*, to depict sunrise and sunset. And similar parallels of Eastern and Western *concetti*, especially in description, could easily be listed at considerable length.

To distill from the Arabic literary achievement the guiding aesthetic assumptions is not to deny the efficacy of other elements acting as contributory causes and confirming or weakening certain implications of the principal trends.

The two hypotheses were well-integrated parts of that general medieval outlook on the world as a static entity whose individual elements obtained their rank and value from their immutable position within the whole which made everything at the same time a constituent and a result of the all-pervading harmony of the universe. There is a cosmic significance in each thing's being thus and no other; willful change upsets and is likely to debase the over-all pattern of unity. This feeling constitutes literary forms or kinds as entities with a life of their own beyond their representation in the individual work and invests their preservation with a certain ethical value. All other motivations of traditionalism, philosophical and psychological, not only strengthen the regard for established form but find in it an embodiment of stability and correctness, as convenient as it is apt.

The failure of Platonism to enter the main stream of Muslim

---

[61] *Poetics* xxiv: 15 (1460a).

[62] Paolo Beni, *Commentarii in Aristotelis Poeticam*, Padova, 1613, p. 4, excellently expounds the theory of ornate poetry as it would be applicable alike to secentistic, late Arabic, or any other concettistic literature. The passage is quoted by Toffanin, *op. cit.*, pp. 235-236.

[63] Under certain conditions, that is: see end of this chapter.

thought is largely responsible for the undisturbed longevity of the two hypotheses. For the last fifteen centuries every revival of the belief in human creativeness, every upsurge of lyrical self-expression or of "romanticism," has almost invariably been wedded to a resurgence of Platonism in some form or other. Arabic and Persian mysticism, permeated to a considerable extent by Neo-Platonic ideas and attitudes, preserved through its belief in man's divine potentialities the artistic productivity of its adepts, providing them at the same time with an overwhelming experience as incentive and theme of self-expression.

The classical critics of the decadent ages as well as the critics opposed to the brilliant inanities of *secentismo* were frustrated in their fight against the playful cleverness of the *concettisti* because they, too, adhered to the theory that had induced the taste they would not share. The Arab critic found himself in the same position. His frequent protests against the excesses of ornamentation, against the aberrations of taste displayed so blatantly even by the best of poets, and against empty verbosity in general[64] were doomed to ineffectiveness as long as he accepted the idea of beauty as an addition from outside, of excellence in style as a plus or minus of varnish applicable to each and every motive, and of lexicological and structural conformity as the primary criterion of the acceptability of a literary product. The helplessness of the theorist in dealing with the original and again the distortion of the notion of originality are well illustrated by the discussion of *mukhālafah*, deviation from traditional motive treatment, as a *Wortfigur*.[65] It is well to note that the Arabs never analyzed the concept of the

---

[64] Al-Khafāji (wrote 1062), *Sirr al-Faṣāḥah*, Cairo, 1932, p. 180, ibn-Khaldūn (d. 1406), *Prolegomena*, ed. Quatremère, Paris, 1858, III, 356 (trans. De Slane, Paris, 1862-1868, III, 399), and others compare the "ornaments" to moles which in small numbers heighten, in large detract from, the beauty of a woman's face. F. Minozzi, *Sfogamenti d'Ingegno* (1641), quoted by C. Trabalza, *La Critica letteraria, secoli XV-XVII*, Milan, 1915, p. 316, uses the same comparison in his argument against the exaggerated use of the *bisticcio*.

[65] *Fawā'id*, p. 233. The fine sense of individual differences between the poets' work *bi-ḥasab ikhtilāf al-tabā'i'*, according to their differences of character, as displayed especially in the ninth and tenth centuries, did not result in literary individualism. The sentiment voiced by critics of this period reminds one of Agostino Mascardi's (1590-1640) fight for the acceptance of the concept of individual style in the Fourth Tractate of his *Dell'arte istorica*, Venice, 1674, pp. 322-95. The passage has been referred to frequently; e.g. by Croce in *La Critica*, XXV, 1927, 9-10, and *Storia della età barocca in Italia*, Bari, 1929, pp. 172-174.

beautiful in literature—in other words, that they never attempted to develop an aesthetic. The sociological fact that criticism, besides being largely inspired by grammatical considerations, actually was for the most part in the hands of grammarians confirmed the paramount position of the concept of correctness in the judging of literature, a concept which is in perfect harmony with the two fundamental hypotheses and the world view within which they retained their authority.

The flowering of Arabic poetry in the ninth and tenth centuries, which molded its style and scope for centuries to come, coincides with the great changes in the industrial and financial structure of the Empire which followed in the wake of, and in part were accompanied by, the change from the patrimonial state of the Umayyads to the "rational" state of the 'Abbāsids (a change, incidentally, which seems to have begun a short time before the accession of the new dynasty). The new state which was to be administered by trained and more or less permanent officials needed literary men to staff the chancelleries. The *kātib* who found himself employed in articulating governmental policies imbued the conduct of state business with a distinct literary flavor. An ornate style of increasing elaboration came to be expected and appreciated in important documents. The *kātib* was an essential part of the machinery of the "rational" state and indispensable to the government as its eloquent voice.

The *kātib*, who was frequently of what might be called bourgeois extraction, had a considerable share in current poetical production. His participation was doubtless an influential factor in the rhetorization of Arabic belles-lettres. In fostering a prosy and oratorical kind of poetry, the *kātib's* contribution closely parallels that of the European humanist, who, too, owed much of his cultural influence and his rise as a member of a class to his indispensability to the emerging rational state in setting up and managing its chancelleries. There is this difference, though, between the *kuttāb* and the humanists—individual *kuttāb* were sometimes guilty of heterodoxy, but as a class they did not back a concerted effort to change the philosophical outlook of their times, whereas the humanists labored to replace church authority by the authority of classical antiquity. The poverty of the classical Arabic, that is, the pre-Islamic heritage when contrasted with that left the humanists by the Greco-Roman age, counts for much in explaining the very moderate inspiration to be derived from that complete return to it which the critics appear to have favored. The disturbing and stimulating effects of the influx of the Hellenic tradition on the Muslim world of the ninth and tenth and the Italian of the fourteenth and fifteenth centuries are clearly comparable phenomena. But in Europe humanism, buttressed by the awakening of science and the renewal of the autonomy of the individual conscience through the Reformation, remained; the Renaissance never passed completely; whereas in Islam, Renaissance—not as renewal of an ancient and supposedly ancestral tradition but as upsurge of humanism, the Greek tradition, the scientific impulse, the historical sentiment, the cultivation of reason over against authority—was short-lived and followed by a period of "medievalism" that exhibited all the traits we are accustomed to associate with the term, among them, of course, traditionalism in literature.

The very refinement of the sensibilities which is as characteristic of the early 'Abbāsid period as of the Baroque Age in Europe, contributed, here as there, to concentration on a purely verbal achievement in literature. Variation of identical themes, indulgence in word-bound rather than visionary imagery, clinging to rules and patterns, surrender to wit—this is the fate growing out of its fundamental structure that overtook Arab belles-lettres as soon as the creative impulse of that spectacular period toward the close of the millennium subsided. Once reason was subjected, foreign traditions brought under control, and the historical sense with its compelling interest in man allowed to wane, there remained but mysticism to threaten the stability of the intellectual scene and to delay the premature withering of Arabic literature.

In the West, science and philosophy, by transforming the static world into one of dynamic motion, forced man to reexamine his position in the universe and to reexamine himself, too. Astronomical anthropocentrism gave way to psychological; consciousness replaced being as the focal problem of philosophy. In this process of reinterpretation, new experiences, new insights into himself, were vouchsafed man. Redefining the universe, he realized his creativeness; groping for a new orientation, he realized a new need for self-expression and new contents to be expressed in new forms. It is fundamentally this psychological experience which in the later part of the eighteenth century reestablished great lyrical poetry in the West; it is its absence in medieval Islam which, in the last analysis, prevented the Arabs from recovering their literary creativeness.[66]

[66] With the obvious modifications, this diagnosis would seem to apply to the withering of pagan Latin poetry in the early centuries of our era as well. Cf. C. N. Cochrane's observations on Seneca's *Moral Essays and Letters* in his *Christianity and Classical Culture*, London, etc., 1944, p. 149.

4

ISLAMIC LITERATURE: PERSIAN

BY ARTHUR J. ARBERRY

It is proposed for the purpose of this essay to define Persian literature as meaning the poetry and prose written in the Persian (Neo-
Persian) language since the Arab conquest in the seventh century A.D., principally in Persia itself but also in the neighboring
Muslim territories, especially of India and Turkey. By this definition the literature is almost exclusively Islamic in character and
inspiration, and writings based on other religions, as well as books
composed by Persians in languages other than Persian, are excluded from the survey.[1] In the recommendations which conclude
the essay nothing is said about pure philology or language-study
in isolation from literature.

Western knowledge of the Islamic literature of Persia dates
back to the first trading missions of the sixteenth century conducted by such men as Anthony Jenkinson, Arthur Edwards, and
the famous Sherley brothers who lived at the court of 'Abbās the
Great (reigned 1587-1628). But though some of these men, and
the later travelers like Herbert, Tavernier, DuMans, and Chardin,
certainly knew Persian well, in their writings we find but sparse
reference to the literature of the country. A wider knowledge of
the language resulted from the establishment by British, French,
and Dutch companies of trading posts in India and from the
activities of Portuguese and other missionaries there, for the domin-

[1] For general bibliographies of works on Persia see M. Schwab, *Bibliographie de la
Perse*, Paris, 1875; A. T. Wilson, *A Bibliography of Persia*, Oxford, 1930. For bibliographies of Persian literature and the history of Persian studies see E. G. Browne,
Literary History of Persia, 4 vols., Cambridge, 1902-1924; P. Horn, *Geschichte der
persischen Litteratur*, Leipzig, 1901; A. E. Krimski, *Die Geschichte Persiens, ihrer Literatur und der Theosophie der Darwishe*, 3 vols., Moscow, 1909-1917; R. Levy, *Persian
Literature*, Oxford, 1923; C. A. Storey, *Persian Literature: a Bio-bibliographical Survey*,
in progress, London, 1926—; A. J. Arberry, *British Contributions to Persian Studies*,
London, 1942; scattered references in J. Fück, *Die arabischen Studien in Europa*, Leipzig,
1944.

ions of the Moghul emperors were administered by men using Persian.

The solitary specimen of printed Persian from the sixteenth century consists of a translation of the Pentateuch in Hebrew characters produced by the Persian Jew, Jacob ben Joseph Tawus, at Constantinople in 1546.[2] Francis Xavier the Portuguese evangelist composed several Christian books in Persian at Goa between 1590 and 1610.[3] The first printed grammar of the Persian language was put out at Leiden in 1639 by Ludovicus de Dieu[4] as a companion to Xavier's *Dastān-i-Masīḥ* (Story of Christ)[5] and *Dastān-i-Sān Pedro* (Story of St. Peter).[6] Five years later the Dutchman Levinus Warner, protesting that Xavier's writings gave an unfavorable impression of the true elegance of the Persian language, published at Leiden a "Century of Persian Proverbs" and so gave Europe its first taste of the genuine idiom of Persia.[7]

[2] Published by E. B. G. Soncino; see Eric M. North, *The Book of a Thousand Tongues*, New York, 1938, p. 271. Persian was one of the languages included in Walton's great *London Polyglot* of 1654-1657, see *ibid.* p. 42, and further, Zenker, *Bibliotheca orientalis*, Leipzig, 1861, II, pp. 102-3. To the manuscripts of Persian translations of the *Gospels* listed in E. Rossi, *Elenco dei manoscritti persiani della Biblioteca Vaticana*, Vatican City, 1948, pp. 27-28, may be added what appears to be the oldest copy of all, one preserved in the library of the London School of Oriental and African Studies; this copy is dated 728/1328, and after passing through Armenian hands was later possessed by the Portuguese missionary Xavier during his residence in Goa and bears his autograph.

[3] In addition to the printed works mentioned below, manuscript copies of the following unpublished Persian writings of Xavier are preserved in the library of the London School of Oriental and African Studies: (1) *Kitāb-i-Zabūr* (The Psalms), translated at Agra from the Vulgate, according to an entry written by Joao Baptista Vechiete: "Psalterio de David conforme a ediçaô Vulgata, tradidudo pelo Pe Gero⁰ Xavier da Compa de Gesu, na cidade de Agra corte do gran Mogol Reis Jahanguir." (2) *Mir'āt al-Quds*, a Life of Christ, completed at Agra in 1602 (copies also in Oxford and Calcutta). (3) *Dastān-i-aḥvāl-i-Ḥavāriyān*, Lives of the Apostles, completed at Agra in 1609 (copies in Oxford and Calcutta). (4) *Directorio dos Reys* (a Christian Guide for Kings), completed at Agra in 1609 and transcribed that year by Yaḥya al-Kātib, a Jew.

[4] Rudimenta Linguae persicae. Authore Ludovico de Dieu. Accedunt duo priora capita Geneseos, ex persica translatione Iac. Tawusi. Lugduni Batavorum, 1639. For an unpublished English-Persian vocabulary, composed by Robert Hughes at Ajmer in 1617, see H. Ethé, *Catalogue of the Persian manuscripts in the Bodleian Library*, Oxford, 1889, coll. 1100-1101.

[5] Historia Christi persice conscripta, simulque multis modis contaminata, a P. Hieronymo Xavier, Soc. Jesu. Latine reddita & animadversionibus notata a Ludovico de Dieu. Lugduni Batavorum, 1639.

[6] Historia S. Petri persice conscripta, simulque multis modis contaminata. Latine reddita, & brevibus animadversionibus notata a Ludovico de Dieu. Lugduni Batavorum, 1639.

[7] Proverbiorum et sententiarum persicarum Centuria. Collecta, & versione notisque adornata a Levino Warnero. Lugduni Batavorum, 1644.

Meanwhile the study of Persian was beginning to attract serious attention in England, where chairs of Arabic were founded at Cambridge in 1632 and at Oxford in 1636; in 1649 the Oxford scholar John Greaves issued at London his *Elementa Linguae Persicae* which he had had ready to print for nine years, following this up in 1650 with an edition of the *Zīj* or astronomical tables of Prince Ulugh Beg.[8] In 1651 we return to Holland to note a most important milestone along the road of Persian studies, the publication at Amsterdam of an edition and Latin translation of Saʿdī's *Gulistān*.[9] George Gentius (Genz) informs us in his dedication to John George II, Duke of Saxony, how he came to learn of this celebrated book. "Praeter spem & opinionem, cum patriis calamitatibus elapsus Orientem peterem, in ROSARIUM hoc incidi, cujus quidem deliciis delinitus patrias clades fortius sustinui." He tells us that he had the assistance of "gravissimorum virorum in Oriente" in establishing and understanding the text; and after remarking on the supreme fame of the *Gulistān* not only in Persia but also in India, Arabia and Turkey, he expresses the hope "quo clarissimum hoc Persidis suae Sidus, quod totum Orientum fulgore suo illustrat, tandem Occidenti nostro quoque affulgeret." This hope was realized in succeeding years to a remarkable degree. A German translation based on Gentius' Latin by the traveler Adam Olearius (Oelschlager) came out in 1654 and was four times reprinted before the end of the seventeenth century;[10] a Dutch rendering by J. V. Duisberg also appeared in 1654;[11] a French version by M. d'Alègre was published in 1704 and reissued in 1714, and 1737.[12] The first English selections were made

[8] Epochae celebriores astronomis, historicis, chronologis . . . usitatae, ex traditione Ulug Beigi . . . primus publicavit, recensuit, et commentariis illustravit Johannes Gravius. Londini, 1650. Another edition and translation, by Thomas Hyde, was published at Oxford in 1665. An English version by E. Ball Knobel was published at Washington in 1917.

[9] Musladini Sadi Rosarium Politicum, sive amonenum sortis humanae theatrum, de Persico in Latinum versum, necessariisque notis illustratum a Georgio Gantio. Amstelaedami, 1651.

[10] Persianischer Rosenthal, in welchem viel lustige Historien . . . vor 400 Jahren von . . . Schich Saadi in persischer Sprach beschrieben. Jetzo aber von Adamo Oleario . . . in hochdeutscher Sprache heraus gegeben, und mit vielen Kupfferstücken gezieret. Schlesswig, 1654.

[11] Perssiaansche Roosengaard . . . in 't Persiaans beschreeven . . . Alles vertaalt door J. V. Duisberg. Amsterdam, 1654.

[12] Gulistan ou l'Empire des Roses, traité des Moeurs des Rois . . . traduit du Persan

by S. Sulivan in 1774, and the first complete English translation, by Francis Gladwin, appeared in 1806. The *Gulistān* has subsequently been put several times again into English, French and German, while versions are available in Provençal, Italian, Polish, Romanian, and Russian. When *persanerie* seized Western Europe in the eighteenth century, and the composing of *contes persanes* became a literary fashion to which even the great Voltaire lent his approval, Persian literature to all intents and purposes *was* the *Gulistān*.

The first half of the eighteenth century brought a widening of the horizon of historical studies, and the brilliant career of Nādir Shāh (reigned 1736-1747) was reflected in biographies published in France, Holland, Spain, Portugal, Italy, and England.[13] The Oxford orientalist Thomas Hyde (1636-1703) included Persian in his wide range of languages, and he printed the first *ghazal* of Ḥāfiẓ with a Latin translation.[14] But the stimulus afforded by the commerce with Persia was now spent, for that country was in a state of political chaos which made trade unprofitable; while the full impact of the Indian connection was yet to be felt. The struggle between Dupleix and Clive, however, focused attention upon the importance of that market, and the last thirty years of the century witnessed an astonishing efflorescence of Persian studies.

Main credit for this new development must be assigned to the Welshman William ("Persian") Jones (1746-1794), a linguistic prodigy who taught himself Persian fifteen years and more before he went to India. Writing in the preface to his *Grammar of the Persian Language* (1771), he had cause to comment sadly on the neglect of oriental studies in Europe. "If pains and want be the lot of a scholar, the life of an Orientalist must certainly be attended with peculiar hardships. Gentius, who published a beautiful Per-

---

par M***. Paris, 1704. For further bibliography of the *Gulistān* see H. Massé, *Essai sur le poète Saadi*, Paris, 1919; E. Edwards, *Catalogue of the Persian printed books in the British Museum*, London, 1922, coll. 562-566; A. J. Arberry, *Kings and Beggars*, London, 1945, pp. 26-29.

[13] For a full bibliography of Nādir Shāh, see L. Lockhart, Nadir Shah, London, 1938; see also V. Minorsky in *Encyclopaedia of Islam*, III, coll. 813-814.

[14] The text is given in: Syntagma dissertationum quas olim auctor doctissimus Thomas Hyde separatim edidit. Accesserunt nonnulla ejusdem opuscula hactenus inedita . . . Omnia diligenter recognita a G. Sharpe. Oxonii, 1767.

sian work called *The Bed of Roses*, with an useful but inelegant translation, lived obscurely in Holland, and died in misery. Hyde, who might have contributed greatly towards the progress of Eastern learning, formed a number of expensive projects with that view, but had not the support and assistance which they deserved and required. The labours of Meninski immortalized and ruined him." But Jones, indomitable optimist as he always was, saw in the activities of the British East India Company reason for the highest hopes of a revival of Persian and other Eastern studies. "A few men of parts and taste, who resided in Bengal, have since amused themselves with the literature of the East, and have spent their leisure in reading the poems and histories of Persia. . . . The languages of Asia will now, perhaps, be studied with uncommon ardour; they are known to be useful, and will soon be found instructive and entertaining; the valuable manuscripts that enrich our public libraries will be in a few years elegantly printed; the manners and sentiments of the Eastern nations will be perfectly known; and the limits of our knowledge will be no less extended than the bounds of our empire." Enjoying at this time the patronage of the wealthy and the encouragement of the learned, Jones addressed an appeal to the princes of Europe to lend their support to the Eastern renaissance which his soaring imagination had already visualized. Reminding them of the part played by the Medicis in the earlier rebirth of classical learning in Europe, he called upon them to stimulate the study of Eastern literature: "Étalez devant tout le monde ces précieux trésors dont vous n'êtes que les dépositaires. . . . Éleves des collèges, des imprimeries; n'épargnez pas les récompenses, les médailles, les lauriers. . . . Ouvrez ainsi les sources cachées de l'érudition, et triomphez de l'Asie en la courannant."

Jones's friendship with the Polish diplomat Reviczki encouraged the latter to publish at Vienna in 1771 his edition and translation of selected poems from the *Dīvān* of Ḥāfiẓ, the second milestone in European studies of Persian literature.[15] Disappointed in his dreams

---

[15] Specimen poeseos persicae, sive Muhammedis Schems-eddini notioris agnomine Haphyzi Ghazelae, sive Odae sexdecim ex initio Divani depromptae, nunc primum Latinitate donatae, cum metaphrasi ligata & soluta, paraphrasi item ac notis. Vinobonae, 1771. For Jones's friendship and correspondence with Reviczki, see my *Asiatic Jones*, London, 1946, p. 9.

of oriental learning in Europe, on his arrival in India in 1783 he threw himself with redoubled energies into the formulation of schemes to achieve the same end in that country. Having founded the Asiatic Society of Bengal in 1784 with the blessing of Warren Hastings, who was himself a connoisseur of Persian literature and art, and thus securing the regular appearance of the first journal dedicated to Eastern studies, Jones conceived an even greater project of having the Persian classics printed at Calcutta, and himself took the first step in that direction by publishing in 1788 *Laylā Majnūn* of Hātifi, the profits of which were assigned to the relief of impoverished debtors. He explains his plan in the preface to this book. "The incorrectness of modern *Arabian* and *Persian* books is truly deplorable: nothing can preserve them in any degree of accuracy but the art of printing; and, if *Asiatick* literature should ever be general, it must diffuse itself, as *Greek* learning was diffused in *Italy* after the taking of *Constantinople*, by mere impressions of the best manuscripts. . . . But no printer could engage in so expensive a business without the patronage and the purse of monarchs or states or societies of wealthy individuals, or at least without a large publick subscription: there are printers in Bengal, who, if they were duly encouraged, would give us editions of Hafiz and Sadi, or, perhaps, of Nizami and Firdausi. . . . I shall ever be ready to promote such undertakings as a subscriber."

Charles Wilkins, servant of the East India Company, who had designed and cut the first printing types of Sanskrit, also applied his ingenuity to the invention of a Persian font. Whereas European printers had taken as their model the *naskh* script and built their Persian types upon the foundations of their Arabic, Wilkins sought to reproduce the beautiful *nasta'līq* hand of Persia which was creditably practiced by the Indian calligraphers. His bold experiment, which involved laying characters at several levels, proved remarkably successful, and it was therefore in Wilkins' *nasta'līq* that the *editio princeps* of Hāfiz came out of Upjohn's Calcutta press in 1791,[16] to be followed by the *editio princeps* of Sa'di's complete works in two folio volumes (1791, 1795).[17] Jones

---

[16] *The Works of Hafez: with an account of his life and writings,* Calcutta, 1791.

[17] *The Persian and Arabick Works of Sadee.* In two volumes. Vol. i containing his Risālehs, Goolistān, Bōstān, and Pund-nāmeh. Vol. ii containing his Dīwan . . . consisting . . . chiefly of Lyrick and Moral Poetry (Calcutta, 1791-1795). This fine edition,

had lived to see some part at least of his dream wonderfully realized. Of Firdawsi a volume of translations was published by
Joseph Campion at Calcutta in 1785 and at London in 1788; Matthew Lumsden planned an edition of the whole *Shāh-nāmah* but
the funds at his disposal sufficed only for the production of one
volume (Calcutta, 1811);[18] it was left to Turner Macan to publish
the *editio princeps* in four volumes (Calcutta, 1829). Niẓāmi was
not so fortunate, and apart from some inaccurate Indian lithographs he was not fully printed until our times and then only in
his native Persia.

While the gaunt scaffolding of our Western appreciation of
Persian poetry was being thus laboriously erected, great progress
was made with the publication and translation of Persian historical texts, though because of the circumstances attending these
affairs almost all the histories studied in the miraculous years
1770-1820 were Persian histories of India; the names of Dow,
Scott, Gladwin, White, Ouseley, Malcolm, Price, Stewart are
among those of many Britons associated with this movement.[19]
The example of the Asiatic Society of Bengal soon fired the
imagination of scholars in Europe; and France, Germany, and
Austria founded their own traditions of Persian studies. By far
the most elegant Persian printing executed during the nineteenth
century was produced by the Imperial Press of the Hapsburgs at
Vienna, whose crowning glories are Rosenzweig-Schwannau's
three-volume interleaved edition and verse-translation of Ḥāfiẓ
(Vienna, 1856-1864) and Graf's text of Saʿdi's *Būstān* (Vienna,
1858). Mohl edited (in seven volumes at Paris, 1838-1878) and
translated into French (Paris, 1876-1878) all Firdawsi, and Vullers
and Landauer brought out another incomplete text (Leiden, 1877-
1884). Garcin de Tassy broke new ground by editing and translating "Aṭṭār's *Manṭiq al-Ṭayr* (Paris, 1857-1863). Niẓāmi's *Makh-*

---

issued by the Honorable Company's Press, was supervised by J. H. Harrington. The
Pand-nāmah had already been edited and translated into English by F. Gladwin at
Calcutta in 1788. The *Pand-nāma* of Farīd al-Dīn ʿAṭṭār was edited and translated into
French by Silvestre de Sacy at Paris in 1819.

[18] For a list of Persian incunabula printed in India during these years, see C. A. Storey
in *Oriental Studies in honour of Cursetji Erachji Pavry*, pp. 457-458; see also my *India
Office Library*, London, 1938, pp. 9-10, 14-15.

[19] Details may be found in my *Catalogue of the Persian Books in the India Office
Library*, London, 1937, under the relevant entries.

zan al-Asrār was edited by Nathaniel Bland at London in 1844, while his *Laylā Majnūn* was published there in an English verse-translation by James Atkinson in 1836; the same scholar while in India had isolated the Suhrāb and Rustam incident from Firdawsi's *Shāh-nāmah* and put it into English verse (Calcutta, 1814), thus preparing the way for Matthew Arnold's famous adaptation of the legend. By far the most fateful event of the nineteenth century in Persian studies was the publication in 1859 of Edward FitzGerald's immortal *Rubáiyát*, which for the first time introduced the name of 'Umar Khayyām to the West. The astounding popularity of this slim work, outstripping in public esteem the whole of what has been done on Persian literature before or since, gave the Occident an impression of Persian poetry and the Persian outlook which can never be effaced.[20]

FitzGerald could never have addressed himself to his momentous trifle had he not learned Persian from Jones's *Grammar*, still reprinted well into the nineteenth century, and had he not had at his elbow John Richardson's *Dictionary* (of Arabic, Persian, and Hindustani, London, 1806).[21] Richardson was presently outdated by Vullers' two-volume Persian-Latin dictionary (Bonn, 1855-1867), which, with the Persian-English lexicon of Steingass (London, 1892), still represents the highwater-mark of Persian lexicography in Europe. Jones's *Grammar* was finally superseded by the more scientific though far less elegant work compiled by J. T. Platts and H. Ranking, who learned their Persian serving British interests in Asia.[22] The nineteenth century saw the birth of Persian bibliography in the full sense of the term, the chief landmarks being Pertsch's catalogue of the Berlin Manuscripts, Charles Rieu's catalogue of the British Museum collection, and Hermann Ethé's works on the India Office and Bodleian libraries.[23] The first com-

[20] See A. G. Potter, *A Bibliography of the Rubáiyát of Omar Khayyám*, London, 1929; V. Minorsky in *Encyclopaedia of Islām*, III, coll. 988-989.

[21] Richardson's dictionary was a welcome replacement of the rare and costly *Thesaurus linguarum orientalium* of F. A. M. Meninski, 3 volumes, Vienna, 1680, upon which earlier scholars had for the most part to rely.

[22] Platts's work was published at London in 1894, Ranking's at Oxford in 1907. Cambridge University Press is now printing a large and excellent Persian grammar compiled by Dr. Ann K. S. Lambton, Reader of Persian in the University of London.

[23] Pertsch's catalog was published at Berlin in 1888. Rieu's catalog was issued at London between 1879 and 1883, with a supplement in 1895; it is a model of its kind. Ethé's catalog of the Bodleian collection was published at Oxford in 1889, while his

prehensive catalogue of Persian printed books was published by Edward Edwards of the British Museum at London in 1922.

Sir Gore Ouseley was the first in Europe to attempt a history of Persian literature, his fragmentary *Biographical Notices of Persian Poets* being published at London in 1846. This worthy but amateur adventure, however, was entirely overshadowed by Ethé's series of learned monographs[24] and Paul Horn's *Geschichte der persischen Litteratur*, Leipzig, 1901. Meanwhile the fashion of admiring Persian writings grew ever more widespread, and while Goethe wrote German lyrics after the style of Ḥāfiẓ and a succession of eminent English poets from Shelley to Tennyson showed an interest in "Persian" themes, the illustrious Ralph Waldo Emerson did not disdain to write a preface to the first American edition of Gladwin's translation of the *Gulistān*. His comments, penned at Concord in 1864, are most important as witness to the standard of Persian literary criticism current in knowledgeable circles of his generation. "The slowness to import these books into our libraries—mainly owing, no doubt, to the forbidding difficulty of the original languages—is due also in part to some repulsion in the genius of races. At first sight, the Oriental rhetoric does not please our Western taste. Life in the East wants the complexity of European and American existence; and in their writing a certain monotony betrays the poverty of the landscape, and of social conditions. We fancy we are soon familiar with all their images. Medschun [*sic*] and Leila, rose and nightingale, parrots and tulips . . . 'tis a short inventory of topics and tropes, which incessantly return in Persian poetry. I do not know but, at the first encounter, many readers take also an impression of tawdry rhetoric, an exaggeration, and a taste for scarlet, running to the borders of the negrofine. . . . These blemishes disappear or diminish on better acquaintance. Where there is real merit, we are soon reconciled to differences of taste. The charge of monotony lies more against the numerous Western imitations than against the Persians themselves, and though the torrid, like the arctic zone, puts some limit to variety, it is least felt in the masters. It is the

catalog of the India Office collection was published at Oxford in 1903, with an index volume (completed by E. Edwards) in 1936.

[24] See *Grundriss der iranischer Philologie*, vol. II, pp. 212-368.

privilege of genius to play its game indifferently with few as with many pieces, as Nature draws all her opulence out of a few elements." In this strain Emerson continues down to the end of his essay: "The Persians have been called 'the French of Asia'; and their superior intelligence, their esteem for men of learning, their welcome to Western travellers, and their tolerance of Christian sects in their territory, as contrasted with Turkish fanaticism, would seem to derive from the rich culture of this great choir of poets, perpetually reinforced through five hundred years, which again and again has enabled the Persians to refine and civilize their conquerors, and to preserve a national identity. To the expansion of this influence there is no limit; and we wish that the present republication may add to the genius of Saadi a new audience in America."

The gratifying sentiments, expressed at a time when FitzGerald's *Rubáiyát* had not yet hit the American continent, for all that they are irresistibly reminiscent—if one may be irreverent enough to say so—of a superior publisher's blurb, can be taken as eloquent witness to the high regard, based albeit on a slight understanding, in which Persian poetry was held these ninety years ago. Would any writer of comparable standing today be able or willing to say so much?

The winding-up of the affairs of the East India Company on the transfer of government to the British Crown in 1858 had the unfortunate result of virtually stopping the flow of patronage which had been in large measure responsible for the development of Persian studies to that date. It is characteristic of all but the most enlightened public administrations that, faced with the dilemma of choosing between the good and the indifferent in literature or art, state officials conscious of their limitations in judgment, are ready to solve the difficulty by helping neither, and so acquire merit as careful spenders to which on the consequences of their policy they are not wholly entitled. So at least things worked out in Great Britain, where nothing whatever was done to stimulate oriental studies until the foundation of the London School in 1917, and nothing thereafter until the Scarbrough Report of 1946 was adopted as a basis of government policy. The situation which William Jones deplored in 1771 and which the East

India Company had done so much to remedy was by 1871 fully reestablished. Persian scholarship subsisted precariously on the accumulated assets of those wonderful years, and the adventitious subvention of FitzGerald's worldwide fame. The position on the continent of Europe was scarcely more favorable, for the attention of Islamic scholars was largely engaged by the numerous important projects connected with Arabic studies then in progress, and little specialist attention was spared for Persian literature. But meanwhile Russia was now becoming a leading center of Persian studies, for the Empire of the Tsars was expanding to the south and east, and the work of such men as Dorn, Rosen, Barthold, and Zhukovsky graced this new school of research with high distinction.[25] In Great Britain the torch of Persian learning was kept from complete extinction by the labors among others of Sir James Redhouse, E. H. Palmer (who in a sadly brief career divided among Arabic, Persian, and Hindustani could but hint at the contributions a longer life would have enabled him to make), and E. H. Whinfield.[26]

This far from promising scene was suddenly transformed by the appearance of a new star in the firmament of Persian studies, a star destined to shine with unexampled brilliance. Edward Granville Browne (1862-1926), who set out to be a doctor, fortunately conceived a boyish passion for orientalism and after a visit to Persia published his *Year among the Persians*, London, 1893, which was the splendid prelude to a life of rich and learned productivity. Convinced, as Jones had been, of the vital necessity of publishing fundamental texts in order to place Persian studies on a firm foundation, he not only himself appeared as editor of a number of important works including the literary histories of 'Awfī and Dawlatshāh, but also founded and in some measure subsidized the short-lived Cambridge Persian Historical Series,

[25] B. Dorn published between 1840 and 1875 a series of books and papers ranging over many aspects of Persian studies; a useful list of these is given in the *Persiche Bibliographie* issued by the Kaveh Press, Berlin, 1920, p. 18. Baron von V. Rosen is best remembered for his 1886 catalog of the Persian manuscripts in the Oriental Institute at St. Petersburg; it was in the festschrift in his honor (*al-Muẓaffarīyah*, St. Petersburg, 1897) that Zhukovsky published his epoch-making paper on the "Wandering Quatrains of Omar Khayyám."

[26] Details of these scholars' careers and publications are given in my *British Contributions to Persian Studies*; see also my *British Orientalists*, London, 1943, p. 22.

whose purpose was superseded when on the early death of the great Turkologist E. J. W. Gibb (1857-1901) the latter's mother established a trust, called after her son, to make possible the publication of texts and translations connected with Islamic studies. Of E. G. Browne's many momentous works by far the most famous and valuable is his four-volume *Literary History of Persia*, Cambridge, 1902-1924; this masterly survey, in which history and biography are skillfully interwoven with abundant illustrations accompanied by accurate and often felicitous translations, despite inevitable omissions (for it is a pioneer study and the virgin territory is vast), will certainly hold the field for many years to come.

Persian studies in the United States were associated in this period with the name of A. V. Williams Jackson who, in addition to his fundamental work on Zoroastrianism and allied subjects, indicated in his *Early Persian Poetry* (New York, 1920) what he could have done in this department of studies had he had the leisure to apply himself to it longer. In Germany Theodor Nöldeke found time to spare from his many other important labors to begin the scientific examination of the sources of Firdawsi; Pizza founded Persian studies in Italy; France served the cause through Schefer, Blochet, and Darmsteter; Denmark produced Christensen. In England the Cambridge school of E. G. Browne was presently reinforced by R. A. Nicholson (1868-1945), who began and ended his richly fertile life with Rūmi; his superb annotated edition and translation of the *Mathnawī* in eight volumes,[27] a publication made possible by Mrs. Gibb's bequest, set a new standard in textual criticism and interpretation. Ḥāfiẓ, always a favorite in the West since the days of Jones and Reviczki, found new admirers through the graceful renderings of Gertrude Bell[28] and Richard Le Gallienne.[29] During many years of exile in Paris the learned Persian scholar Mīrza Muḥammad Qazvīni, friend of E. G. Browne, collaborated with a number of European scholars and taught Western methods of criticism to his own

[27] The first volume appeared in 1925, the last in 1940. I have given a complete bibliography of R. A. Nicholson's writings in the introduction to my *Pages from the Kitāb al-Luma'*, London, 1947.

[28] First edition published at London (William Heinemann, Ltd.) in 1897.

[29] Published at Boston (L. C. Page & Co.) in 1905. For other translators of Ḥāfiẓ into English verse, see my *Fifty Poems of Ḥāfiẓ*, Cambridge, 1947, where specimens by fifteen different hands are given.

countrymen; while the Kaviani Press in Berlin, which served German propaganda during the First World War, afterwards issued a valuable series of Persian texts.[30]

India during the nineteenth century, after the collapse of printing in types—one of the last ambitious enterprises was the King of Oude's dictionary *Haft Qulzum* in two folio volumes (Lucknow, 1822)—poured forth an unceasing stream of cheap lithographs which despite their many faults served a valuable purpose in making available many texts which would otherwise have remained in manuscript; a superior tradition was still maintained by the *Bibliotheca Indica* of the Asiatic Society of Bengal in which the products of British and Indian scholarship were periodically issued. Persia had a short bout of type-printing early in the century but later also turned to lithography. Some Persian works were printed in Turkey and Egypt during this period, though the output was naturally never very large.

It was not until after the end of World War I that Persia really came into her own as a center of scholarly publication. Between the two wars a most valuable and important series of texts, adequately edited, came out of the printing presses of Tehran; unfortunately the dislocation caused by World War II considerably diminished this output and a full recovery is not yet in sight. Nevertheless, it has been amply proved during the past thirty years that Persia is fully able, given favorable circumstances, to produce the scholars competent to undertake all that may be required of fundamental editions and critical studies on the national literature; while the dictionaries of Nafīsi and Dihkhuda, still in the course of publication, show to what extent lexicography may be expected to benefit at the hands of learned Persians.

Before turning to a discussion of what may be the most useful and profitable lines of research and publication on Persian literature during the coming decades it will be convenient to glance backwards at the general perspective of what has been accomplished thus far. The foregoing partial review sufficiently indicates that the magnitude of past achievement is very considerable.

[30] Kaviani publications included Nāṣir-i-Khusraw's *Safar-nāmah*, *Vajh-i-dīn* and *Zād al-musāfirīn*; Sa'di's *Badā'i'* and *Gulistān*; the *Munājāt* of Anṣāri; the *Rubā'īyāt* of 'Umar Khayyām; three plays of Malkum Khān; and a student's edition of Niẓāmi's *Chahār Maqālah*.

A notable proportion of the major poets, historians, biographers, and theologians has been published, though for the most part quite inadequately; anything approaching final or even standard editions is sufficiently unusual to be a great rarity, and little has been properly indexed. Some poets have been studied more or less critically, but detailed analysis and criticism are still in their infancy. No scientific history of Persia has been written in any language, and some of the most vital sourcebooks are as yet in manuscript. There exists no adequate dictionary of the Persian language in any shape or form whatsoever; nothing to compare, for instance, with Lane's Arabic-English lexicon and Dozy's supplement.

Meanwhile it is a most unfortunate circumstance that the costs of printing in Persian have risen so steeply in Europe and America that it is extremely doubtful whether any major project of publication could be undertaken with the subsidies at present available. It is impossible to exaggerate the seriousness of this situation, which threatens to cut the very arteries of Persian studies in the West; for no linguistic and related research can flourish and remain vigorous unless it springs out of the roots of sound editing. Textual work in Persian in any case presents peculiarly difficult problems because of the great divergencies that exist in the main manuscript traditions, and certainly cannot be wholly satisfactory until much more precise information is forthcoming about the contents of the splendid libraries of Persia and Turkey. For while C. A. Storey's bio-bibliographical *Persian Literature*, in progress since 1926, has proved itself the editor's most precious aid—and the slowness of its completion is entirely due to printing difficulties—there is scarcely one text awaiting scientific editing of which vitally important manuscripts are not known or credibly rumored to exist inaccessibly in the East or elsewhere. What more striking example of the truth of this statement could be imagined than the fact that of the *Rubā'īyāt* of 'Umar Khayyām—an author who has enjoyed the quite exceptional attention of editors, to a degree far exceeding any other work in Persian—two manuscripts exist in private ownership which antedate all known copies by two centuries, so that their contents if ever made available will entirely overthrow the elaborate structure of textual criticism built up during forty years of intense study by many experts?[31]

The most urgent task confronting Persian scholarship today is the compilation of an index of all the Persian manuscripts contained in the public and private libraries of the world; it would be an immense advantage if, associated with this very great task—which would call for the cooperation of governments, institutions, collectors, and scholars on an unprecedented scale—a scheme could be prepared and financed for the making, for deposit in a number of centers, of microfilms of all the most important codices. To organize such a double enterprise would require the establishment of a central bureau of Persian research, which might most properly be established in one of the great libraries or universities having Persian interests. It should be feasible for a small and efficient directorate to plan and execute this work over a number of years; perhaps two decades would suffice, though having regard to the intrinsic difficulties of such an undertaking and the present unsettled state of the world the labors might well occupy a considerably longer period.

Next in order of priority one would be disposed to recommend the formation of an international committee of publication with the assignment of drawing up proposals—and, given the finance and technical arrangements, of seeing them executed—to secure the scientific editing of all the most important, fundamental works of Persian literature. This committee would best work in close association with the central bureau of research, but it would be essential for it to have its separate directorate and budget for maximum efficiency. The steep rise in production costs already mentioned, and the seeming improbability of a return to former conditions, are among many factors calling for a rational, concerted approach to this question of publication. The work of printing could best be divided among a number of countries and centers, with all possible regard for private enterprise; but private enterprise must be encouraged not only, or not so much, by financial

---

[31] EDITOR'S NOTE: Since this was written Professor Arberry himself has helped to fill this gap by his excellent edition of the A. Chester Beatty MS (*The Rubā'īyāt of 'Umar Khayyām*, ed. from a newly discovered MS dated 658 H. [1259-1260] . . . London, 1949) in which he has added to the text the English verse translations of FitzGerald and Whinfield, and his own prose rendition.

help but still more by the prospect of steady employment and guaranteed sales. It is hardly necessary to go into purely technical matters in a short paper, but all familiar with recent developments in printing technique are aware of the advantages of the new machine-setting processes, provided the machines are economically handled. A long-range program of the kind here advocated would desirably involve tne installation of such plant in Persia itself and the training of Persian technicians to use and service the machines. It is further greatly to be wished that the other processes of book production, such as imposing, sewing and binding, should be thoroughly learned by Persian craftsmen so that their books may stand up to the rough handling they are likely to experience in lending libraries and on scholars' worktables. Above all, let the paper be good and strong.

While laying this heavy emphasis on the publication of texts, the necessary prelude to all other work, we do not lose sight of the importance of translation, both for its own sake and as a means of stimulating and assisting the researches of scholars in other fields who may wish to use Persian sources but have not the time to learn the language. Translation is a much underrated activity, and it is folly to leave this important instrument of scholarship to the hazards of chance initiative. An international committee of translation is therefore greatly to be recommended, to work alongside the two other bodies already proposed.

Fourthly and lastly—for space is limited and much must be left for development elsewhere—we need a program of detailed research on particular aspects of Persian literature, and individual problems and figures. It is fair to say that the condition of studies in this field—and this applies pretty generally over the whole territory of orientalism—is not far removed from that of Greco-Roman studies at the Renaissance. If we are to catch up the lag of four centuries and raise our scholarship to the same level as that ruling in other language work (we mean of course on the literary and not the purely philological side), we require to press forward strenuously with the assembling of knowledge and the coordination of current discovery, putting a considerable team of students to work, to function as a team, upon a well conceived program of research. This needs full exchange of information between universities and other centers of study, and before all else it calls for a true spirit of international comradeship such as we have seen to exist in the past on a small scale, but which is today scarcely to be found. This spirit can perhaps be greatly fostered by the holding of conferences where social intercourse may reinforce the sympathy of common scholarly interest; the experiment is at all events worth trying; it would be most helpful surely if young scholars and even students could participate in such discussions, for the ambitious projects here adumbrated will have to be carried out in the main by future generations, and this getting together cannot begin too early.

These are far-reaching proposals, and would require a great expenditure of thought, energy, time, and money, but they are indispensably necessary to the full development of Persian studies. Even a partial realization of our programs—which are but the logical continuation of what William Jones and others pleaded for so long ago—would transform the present scene beyond recognition. If nothing is done on these lines, and matters are left to drift, it can be safely predicted that Persian, and indeed all oriental studies, will suffer a gradual recession until they become once more the eccentric amusement of a few individuals starved of public interest and striving heroically to accomplish isolated projects of research as means provide or fancy may dictate. And that drift will end in stagnation and death.

5

ISLAMIC SCIENCE

BY GEORGE SARTON

THE SCIENTIFIC BOOKS written in Arabic during the Middle Ages were, for a few centuries, the main vehicles of the living science. They have been edited, translated, or analyzed and discussed, by a good many scholars who were primarily arabists, orientalists. Now that the history of science is slowly growing to maturity and begins to be recognized as an independent discipline, the situation is changing. There is now a new kind of scholars, professional historians of science, who, if they would understand the transmission of ancient science to the modern world, must obtain some knowledge of Arabic science. Their position is a very difficult one. Let us consider it for a moment.

I

Of course, the teachers in our scientific departments cannot be expected to know much about Arabic science, because it is a thing of the past, and they are looking toward the future; keeping abreast of the living science is as much as they can do. On the other hand, the instructors of Arabic can hardly be expected to know science; their business is to know the Arabic language, Arabic literature (not the literature of science), perhaps Arabic history, Islamic theology, and many other things, but not astronomy, medicine, or chemistry. I have not yet told you the worst. Even the professional historian of science can hardly be expected to know much about Arabic science, and we should hesitate to blame him.

The history of science is an immense field. Our teachers of history (plain history, political history) are not supposed to be familiar with every period of the past—they are classified as historians of antiquity, or of the Middle Ages, or of America, or of modern Europe and Asia. On the other hand, if the historian of science is alone of his kind in the faculty, as he usually is if he be there at all, he must be acquainted with every period and with every clime, and, in addition, with the whole of science, the science of yesterday and today, and the trends of tomorrow! A pretty big order. The results are disastrous.

Open almost any general book devoted to the history of science or even to a particular science such as medicine, and you will find chapters dealing with Egyptian science, Babylonian science, Chinese science, the story being told in each case as if it were localized in time and space, and as if it could be neatly separated from the rest, like each department in a world fair, the Chinese pavilion, the Russian pavilion, and so on. The same books may have a chapter, tucked in before or after the medieval section, entitled "Arabic science" or "Arabic medicine," as if that were a single homogeneous thing, which happened in one place and one period. Well, that is not *quite* wrong. Arabic science was more or less localized, but its locality was the best part of the world, and the period was limited, much shorter than the Egyptian, Babylonian periods or even than the Greek one, yet much longer than the whole of American culture down to our own days.

The study of Arabic science is so vast a subject in itself, so heterogeneous and so rich, that a man of great learning and zeal, devoting all of his time and energy to it, could not investigate deeply the whole of it. He would have to choose between embracing the whole field, as I have tried to do, or excavating more thoroughly a small part of it.

II

My charge is not to give an account of Arabic science which would be impossible and almost meaningless in so short a time, but rather to indicate new approaches in the exploration of that field, to explain what should be done in the near future. It is best, however, to introduce those recommendations with a few general remarks describing the peculiarities of the field.

One may speak of the miracle of Arabic culture as one speaks of the miracle of Greek culture, the meaning of the word miracle being the same in both cases. The things that happened were so extraordinary that there was no way of accounting for them in rational terms. Well might Muslim historians explain the development of Islamic power and faith, the immense extension of the Arabic language as providential.[1] The Prophet built infinitely better than he knew because (so say those historians) he was the instrument of Providence. He established a faith so generous and yet so simple and so moderate that every man could understand and accept it at once; his own tribal language happened to be one of great beauty and flexibility, ready to be adapted to any rational use; the priority which he gave to it caused it to become for a few centuries almost universal; the obligation of the Pilgrimage secured the unity of Muslim culture, in spite of tribal jealousies which were intense and never abated for very long; the Prophet's injunction against the use of alcohol was a blessing of which nobody could foresee the amplitude at a time when concentrated alcohol was not yet obtainable. In short, the Prophet published a unitarian faith almost nine centuries before the Christian Unitarians; he declared the superiority of Arabic without knowing any other language; he created a cultural center for Islam without suspecting how much such a center would be needed when his followers would be reunited from many races and nations; he forbade the use of intoxicants long before alcoholism was (or could be) the scourge which it has become in our own days.[2] No prophet has ever been as completely vindicated as he was.[3]

[1] Or as a logical development inherent in the human realities. This paradoxical point of view dominates the philosophical romance entitled *Fāḍil ibn-Nāṭiq* composed by 'Ali ibn-abi-al-Ḥazm ibn-al-Nafis (XII-2), in imitation of the *Ḥayy ibn-Yaqẓān* of ibn-Ṭufayl (XIII-2). *Fāḍil ibn-Nāṭiq* is not a historical romance in the ordinary sense; it is a clever attempt to show that the concatenation of the events of the Muslim past was of such an unavoidable nature that it could be reconstructed imaginatively a priori. Muslim power and glory in the eyes of a mystical historian of the thirteenth century were not accidents but logical necessities. That fantastic point of view is not very distant from the one which dominated Christian historians like Eusebios of Caesarea (IV-1) and even Bossuet. When men are in power, or when their ideas are generally accepted, they like to think that their success is simply the fruit of inherent superiority. The *Fāḍil ibn-Nāṭiq* is represented by a single MS in Istanbul the edition of which seems very desirable. See M. Meyerhof (*Isis*, 23, 108); Joseph Schacht: *The Life and Works of Ibn al-Nafis* (*The Arabic Listener*, vol. 7, no. 17, London, 1946), in Arabic; Brockelmann, suppt., vol. 1, 900.

A symbol like (XIII-2) used above means two things: (1) Ibn-al-Nafis flourished in the second half of the thirteenth century, (2) an article is devoted to him in G. Sarton's *Introduction*.

[2] "O you who believe! intoxicants and games of chance . . . are only an uncleanness, the devil's work; shun them therefore that you may be successful" (Koran 5:90 or 92). The word translated as intoxicant is *khamr* which means not only wine but everything

The rude Arab invaders of the Mediterranean world triumphed not so much because of their own strength as because of the weakness of their adversaries, and not only because of their own faith and unity but also because of the lack of unity and the disillusionment and despair of the outsiders. Yet it was not enough to conquer, it was at once necessary and far more difficult to administer the conquered lands. The Arabs were at first incapable of doing that; they had hardly learned to be at peace among themselves when they were called upon to pacify other nations; their experience of war was great but their ignorance of administration much greater. The simple-minded children of the desert, knowing but one language, were soon faced with the problem of governing multitudes of men speaking other languages, and whose lives were guided by different religions and traditions. In spite of their self-conceit, which was extreme, the most intelligent among them must have realized that the foreigners whom they had vanquished—Greeks, Syrians, Persians, Egyptians, Spaniards, etc.—knew many arts which were unknown to themselves. To say that the Arabs needed the help of some of those foreigners would be an understatement; they could have done nothing without that help. The Muslim empire was created with the willing collaboration of Greeks, Persians, Copts—Christians, Magians, Sabians, and Jews. They needed no help, or so they thought, in religion and literature, but they realized with astonishing speed that the cultural superiority of some foreigners was largely due to their technical or scientific equipment.

This introduces what might be called the miracle of Arabic science, using the word miracle once more as a symbol of our inability to explain achievements which were almost incredible. There is nothing like it in the whole history of the world, except the Japanese assimilation of modern science and technology dur-

---

that stupefies or intoxicates the mind. The Prophet said, "Every drink that intoxicates is forbidden" (Bukhāri, 74:3) and again, "Of whatever thing a large quantity intoxicates, even a small quantity is forbidden" (Abū Dā'ūd, 25:5).

[3] The reader may appreciate the situation better if he asks himself what would have happened if the Prophet had not laid so much stress on the Pilgrimage, or on the dangers of intoxicants, and above all if he had not attached more importance to his language than Christ did to Aramaic. While the Christians permitted the Syriac and Coptic languages to die out, the Prophet made his an essential part of his religion and thus established it on an eternal basis. Therefore, he is the Prophet not only of Islam but also of the Arabic language and of Arabic culture, irrespective of race or faith.

ing the Meiji era.[4] The comparison is useful, because the situation was fundamentally the same in both cases: the intellectual leaders of the Arabs realized the need of Greek science as urgently as the Japanese of two generations ago that of European science. Both had the will and the kind of spiritual energy which overcomes insuperable difficulties; indeed they had not sufficient experience nor enough patience to consider difficulties and be frightened by them; they simply rushed through. Everything becomes easier if you don't even imagine how difficult it is!

It should be noted that the almost unbelievable development of Arabic science did not begin until the second half of the second century of the Hijrah. The Prophet was too deeply concerned in the hereafter and, as far as this life was concerned, in ethical and religious issues, to be interested in science. Some modern apologists have tried to read scientific ideas in the Koran, but they can do this only by giving some words of it connotations which could never have occurred to the Prophet or to anybody else for centuries. The orthodox caliphs were not more scientifically-minded than he was; it is probable that the Greek clerks whom they employed were more familiar with business administration than with science, and that they were no longer capable of appreciating the intellectual achievements of their own ancestors. In short, there was no science to speak of in Medina or Mecca, or even in Damascus. The miracle of the Arabic renaissance did not manifest itself before the establishment of the Caliphate in Baghdad. What happened there? The Arabic genius was actuated by the Iranian ferment; the Arabic and Persian qualities (and defects) were complementary. The miracle of Arabic science was largely due to the catalyzation of Arabic vigor and earnestness and of Islamic faith by Persian curiosity and sophistication. To put it in more general terms, Arabic science was the fruit of the Semitic genius fertilized

[4] The reign of the emperor Mutsuhito (1868-1912) lasted less than half a century. The period is much shorter than that of the Arabic assimilation of Greek culture, but that was natural enough. Everything was much slower in the Middle Ages, and the Arabs did not have the marvelous tools which accelerated every educational process (printing, steam engines, telegraph, etc.). The earlier Japanese assimilation of Chinese culture was comparable in length to the Arabic assimilation of Greek culture, but it stopped there, while the Arabic achievements were only a link in the development of our own culture. For that reason we may neglect the Japanese culture, but we cannot overlook the Arabic without loss.

by the Iranian genius. This may be too general a statement for strict accuracy, but it helps us to understand roughly what happened in Baghdad. Within a couple of centuries (c. 750-950) the Islamic rulers, using their polyglot subjects, most of them Christians and Jews, caused the best of Greek knowledge to become available in the Arabic language.

Some historians have tried to pooh-pooh those immense achievements by claiming that there was nothing original in them and that the Arabs were nothing but copy-cats. Such a judgment is all wrong. In a sense, nothing can be more deeply original than the genuine hunger for knowledge which possessed the Arab leaders. Of course, some of that knowledge was immediately needed for administration and government, but they passed quickly from that utilitarian stage to a higher one. Medicine, one might say, was practical knowledge, and so was astronomy, if only because of astrological needs, but the Arabs translated much else in mathematics and philosophy which was not useful except in the highest Platonic sense. One might object also that the dragomans were most of them foreigners, non-Muslims and often non-Arabs, and hence that whatever credit is due for the translations should go to them rather than to their employers. No, the merit must be shared. The translators were most of them foreigners for the simple reason that the task required a degree of polyglottism which the invading Muslims could not have. In order to translate from one language into another one must know both languages well. Such qualifications as the foreigners had were necessary but not sufficient. In general, no work, especially not one which is long and exacting, can be done unless somebody wants it badly enough and is willing to maintain the scholars engaged in it. The Arab leaders were generally anxious to have the work done and ready to make its performance possible; there often was a generous emulation between them about that. The initiative was theirs.

The vast majority of the translations were made from the Greek, either directly, or through Syriac versions; some were made from the Sanskrit and possibly from other Oriental languages. Our knowledge of the Sanskrit and other Oriental borrowings is still very imperfect, because very few scholars are equally familiar with Arabic and with Sanskrit (Old Persian, Chinese, etc.). This evidences another aspect of the Arabic originality and initiative. They not only exploited the Greek source (and I suspect they did not at first realize its overwhelming superiority); they were eager to drink from every source. Nor did much time pass before they began to assimilate that knowledge and transform it into something new.

The two greatest Arabic innovations in mathematics and astronomy are the new arithmetic and the new trigonometry. It is significant that both were established on a double foundation, Sanskrit and Greek. Even so, medical borrowings from India as well as from Greece are acknowledged in the *Paradise of Wisdom* of 'Ali ibn-Rabbān al-Ṭabari (IX-I).[5] A few centuries later Rashīd al-Dīn (XIV-I)—writing in Persian, it is true, rather than in Arabic—would extend the field of borrowing to China. Those who would begrudge and belittle Arabic merits, object again that borrowing from many sources is hardly better than borrowing from one. This manner of argument is certainly very misleading, especially in mathematics. In the two cases mentioned above the Arabic mathematicians did not copy the Greek and Sanskrit sources—that would have been almost useless—they brought them together and fertilized the Greek ideas with the Hindu ones. If these were not inventions, then there are no inventions in science. A scientific invention is simply the weaving together of separate threads and the tying of new knots. There are no inventions *ex nihilo*.

One may object also that the Arabic scientists did not completely understand their discoveries. For example, I have shown[6] that they did not use Hindu (Arabic) numerals in the very occasions when those numerals would have been most useful, in astronomical and geographical tables. But what of it? The implications of any scientific discovery, if it be really an important one, are so varied and so far-fetched, that no man of science, however great his genius may be, ever understands completely what he is doing.

---

[5] This 'Ali al-Ṭabari should not be confused with the more famous Muḥammad al-Ṭabari (X-I), author of an elaborate universal history and of an immense *Tafsīr*. My account of him (*Introd.*, 1, 574) is very insufficient because his *Firdaws al-ḥikmah* was still unknown to me in 1927. It was edited in the following year by M. Z. Ṣiddīqi (Berlin, 1928); see the long analysis by Max Meyerhof (*Isis*, 16, 6-54). My account of Rashīd-al-Dīn, appearing twenty years later, is far longer and more satisfactory (*Introd.*, 3, 969-976).

[6] *Introd.* (3, 133, 797-98).

The fructification of deep ideas is generally accomplished by other men, smaller but more practical. Thus were the ideas of Faraday fructified by Zénobe Gramme and those of Clerk Maxwell by Marconi.

To return to medieval Iraq, the singularity as well as the pregnancy of Arabic science lies in the fact that it brought together Greek and Oriental elements and created a new synthesis, or made such creation possible in the future. Greek science might have been transmitted more simply to the Latin West if Catholic Christianity had not been almost completely separated from Orthodox Christianity by a wall of intolerance, distrust, and hatred. As that wall unfortunately existed, there was no way between the Greek science of the past and the Latin science of the future except by the Arabic detour. Looking at it from the point of view of the development of mankind as a whole, the Arabic-Islamic culture was of supreme importance, because it constituted the main link between the Near East and the West, as well as between the Near East and Buddhist Asia. The Near East was really the Middle East.

III

When we observe the occurrence of a large body of translations from one language into another, we may assume that this represents a fall of energy from a higher level to a lower one; that fall may be followed, and generally is, by a new rise. This happened in the two cases which interest us most, the transmissions of knowledge from Greek to Arabic, and later from Arabic to Latin. There is, however, a fundamental difference between these two cases the appreciation of which will help us to see the Arabic efforts in a new light.

The Arabic translations began to appear only by the end of the eighth century, that is, almost four centuries after the final climax of Greek science. It may be objected that Byzantine culture continued to some extent the Greek one and that some Byzantine scientists like Joannes Philoponos (vi-1), Aëtios of Amida (vi-1), Alexander of Tralles (vi-2) and Paulos Aegineta (vii-1) helped to transmit Greek learning to the Arabic-speaking world, but on the other hand the very best of Greek culture had been published, not four centuries but six centuries and even a whole millennium and more before its decantation into Arabic was attempted. It is substantially true to say that the treasure of Greek wisdom and knowledge had been gathered many centuries before the Arab leaders became aware of its existence and undertook its systematic exploitation.

The Latin translations from the Arabic began with Constantine the African (XI-2) in the third quarter of the eleventh century, at a time when the Greek-Arabic transmission was almost completed and the Arabic work of assimilation and creation was in full swing. In other words, while the Greek and Arabic periods are almost entirely separated, and widely so with regard to the essentials, the Arabic and Latin periods are partly contemporary. Arabic men of science were late epigoni of their Greek models, while the early Latin ones were younger contemporaries of their Arabic colleagues. Many illustrious Arabic authors, like ibn-al-Haytham, ibn-Sīna, al-Bīruni, al-Ghazzāli (not to mention earlier ones) were already dead when Latin science began to flourish; on the other hand, some others were posterior even to the golden age of Catholic learning. Ibn-Baṭṭūṭah was posterior to Marco Polo and ibn-Khaldūn died one hundred and thirty-two years after St. Thomas.

This difference between the two traditions, Greek-Arabic and Arabic-Latin, had far-reaching consequences. The Muslim rulers (and their advisers) could contemplate Greek science from a long distance, when much of that science had become classical and the masterpieces were fully recognized. In general, they translated the best and neglected what was worthless; by the end of the tenth century or even of the ninth the treasure of Greek knowledge could be read in Arabic.

Many of the Greek books thus translated are lost in the original. Some have been recovered in Arabic, the best known being Books v to VII of Apollonios and small treatises of Archimedes.[7] The collections of Greek MSS, even of palimpsests, have been so thor-

---

[7] Books v to VII of the *Conics* were translated into Arabic by Thābit ibn-Qurrah (IX-2) and revised by abu-al-Fath Maḥmūd ibn-Muḥammad al-Iṣfahāni (X-2); that Arabic text has not been edited but a Latin version was first published by the Maronite Abraham Ecchelensis and by Giacomo Alfonso Borelli (Florence, 1661), then again in Edmund Halley's monumental edition of Apollonios (Oxford, 1710). A translation of Archimedes' memoir on the regular heptagon was made by the same Thābit ibn-Qurrah and published by Carl Schoy, not in Arabic but in German (*Isis*, 8, 21-40, 1926).

oughly investigated that the hope of finding more Greek originals is very small; on the contrary, there is much hope of finding Arabic translations of them. The paradoxical consequence of this is that the study of Arabic MSS is at present our most promising method for the improvement of our knowledge of the Greek scientific literature.[8]

The Latin translators did not have enough perspective always to recognize the best of Arabic literature. They translated some of the most important works (e.g. in medicine and astronomy) but also a considerable amount of rubbish. At the very time when Latin learning was in the ascendant, Arabic learning was beginning to decline, being smothered by theological obscurantism and by superstitions. It happened that some medieval Arabic writers enjoyed a popularity which they did not deserve but which reached the ears of their Latin imitators. This remark applies especially to astrological books which were considered the last word of Arabic wisdom and the key to Arabic power and were eagerly translated—the same texts being sometimes repeatedly translated not only into Latin, but also into Hebrew and sundry vernaculars.

Some of the greatest Arabic writers such as abu-al-Fidā', ibn-Baṭṭūṭah, ibn-Khaldūn came too late to be translated into Western languages[9] and hence in spite of their value for the study of Arabic culture, they are relatively negligible in the history of Western culture.

The case of ibn-Khaldūn, who was perhaps the greatest historian and sociologist of the Middle Ages, is particularly curious. Ibn-Khaldūn came too late not only to be translated into Latin and thus to fall in the stream of Western learning; he came too late even to be appreciated by his own people. Strangely enough, the first foreigners to appreciate him were the Turks, and that happened only in the sixteenth century.[10] They were interested in

---

[8] The most noteworthy recent finds refer to Galen (II-2). Galen's anatomy was published in Arabic and German by Max Simon (2 vols., Leipzig, 1906); his treatise on medical experience was published in Arabic and English by Richard Walzer (London, 1944. cf. *Isis*, 36, 251-255).

[9] I am thinking only of medieval translations, of course. Translations made in the seventeenth century or later by Western Orientalists do not count here for they did not help to transmit scientific knowlege to the West, but were made largely to gratify the retrospective curiosity of scholars.

[10] Curious details concerning this may be found in my *Introd.*, 3, 1776.

him, I imagine, because of his political views at a time when they themselves were the greatest power of the Mediterranean world and the feudal lords of his native land.

Arabic science declined rapidly after the fourteenth century. As their political power decreased, the Muslims fell into a kind of sluggishness and despondency which made further progress impossible; this meant that they became really more and more backward in a progressive world. Their scientific mission in the East and North Africa was continued for a while (from the sixteenth to the eighteenth century) by the Turks,[11] but even during the golden age of the Ottoman Empire Turkish science and philosophy were but feeble imitations of the Arabic achievements. The highest Turkish level was never as high as the highest Arabic one had been centuries before, and meanwhile the Western world having discovered the "open sesame" of experimental method, science rose with increasing speed to such new heights that medieval achievements, whether Arabic or Latin, seemed negligible in comparison.

The contempt of medieval thought and especially of medieval science was an error of the youthful Renaissance, an error which was aggravated as Western science grew by leaps and bounds in the seventeenth century and later. It is only in our time that medieval science was reappreciated at its true value. This implied, first of all, a revaluation of Arabic science, for that was the very core of medieval science before the twelfth century and remained an essential part of it until the fourteenth.

Western scholars of many nations have devoted much time and energy to exploration and study of Arabic scientific MSS. These MSS are so abundant that the task is immense and very much remains to be done. We may be almost certain that as it is continued many discoveries will be made. It is a very tempting field, but like any exploration it is much of a gamble, and the most in-

---

11 Ṣāliḥ Zaki: *Āthār-i-bāqiya* (2 vols. in Turkish, 512 pp., Istanbul, 1911; *Isis*, 19, 506-515). Abdulhak Adnan: *La science chez Turcs Ottomans*, Paris, 1939 (*Isis*, 32, 186-189); revised and enlarged translation into Turkish, Istanbul, 1943 (*Isis*, 38, 121-125). Aydin M. Sayili: *Turkish Medicine, Isis*, 26, 403-414, 1937. Q. Ḥ. Ṭūqān: *Turāth al-'Arab al-'ilmi fī al-Riyāḍīyāt wa-al-Falak*, 268 pp., Cairo, 1941 (*Isis*, 36, 140-142).

telligent and systematic investigation will not necessarily be the most successful.

I receive from time to time requests for the indication of Arabic MSS the edition of which would be particularly desirable. I cannot answer those requests except in a general way as will be done now. Let me remark first that if I were certain that a MS available to me (in one form or another) were extremely important, I would probably stop any other activities and devote my whole time to its study; if I could not do that myself, I would entrust the MS to a special friend of mine or to a favorite student, to whom I would thus give a unique chance of distinguishing himself among other scholars; I could not make him a greater gift.

As a matter of fact, I have no such certainty, only guesses, which may be happy or not. If my time were not completely mortgaged to other undertakings and if I wanted to edit a MS, I would have to hunt for a suitable one like everybody else. How would I go about it?

IV

Let us first consider the main tools without which the task would be, if not hopeless, at least far more adventurous than it already is. These tools are the catalogues of the great collections of Arabic MSS preserved in some eighty cities of the world.[12] The scholars who prepared those catalogues (some of which are very elaborate and deal with many thousands of MSS) were the true pioneers of our studies. They cannot be praised too highly, especially because their merit remains necessarily unknown except to a very few students. Our highest praise must be reserved perhaps for the scholars who published the earliest of those catalogues, for they were really breaking the ground. Their followers could take advantage of their work in many ways, and prepare better catalogues, containing much of the information available in the earlier ones and avoiding their blunders.

We might pause a moment to express our gratitude to those

[12] Lists of them will be found in Giuseppe Gabrieli: *Manuale di bibliografia musulmana*, 189-245, Roma, 1916 (*Isis*, 5, 449-450), and Carl Brockelmann: *Geschichte der arabischen Litteratur, Supplement*, vol. 1, 5-11, Leiden, 1936; vol. 3, 1191, 1939.

early pioneers who built so well and did so much for us. It is interesting to note that they were all, with one exception, Lebanese Maronites: Abraham Ecchelensis (Ibrāhīm al-Ḥāqilāni, 1605-1664), and his nephew Giovanni Matteo Naironi (al-Namrūni), then the two Assemani (al-Samʿāni): Giuseppe Simone Assemani (1687-1768) and his nephew Stefano Evodio ('Awwād) Assemani (1711-1782), and finally Miguel Casiri (al-Ghazīri, 1710-1791).[13] Between them those learned Maronites inventoried the wealth of Arabic MSS preserved in the Italian and Spanish libraries. The one exception which occurs to me is the Hungarian Joannes Uri,[14] who published the first catalogue of Oriental MSS in the Bodleian.[15]

The richest collection of Arabic MSS of the New World is the one of Princeton University. One half of it has already been catalogued by Professor Hitti and his assistants, and we are anxiously waiting for his catalogue of the very large remainder.[16]

In all these catalogues, the scientific MSS are generally separated from the others, but one cannot depend too much on that classification (especially in the earlier catalogues), and the composite MSS (MSS containing many texts) are not always as well analyzed as they should be. The cataloguers were generally theologians and historians without scientific education and without means of appreciating the real value and originality of the scien-

[13] According to Professor Hitti, Casiri's original name was Mīkhā'il al-Ghazīri, his *nisbah* being derived from the place Ghazīr, a small Maronite village in the Kisrawān, Lebanon, a little to the north of Beirūt, overlooking the sea.

[14] Joannes Uri was born in 1724 in Nagykörös, Hungary, that is, not in the same place as the more famous Alesander Csoma de Körös (1784-1842), whose birthplace is in Transylvania. He studied in Leiden and was invited to go to Oxford in 1766 in order to catalogue the Oriental MSS of the Bodleian. The first part of that catalogue, published in Oxford 1787, contains the description of 2,358 Oriental MSS, 1,476 of them in Arabic. Uri died in Oxford in 1795 (*DNB* 58, 42). The second part of the catalogue, much smaller than the first, was published by Alexander Nicoll (1793-1828) in Oxford in 1821; it contains the description of 234 MSS, 156 of them in Arabic. Uri had done the lion's share of the work. For more information on Uri see article by Joseph de Somogni in *Isis* 39, 61-63, 1948, correcting various errors in *DNB*.

[15] Pioneers are always preceded by other pioneers just as fathers are preceded by other fathers. The early cataloguers were naturally preceded by the early collectors, and the authors of published catalogues were preceded by the authors of catalogues which never reached the printed stage. We cannot go into that. The difficulty and complexity of such stories may be judged from one of them well told by Giorgio Levi della Vida: *Ricerche sulla formazione del più antico fondo dei manoscritti orientali della Biblioteca vaticana*, Vaticano, 1939 (*Isis*, 36, 273-275).

[16] Philip K. Hitti, Nabih Amin Faris, Buṭrus 'Abd-al-Malik; *Descriptive Catalogue of the Garrett Collection of Arabic MSS*. Princeton, 1938-1939 (*Isis*, 31, 558).

tific texts falling under their eyes.[17] Happily the historian of science has another method of approach, the main steps of which are as follows:

1. First take Sarton's *Introduction to the History of Science*, and read carefully, with pencil in hand, the Arabic sections of the chapters which appeal to your curiosity, say, the geographical chapter or the medical one. Thus, your attention may be focused upon this or that author, say, al-Bīrūni (XI-1), al-Idrīsi (XII-2), al-Jildaki (XIV-1). In many articles (but not always), unpublished texts are mentioned.

2. Consult Brockelmann's history of Arabic literature. The reference to the early volumes is generally given by Sarton, and from the early volumes it is easy to pass to the supplements. This will enable you to find where MSS of the unpublished texts of this or that author are kept. If one of these texts was mentioned by Sarton, it is possible to form some idea of its importance from the context of his article.

3. When a definite text has been tentatively chosen on the basis of Sarton's and Brockelmann's indications, examine the catalogues of the libraries where MSS of it are kept (those libraries are listed in Brockelmann, and the number of each MS in their catalogues given by him). These catalogues describe the MS and sometimes analyze the text, discuss it and may even quote extracts from it.

4. Consult for the same text or the same author the catalogues posterior to Brockelmann, e.g. the Princeton one prepared by Hitti or the Istanbul lists issued by Helmut Ritter and his associates.

5. Photostatic copies of one or more MSS of the selected text are ordered. A long time will probably elapse before the photostats arrive but that interval can be profitably used for the study of other works of the same author already edited and of the memoirs already devoted to him. A fairly complete list of them will be found in Sarton's *Introduction* or in the corresponding

[17] Thus the exceptional importance of a mathematical MS was overlooked by such great scholars as Adolph Neubauer and Ernest Renan in 1893. This was a Hebrew MS, but the situation would have been the same with an Arabic one (*Isis*, 25, 16-45, 1936; *Introd.*, 3, 1518). Scientific sections of modern catalogues may be entrusted to scientists; this is done for the new catalogue of Escorial MSS in the course of publication. The part devoted to medicine and natural history was prepared by our late friend, Dr. H. P. J. Renaud of Rabat, Paris, 1941 (*Isis*, 34, 34-35).

chapters in the *Critical Bibliographies* which appear from time to time in *Isis*.

6. When the photostats are finally available a rough decipherment of them and analysis of their contents will determine the final decision as to whether you find it worthwhile to spend considerable time editing it and perhaps translating it, or not.

We need not explain here the long process of edition; that is a philological matter. It might happen that you did not care to edit the whole text, but would rather restrict yourself to an analysis of it, together with extracts in Arabic or translation. Even if you rejected the text, the time spent in the preliminary investigations would not be by any means lost; much knowledge would have been obtained which would be of use for similar investigations at a later time.

When the text has been edited in Arabic, the task is very far from completion. The scholar having the required paleographic and philologic aptitudes for critical editing, may not have the training necessary for the correct appreciation of the contents. Indeed, this implies a sufficient knowledge of the branch of science concerned, past and present, and a sufficient familiarity with other texts of the same kind and period, as well as with other texts written somewhat earlier or later in the same language (to clarify the terminology).

This process of interpretation requires almost always the co-operation of many scholars working together or (as is more usually the case) in successive shifts. For example, one scholar may attempt to translate the text into English (or into another vernacular) or to analyze it. This opens the field to a new set of scholars, knowing less Arabic (or none) but more familiar with the contents.

The length of the whole procedure is easily illustrated with reference to particular cases. Take any of the longer articles in Sarton's *Introduction*, where the available texts and translations are enumerated in one section and the modern studies are listed in chronological order in another. In the case of an astronomer like abu-al-Wafā' (x-2) we find a succession of orientalists, mathematicians, astronomers undertaking the varied tasks of edition, translation, elucidation, the one after the other, sometimes after long intervals of silence.

The establishment and explanation of a new text and the ascription of a new discovery to this or that author require efforts which are not only considerable but also of great variety. The text must be discovered, suitable MSS located, collated, edited, translated, explained; the explanations may involve the comparative study of other texts and evoke the criticisms of men of science; then a better text may be found and the whole work may have to be done over on a new basis. The possibility of all this (or most of it) being done by a single man is not excluded but will always be rare. In general, the task is a collective one involving the cooperation and the emulation of many scholars, often of many nations, and its completion may take a century or more. In a sense the task is never completed, for other texts may entail a revision and reappreciation of the first one and so on.

The main burden of my remarks is to show that our studies are necessarily slow. In spite of the possibility of accidental discoveries, the way to knowledge is a very long one, and we should be patient. An enormous amount of work remains to be done by our generation, and when it is done, plenty more will be left for the following generations. Let us say *al-ḥamdu li-Allāh*!

In conclusion, we could not be too grateful to our Arabic-speaking forerunners, especially the pioneers of the eighth to the eleventh century, who brought to us the treasures of Greek wisdom and part of the Iranian and Hindu treasures and added to them much knowledge of their own. They helped us to build our own traditions, the most valuable part of our heritage. The best that is in us we owe to our spiritual ancestors of many races, of many faiths, of many climes. They were not thinking of us, of course, but are we thinking overmuch of our distant progeny?[18] The best way of thanking and praising our spiritual ancestors is to continue their work, our work, without impatience, slowly, steadily, honestly.

[18] There is one thing which we can do for our descendants and which our ancestors fortunately could not do for us. Our financial organization is so remarkable that we are able to burden our progeny with our own enormous debts! Let us hope that we may be able to bequeath to them other things than unpaid bills!

6

ISLAMIC RELIGION

BY EDWIN E. CALVERLEY

TRADITION says that Muhammad, the Prophet of Islam, received his special interest in religion first from Christians. It was the devotional life of hermit Christians that set them apart from the pagan Arabian life he knew and that attracted his attention. The Koran itself shows that he remembered the deep impression these monks of the mountains made upon him.

Moreover, when Muhammad, about forty years old, yielded to the call of Allah and began to call others to the same obedience, he enjoyed the friendship and good will of Christians. At Mecca a few Christians accepted his religious leadership. That others did not caused him sorrow rather than anger. He believed that most Christians had strayed from the true teaching of Jesus, but he did not break away from their friendship nor did he deny their worth.

When Muhammad went north to Yathrib, which thereby became al-Madīnah, the City of the Prophet, he became not only the religious leader of a larger community, but also the political ruler of a city-state.

At Yathrib there were tribes of Jews. Muhammad tried to induce them to accept completely his religious claims as well as his political authority. Muhammad and his followers acknowledged Abraham, Moses, and the prophets of Israel; why should not the Children of Israel accept Muhammad as a prophet of the same God sent to the Arabs? He was angered by their rejection of him as an Arabian Apostle and by their refusal to recognize the religion he taught as a new and later version of the same religion. He turned against the Jews and changed the direction of worship from Jerusalem to Mecca, giving Arabian loyalties, which were the contemporary form of what is now called nationalism, a permanent and important place in his religion.

To his Arab fellow countrymen Muhammad gave a new doctrine of God, a new place and part in sacred history, a new line of prophets and a new book of revelation. But when Muhammad made Mecca and the Ka'bah the religious center of Islam and the place of pilgrimage for his followers, he incorporated in his religion what was most precious to the Arabs and so ensured its success.

During Muhammad's lifetime, then, there was a vital difference of conviction about Muslim and Christian doctrines of God and Jesus Christ, but no communal disaffection or conflict.

It was only at the very end of Muhammad's life and after his death that active Muslim-Christian antagonism arose. Islam, starting as a minority religion, needing and teaching toleration, had become an increasingly powerful political community with religion as its cohesive and impelling force. In all Arabia there was no tribal society, and no political or religious group strong enough to stand against the new Muslim movement. The combination of religious zeal and the advantages of governmental control made Islam victorious wherever the Muslim armies marched.

They went northward into Syria, defeated the army of Heraclius at Yarmūk, and captured Jerusalem and Damascus. They went eastward into Iraq, defeated the Persians at Seleucia and controlled the Fertile Crescent. They went westward and took Egypt away from the Byzantine Empire. In all this expansion, there was no forcible conversion of Jews or Christians to the Muslim religion. There was freedom for "the People of the Book" to continue in their own religious beliefs and practices. It was required of them to yield civil and political sovereignty to the Muslim state.

In Arabia the communal organization of the Arabs had been tribal. The bond of cohesion and allegiance had been blood relationship. Muhammad's new movement made religious belief rather than birth and lineage the tie that bound people together. In the countries around Arabia, such as Syria, Egypt, Iraq, and the rest of the Byzantine Empire, as well as in Persia, the politico-religious type of government had long been normal. Communities which were not paramount in numbers and political power retained their own religious rights and privileges, but had inferior civil status. Those accepting the religion recognized or established by the state received great material advantages not enjoyed by the other religious communities. This increased the importance of religious differences. Controversy over religious questions was the natural consequence. Such controversies had been common in occurrence, momentous in subjects, and lasting in their effects in pre-Islamic Christendom. The results of those conflicts of belief and teaching were not agreement and unity, but rather, in nearly every case, the crystallization and perpetuation of both the majority and minority opinions. The doctrines of the majority became orthodox for the majority, and all else was heresy. But to each minority its own views remained right. Many of these minorities retain their ancient positions to this day.

Into Christendom's arena of doctrinal differences came Islam. Unquestionably the hostility of the Christian sects towards one another facilitated the conquest of the Christian lands by the Muslim armies. Then flamed anew the Christian-Muslim doctrinal conflict which had started in the Koran and which has never ceased.

In Dr. H. G. Dorman's recent book, *Toward Understanding Islam*, an excellent résumé of the Muslim-Christian polemic through the centuries is presented. It describes "the very first recorded controversial discussion" between the Jacobite patriarch, John, and 'Amr ibn-al-'Āṣ, the conqueror of North Syria, and later of Mesopotamia and Egypt. When John of Damascus in his defense of the Greek orthodox church gave his account of one hundred heresies, he added one more, and described the errors of Islam, using only four or five surahs of the Koran. Living in what was then the political capital of the young but mighty and far-flung empire, he had the courage to prepare and the freedom to publish a question-and-answer catechism to enable a Christian to refute a Saracen in religious disputation. John wrote in Greek, not Arabic, but that does not detract from his courage, nor does it decrease respect for the toleration of the Muslims. When Arabic, the sacred language of the Muslim rulers, became also the language of all culture in the Empire, then the controversy was carried on in that language. More than one Muslim emperor showed interest in the discussions. In 861 at the court of the 'Abbāsid Caliph, al-Ma'mūn in Baghdad, the Christian, 'Abd-al-Masīḥ ibn-Isḥāq al-Kindi, and the Muslim, 'Abdullāh ibn-Ismā'īl al-Hāshimi, conducted well mannered and serious defenses of their own religions. All too often, before and since, adjectives and epithets have taken the place of facts and reason in such arguments.

In later centuries when Islam and Arabic had become well established in Spain the Muslim-Christian religious controversy flourished there. But there the adherents of the two religions spoke different languages. The educated Christians used Latin which the Arabs have never taken the trouble to learn. Some few of the Christian religious leaders learned Arabic and later on established Arabic courses in the universities. But for the most part, the Christians depended on the translations from Arabic for the subjects they wanted to study. Those subjects were chiefly the Greek medicine and the philosophy of Aristotle and others. As is well known, the works of al-Fārābi, al-Ghazzāli, ibn-Sīna (Avicenna), and ibn-Rushd (Averroes) were translated into Latin, sometimes directly from the Arabic, but often through the medium of Hebrew. The translators were chiefly Jews who often knew and spoke Arabic better than their own sacred Hebrew. Frequently also translators worked in pairs, one specializing in explaining the original and the other in expressing the meaning in the Latin.

Meanwhile the Crusades had begun. They were conducted in the name of religion, but it must be remembered that all the activities of medieval life were religious in their motivation and expression. The term "secular" did not mean what it has come to mean in our time. Then "secular" meant non-ecclesiastical, not non-religious. But for us to understand the Crusades we should think of them not as wars to spread the Christian religion among non-Christian peoples and to win converts by force of arms; rather they were to conquer lands ruled by Muslims and to establish Christian rulers in their place.

To secure support for such political and military objectives the propaganda used religious motives. Nothing too harsh or too false could be said to excite hostility against the Muslims, both when the armies and the funds were collected and when the Crusaders reached Western Asia. The centuries of the Crusades are the most shameful and the most disastrous in the history of Christianity.

The half of a millennium that has since elapsed has not removed the dishonor or the distrust that the Crusades left behind in the Orient.

The false information poured out for several centuries to all people of Europe who supplied the men and the means for the Crusades, and the false reports brought back by those who returned from the wars filled the West with popular misinformation about Islam that Western mass education has not yet been able to remove.

One needs only to examine the early vernacular literatures of Europe from Italy to England to find innumerable instances of inaccurate statements about Muslim beliefs and customs in general and about Muhammad in particular. Muslims may still justly object to statements repeatedly made in our daily newspapers and monthly magazines, our church weeklies and even our missionary addresses, our stories and novels and even our text books. This is the heritage in the West of the Crusade propaganda.

But it was also during the centuries of the Crusades that a beginning was made in the West to learn about Islam, the Koran, and Muhammad, not from propaganda and hearsay, but directly. In the twelfth century Peter the Venerable (1094-1156) had the Koran translated for the first time from Arabic into Latin. The purpose was the refutation of Islam, but the method was honest and without compulsion. The study of Islam as a religion in the West may be said to have begun with that translation.

In the tenth and eleventh centuries in both East and West a class of religious literature was produced that carried on the Greek and Latin custom of describing varieties of philosophical thought. Plutarch in Latin and Diogones Laertius in Greek are representatives of such classical histories. When theology replaced philosophy as the main interest of thinkers, then descriptions of creeds and deviations from them carried on the tradition. In the East al-Ash'ari (c. 933), al-Baghdādi (d. 1038), and al-Shahrastāni (d. 1153), and in the West ibn-Ḥazm (d. 1044) are the chief Muslim representatives of this class of literature, but they had predecessors and imitators. In some cases, non-Muslim religions were included in the surveys. Since these works were written to show the superiority of Islam, or a special branch of Islam, to the religious thought of others, it naturally produced defensive works. On the Christian side Raymond Martin is one of the prominent names of this period.

The same period produced two men, Francis of Assisi (c. 1181-1226) and Raymond Lull (c. 1232-1316), who furnish medieval Christian history with brighter pages of Christian-Muslim relationships. The motives of both were religious, but their spirit was service for, not against, the Muslims. St. Francis sought to express Christian good will and appealed to the hearts of Muslims by his active, harmless, and helpful service. He received from responsible Muslim leaders a courteous welcome, respect and friendship. Lull was a scholar who sought to understand Islam directly and to appeal directly to the mind of the Muslims. He promoted the study of Arabic in the universities of Europe. He prepared literature in Arabic especially for Muslim readers. He visited North Africa to reach Muslims personally and in all probability died a martyr at the hands of a Muslim mob. The witness of Francis and Lull, however, was too weak to count in the face of the wars that nearly every generation of Christendom was then waging against Islam.

At the end of the Crusading period there were two results of vital importance for the future: the Koran had been translated into Latin and the Arabic language was being taught in several universities in southern and western Europe.

From that time on two streams of knowledge about Islam have flowed through Western history. One stream has been a broad shallow river of misinformation, received not from Eastern Arabic sources but from Crusader or other propaganda and embodied in the popular literature of the Western peoples. The other stream has been that flowing from the schools and universities, where first-hand studies of the Arabic sources have provided accurate knowledge of Islamic beliefs and practices, together with the manners and customs of Muslim peoples everywhere.

Both these streams of ideas about Islam, the popular but incorrect ideas, and the scholarly, accurate knowledge, have been moving together through Western Europe down the generations, but usually in different strata of the population and in works appealing to different audiences. Of the former of these two types of books, quite a number of studies have been made for English and

French literature. These show that in England from Chaucer to the present time, poets, dramatists, novelists, travelers, and essayists have been themselves interested in the East and have reproduced in their works the information learned by reading or hearsay without bothering to check for accuracy what they themselves wrote.

There are several full studies of the popular literature of particular periods in England. One is Samuel C. Chew's *The Crescent and the Rose* (New York, 1937) and his supplementary article, "Islam and England During the Renaissance," in *The Moslem World*, vol. 31, 1941. This study of Elizabethan literature is continued, in Byron Porter Smith's *Islam in English Literature* (Beirut, 1939), to the publication in 1840 of Thomas Carlyle's excessively favorable and quickly modified lecture on "The Hero as Prophet. Mahomet: Islam." Another work dealing chiefly with the English drama of the eighteenth century which might be overlooked because it was published in Shanghai (1939) is *Oriental England* by T. Blake Clark. It is not overlooked in the admirable chapter on "The Sense of the Past," by the late Arthur E. Christy in the book he edited on *The Asian Legacy and American Life*, New York, 1945.

A somewhat comparable account of Islam in French literature is given in *The Turk in French History, Thought and Literature* (1520-1660), by Clarence Dana Rouillard, Paris, 1940, reviewed in *The Moslem World*, vol. 37, 1947, by the late Professor Walter L. Wright, Jr.

Attention may be called here to a work first published in 1911 with the title, *An Account of the Rise and Progress of Mahometism with the Life of Mahomet*, edited with an Introduction and Appendix by Ḥāfiẓ Maḥmūd Khān Shayrāni. It was published by private subscription under the auspices of the Islamic Society and by Luzac & Co., London. The work is ascribed to Dr. Henry Stubbe, M.A., of Christ Church, Oxford, who died in 1676. It is thought to have been written about 1672 or 1673. It is the first vindication and defense "of his religion from the Calumnies of the Christians" to have been written in English. The Muslim editor found it advisable to omit some passages offensive to modern taste and expressed regret for serious errors of the author, and he excused them because of the state of knowledge about Islam in seventeenth century England.

The book is interesting because it shows the attitude of at least one rationalist rebel to the fables and legends about Muhammad and Islam then flourishing in Western Europe. The editor added an appendix of his own on "Early Christian Legends and Fables Concerning Islam," which he also printed separately, deriving his material and references from standard and common English works.

These few but valuable accounts of literature in only two countries are enough to reveal a deplorable amount of misinformation all too common among writers for the public. The same errors about Islam are still found throughout the Western world. This lack of knowledge has not yet been remedied by popular education, because the Orient has not been included in the curriculum of the public schools.

To this day Oriental languages receive little or no recognition or attention in our modern language associations and schools. The Orient, and especially the Muslim East, remains amazed that so much wrong information about Eastern peoples exists everywhere in the West. The prevalent misunderstandings hurt the sensibilities of Orientals and endanger the welfare of the West.

Yet the impression must not be given that all the knowledge about Islam and the Muslims in Renaissance Europe was merely misinformation and suspicion. Some there were—and the number included Martin Luther, whose fanaticism Mr. Shayrāni mentions and illustrates—who were well acquainted with the facts and tenets of Islam, but who were too close to the propaganda of the Crusades to free themselves of prejudice and antagonism.

Furthermore, there is another aspect of the whole subject that needs to be kept in mind, especially by people whose heritage, environment, and education have accustomed them to the idea and experience of the separation of organized religion and government. Adherents of Western Protestantism tend to take it for granted that the separation of church and state is the right and normal institutional relationship. Usually those people have not had occasion to realize that such separation of ecclesiastical and civil authority is a comparatively modern minority movement in Christendom and is practically unknown to Islam and the other world religions. As an historical fact, until the Protestant Reformation in Europe reaffirmed what it held to be the New Testament teaching that the personal, spiritual, and voluntary nature of religion was more important than the communal, institutional, and imposed aspects of religious observances, Christianity, or rather one branch of the Christian Church, was integrated with the system of government of its area. That integration, begun in the time of Constantine, was made official for the Byzantine government by Theodosius in 380; it spread throughout Europe during the Dark and Middle Ages and persists in all the countries there with varying modifications until the present time. It was because society was a unified political and ecclesiastical system that the Crusades, the Wars of the Cross, which were basically international and intercontinental political and economic conflicts, included and expressed religious motives and attitudes.

Similarly the rulers of Islam, by means of their *jihād*, had spread their empire and consequently, to some extent, their religion by the conquests of their armies. The rivalries, antagonisms, hostilities, and hates which were aroused and expressed by worldly desires and means, influenced and indeed determined the religious attitudes of races, nations, and communities toward one another. The resultant war and battle feeling and psychology of the adherents of one religion toward those of another have not yet entirely disappeared. There is need in nearly all religious groups for forgiveness for the wrongs of the past, for understanding of the deficiencies of the present, for appreciation of all that is right and good, wherever they exist and for the spirit of humble, helpful fellowship in the service of man, God, and true religion.

We have seen that it was Islam that brought intellectual light and life to southwestern Europe. We have noted that it was the translation of the Koran into Latin and the study of the Arabic language that made a more accurate knowledge of Islam as a religion possible in Western Europe.

But Christians received more than knowledge of Arabic and Islam from the Muslims. It was Islamic and Arabic culture that provided the subjects and content which engaged the attention of educated medieval Christendom. It is true that those who put the legacy of Greek culture into Arabic were Christian scholars, but these Christians worked for Muslim patrons and produced Muslim scholars. It was the Muslims who absorbed this heritage, transmuted it into a Muslim culture and civilization, and then transmitted it as their treasure and legacy to the West. More specifically for our present purposes, the Muslims had learned the Hellenistic sciences and philosophy. Then they modified that philosophy, adapting it to their own Koranic theology. They accepted the Hellenistic description of the system of the universe, and then made Allah the Creator and Ruler of that system.

Then, following the example of some Neo-Platonists and the Christian thinkers generally, they also insisted on the necessity of divine revelation to supplement the attainments of philosophical speculation. Their theology made Muhammad and the Koran Allah's final revelation and messenger to mankind. That theology the Muslims took with them to the lands they conquered. The science and philosophy which they had accepted when they first became cultured themselves, they also taught when they became bearers of that culture to Western Europe and elsewhere. Then, in its turn, the substance of Arabic and Islamic scientific and philosophical culture became the content, with a different theology, of the Christian culture of the West.

There is a tendency on the part of some Christian scholars to minimize the extent of the influence of Muslim philosophical theologians upon Christian scholastic theology: the very labor of explanation and discrimination is itself evidence of the closeness of the relationship.

The few Christian leaders of the twelfth and thirteenth centuries who knew Arabic and the beliefs and practices of Islam were hindered, by their environment and the spirit of the age in both communions, from working with or for the Muslims with mutually acceptable success. There is still need for a different spirit for the peoples of Christendom and Islam to get along well together.

Thus far our account has stressed the antagonistic and deplorable attitudes that have existed through the centuries between Muslims and Christians. Some notable exceptions have been mentioned to show that Western interest in Arabic and Islamic literature and culture was not exclusively intolerant. In Spain and Southern

France there was a considerable knowledge and appreciation of Arabic poetry which resulted in the conscious adoption and imitation of Arabic poetic forms and subjects. The best and fullest report of this influence is to be found in *Hispano-Arabic Poetry and its Relations with the Old Provençal Troubadours*, by A. R. Nykl, Baltimore, 1946. Dr. Nykl's book gives abundant evidence that there was a closer and more sympathetic relation between Arabic and European cultures in the field of imaginative literature, apart from the drama, than in religious and philosophical concerns and studies. It is curious that Arabic literature until the last century never included dramatic works, although shadow and puppet plays flourished in Constantinople and Cairo before then. But interest in Arabic story literature and poetry began early in Europe and has never ceased. For instance, both Dante and Chaucer used much Islamic story material. Translations of Arabic poetry into English began in 1750 with the publication by Sir William Jones of *The Moallakat or the Seven Arabian Poems which were suspended on the Temple of Mecca*. Translations of other Arabic poetry have appeared in every generation since. Long and short poems, using Arabian incident and idea and even meter, by prominent and other English and American poets, have become innumerable.

It was the appearance of Antoine Galland's French translation of *Les mille et une Nuits* early in the eighteenth century, that gave a new and strong impetus to widespread interest in Oriental life and thought. The retranslation of the French version into other languages of Europe followed immediately and also stimulated imitations of the Arabic tales in many Western literatures.

These prose and poetic examples of Arabic literary ability, with their accounts of the thoughts and conduct of Islamic peoples as revealed by themselves, gave enjoyment to adults and children alike. Now, with multitudes, the new information about Muslim lands and Arabic civilization produced appreciation and admiration that before had been confined largely to scholars and to all too few of them. Then in 1734 there was published not the first translation of the Koran in English, but the first good translation, that by George Sale, whose quality is so evident that in spite of later and better translations, reprintings of it are still in regular demand.

From then on, the public had access to adequate and authoritative information about Muhammad and his Book, and the number of those seriously interested in Islam greatly increased. Probably the best example of the sympathetic interest that the new knowledge of the literature of the Muslim East produced is Sir Edwin Arnold's *Pearls of the Faith*, which put into poetry the ideas expressed by the Ninety-Nine Most Beautiful Names of Allāh.

But it has taken over eight centuries of learning, research, and teaching by hundreds of scholars in the universities of many countries of Europe to provide the tools and the materials for study that have enabled amateur and professional orientalists to translate and emulate Arabic authors in the poetic, religious, and other fields. Not the least indication of the growing appreciation of the cultural interrelations of even the modern West to the medieval East is the large bibliography of books and articles dealing with the subject. One of the best brief discussions is to be found in Professor T. Cuyler Young's "Christendom's Cultural Debt to Islam," in *The Moslem World*, vol. 35, 1945, with a full apparatus of references. Since then Professor DeLacy O'Leary has published a book of 196 pages entitled *How Greek Science Passed to the Arabs*, London, 1949. In spite of many mistakes it provides much background for the earlier article by R. Walzer on "Arabic Transmission of Greek Thought to Medieval Europe," which appeared in the *Bulletin of the John Rylands Library*, Manchester, 1945, which, of course, was not listed in Professor Young's article.

Among the accounts that have been published dealing specifically with the progress of Oriental studies in Europe, the fullest—but of course now out of date—is that of Gustave Dugat, *Histoire des orientalistes de l'Europe, du XIIe au XIXe siecle, précédée d'une Esquisse Historique des Études orientales*, Paris, 1868, 1870. This essay deals with the three main Islamic languages, and others also. It mentions the important translators and dictionary-makers, whose works gave solidity and confidence to the few who wanted valid first-hand knowledge about the Turks, Persians, and Arabs and their literatures.

Now the most accessible and best brief information about the earliest Arabists—such as, to mention British orientalists only, Abelard of Bath, "the first Englishman to learn Arabic," Robert of Chester, who participated in making the first Latin translation of the Koran (cf. *Al-Andalus*, vol. XIV, 1949, pp. 154 ff.), Michael Scot, Roger Bacon, and their successors down to the fifteenth century—is of course the *Introduction to the History of Science*, by George Sarton, 3 vols., 1909, 1927, 1949. Later orientalists and their works receive mention but not extended attention in *La science Arabe*, by Aldo Miele, Leiden, 1938.

Dugat's volumes mention the first edition of the Arabic grammar published at Leiden in 1613 and the very hostile Du Ryer French translation of the Koran in 1649, "Englished" the same year, possibly by Alexander Ross, with the same hostile attitude. Golius, in 1653 at Leiden, published his Arabic-Latin Dictionary and Meninski in 1680 his *Thesaurus linguarum orientalium*. In 1697 d'Herbelot published at Paris his *Bibliothèque orientale*, "a magnificent work for the time when it was composed." This encyclopedia had many editions and provided scholars and authors of Europe with their most convenient if not always most reliable sources of information about Muslim history, government, religion, science, and personalities.

After completing his general survey in fifty-one pages, Dugat proceeds to give short or long biographical sketches of thirty later orientalists of England, France, Germany, Italy, Russia, Spain, Sweden, and Switzerland, from Kosegarten to Wüstenfeld.

Most, but not all, of these scholars dealt with Western Asia, but a much longer list has since been made, of British scholars alone, who specialized in the Islamic languages and literature. During World War II a brochure on "British Orientalists" was prepared by Professor A. J. Arberry. It includes an account of William Bedwell, the father of Oriental Studies in England. It expresses only the highest appreciation of Oriental literary and cultural values. It makes up in part for the uninformed and prejudiced depreciation of Islamic peoples and principles far too prevalent, earlier and even now, in the West.

Even though it may be assumed that this brochure and other booklets and magazines in English and other languages may have been written as propaganda to enlist the sympathy and aid of Muslim and other peoples, still, in so far as the statements in them are true and just, they impart interesting information that should be widely known. The result should be better understanding and greater appreciation and cooperation for the common objectives and benefits between the West and the East, and ultimately between all areas and peoples of the world.

In the past, as we have seen, the spirit of Islamdom and Christendom has been excessively partisan and unsympathetic. The attitudes of both resulted from fundamental differences of doctrines in Islam and Christianity as religions. The two religions are indeed basically different in many respects. Their claims of allegiance are mutually exclusive. But there is no reason inherent in either religion as such why the difference in basic religious beliefs and principles should result in personal attitudes of enmity and in overt actions of conflict. Warfare and compulsion belong, if anywhere, to secular life and worldly concerns. The Koran contains a verse gloriously true. It is known to all Muslims and should be known to all other people in the world. The verse says, "There is no compulsion at all in religion" (II, 257). It is unfortunately but historically true, that most Muslims have held that the period of authority of this statement was terminated or abrogated by the numerous "verses of the sword" in the Koran which were proclaimed at al-Madīnah when Islam became a political as well as a religious movement. Six centuries earlier Jesus Christ had taught the same fundamental principle that religious duties were to be kept separate from any governmental obligations in the words, "Render to Caesar the things that are Caesar's and to God the things that are God's" (Mark 12:17).

Historically Christianity remained primarily a religion until under Theodosius at Constantinople in 380 it became officially the religion of the Eastern Roman Empire. Islam also began simply as a religion until in A.D. 622 political and legislative powers were added to Muhammad's religious role. Nevertheless, for both communions, for all people, at all times, religion is, in its essential nature, purely a matter of the spirit. It is the spirit that must have authority over the outward acts of man, if those acts are to have religious value.

Religions in their formal statements may and do make exclusive claims. They may and do claim the exclusive allegiance of all men. But no religion, as such, has any inherent right to use political, economic, or social compulsion to secure acceptance or observance. The only motive, the only authority, valid in religion as such is spiritual, voluntary, personal and sincere.

If these statements are true in fact and valid for conduct, then it should be possible for people East and West and everywhere to study and discuss together any subject of interest, and especially religion, without fear of any unfairness and with all good will and appreciation and with every hope of finding truth, goodness, and God together.

It is admitted that in the past the study of Islam by Christians, and of Christianity by Muslims, has largely been controversial. The results have been negative for the most part. A new attitude and method are needed in the West for an accurate and adequate knowledge of Islam. A method and attitude were presented in a paper on "Arabic Religious Literature, New Approaches in Research," read at the Princeton University Bicentennial Conference on Near Eastern Culture and Society, March 26, 1947. The paper was published in full in the *Ignace Goldziher Memorial Volume, Part 1*, Budapest, 1948. The final section is reproduced here by the kind permission of the editors of the Goldziher volume and at the request of the editor of this Symposium.[1]

Our third and final classification of the ways to study theological literature calls attention to some new personal attitudes and psychological factors in religious research.

It is not necessary to describe the supreme importance of religion in the culture and society of the Orient. The history and literature of every Eastern country reveal that religion not only permeates every interest and activity of the people, but also that it is the most dominant element in the life of most men and women of the Orient. It cannot be said that any noticeable proportion of the people of the East are indifferent to the religion of their community. It is quite impossible for Westerners to understand the culture and society of the East without learning about the religions of the communities there. The Sacred Books of the East, the Bibles of the World, the theological literature, the religious

---

[1] The first two categories suggested in connection with new approaches in research in this field were: (a) the mechanical, or instrumental means and facilities available to the student; (b) the methodological, or system and scheme followed by the student.

history of the Orient, all have a proper place in every cultural conference and academic course dealing with the Eastern world.

But there is need for something new and different in the approach to the study of Oriental religious life and literature. Lucretius in his time indicted religion for the most and the worst of the evils of man's inhumanity to man. The Crusades of the Middle Ages increased to continental scale the evils of wars in the name of religion. The literatures in the languages of ancient and medieval times preserve the hate, the falsehood, the evil, sanctioned, and indeed taught, by some leaders of one religion against the adherents of other faiths.

The wars of this century have been more extensive, more intensive, and worse than the wars of the past. But in one respect at least they have been better. They have not been wars of religion. Even though religious principles have had a part in their motivation and conduct, our modern wars have not been fought to win converts or extend the dominion of any religion.

Religious freedom for the individual is the new element in the life of our modern world. In the past the individual, whether he was a Socrates in Athens, a Jesus in Jerusalem, a Hypatia in Alexandria, or a Latimer at Oxford in the sixteenth century, had to conform to the religious pattern of the community—or else suffer. The non-conformist who criticized or rejected the communal religion was treated as a traitor to his nation. When religion and government became separate departments of public life, liberty of conscience in religion became an individual right, and the modern world was born. It is encouraging to know that a prominent Indian Muslim has recommended to his fellow-Muslims that they study the history of Christianity, the Renaissance, and the Protestant movement which resulted in the separation of the church from the state.[2] When the Eastern peoples free their personal religion from the compulsions exercised by government, they will move from their medieval state into the modern world.

It is this element of liberty of conscience in personal religion that should characterize all modern research in the religious literature of the past, the present and the future. The canons of

[2] See *Islam Today*, edited by A. J. Arberry and Rom Landau (London, 1943), chapter on India by Sir Hassan Suhrawardy, p. 208.

criticism must not be conformity to any system, but should be the same as the canons of criticism in any other department of human interest, where the standards are truth, goodness, right, and beauty.

Freedom of religion implies that the individual need not conform to the pattern of the majority in religious thought and purely private practice. It is not so generally recognized that it also implies that conformity to majority conduct should be a conscious and voluntary attitude, definitely adopted by the individual.

When any student of religion, whether an adherent or a nonadherent of that religion, examines any piece of religious literature, and studies it from the standpoint of the general principles of beauty, goodness, right, and truth, then he is abiding by the principles that characterize the modern scholar and which distinguish him from the medieval scholastic.

A good example of this approach to religious literature is found in a review of a recent English translation of the Koran made by A. Yusuf Ali. The Arabic text and English translation with copious notes were first published at Lahore in 1938. The review of that translation by Professor Arthur Jeffery appeared in *The Moslem World* in January 1940. The review is a model of appreciation by one conscientious gentleman of the spiritual values of a sincere and worthy adherent of another religion. The personal attitude expressed in that review represents (to me) the new approach that should mark all individual work on the literature of any religion.

Still another new procedure that will improve the quality of research in religious literature is cooperative study of a theological subject or book by two students, one from the Orient and the other from the West. Such personal collaboration should be extended to include the association of an orientalist trained in scholarly method, with one or more Orientals as co-workers investigating modern religious problems and movements. Such sharing of techniques and experiences, with joint responsibility and credit for results, would produce reliable studies and mutual understanding which would tend to unify the culture of the East and West.

With all having access to all knowledge, with all free to think, with all having the training and encouragement to accept what is true and right and good, there is the possibility that one religion may ultimately prevail in the world.

Certainly I, for one, shall be glad to follow and recommend one world religion which, among other things, is based on what is historically true, which promotes social righteousness, which inspires the highest moral goodness and which gives beauty for ashes and love for hate.

PART II

The East Meets the West: Current Problems
of Near Eastern Peoples

7

INTERACTION OF ISLAMIC
AND WESTERN THOUGHT IN TURKEY

BY ABDULHAK ADNAN-ADIVAR

THE INTERACTION OF ISLAMIC AND WESTERN THOUGHT, a subject of peculiar importance at the present time, is a process begun more than a thousand years ago. It presents a problem which has concerned the Turks no less than the Arabs, since the Turks occupied the forefront of the Islamic world for over five centuries. Foreign, in a sense, to both Islamic and European cultures, the Turks were well placed to effect some form of synthesis of the two civilizations. In this they largely failed, primarily through an inability to shake off the dogmatism of Islam. The attempt is still in process, however, possibly now with greater urgency and promise of success than in any time of the past.

The Turks of Central Asia first came in contact with Islam at the beginning of the eighth century, at a time when among the Arabs themselves Islam was no more than a series of rituals to be performed without discussion of the faith required of its followers and the heaven-sent Koran a book to be learned by heart. Although the Turks were for long frankly skeptical of Islam's continued success, the increasing ability of the Arab State to organize its economic and social affairs greatly impressed the Turks. Moreover, the monotheistic, realistic, military character of Islam suited the Turkish temperament. As the Turks were followers of Shamanism or Buddhism, their conversion was sporadic and it was not until the eleventh century that their adherence to Islam became global. Once effected, however, this conversion of the Turks to Islam proved to be one of the most important events of Islamic history, if not, indeed of world history as well. Once converted, the Turks became not only passionate defenders of their new faith against other religions, but at the same time opponents of all heterodox sects and schisms within Islam itself.

It was only after this global conversion that the Turks came in contact with Greek, that is Occidental, thought and then only through the work of philosophers who wrote in Arabic. According to al-Bīrūni (d. 1048)—of whose origins I am uncertain in spite of the enthusiastic declarations of Turkish historians and scholars—Islamic culture was then becoming an extension of Greek culture. Nevertheless, it must be admitted that this Greek influence was largely sterile; philosophers talked, wrote, discussed theological and philosophic problems, but Islamic thought did not develop in any notable way except among certain heterodox sects, and among those liberal spirits known in the history of Islam as al-Mu'tazilah, or rationalist schismatics.

Of the Islamic philosophers who attempted to reconcile Islamic concepts, as expressed in the Koran, with both Aristotelian and Platonic philosophy, mention must be made of al-Fārābi, whose Turkish origin is incontestable. He was the first Muslim philosopher to give a high place to Neo-Platonism in Oriental philosophy; he was the first, moreover, to present the problem of the relation of revelation to scientific reasoning. He was the first as well to recognize the part played by mystical experience in religion, thus exhibiting interest in both major aspects of Islamic thought: orthodoxy and mysticism.

Al-Fārābi's own teaching took a dogmatic turn and aided in the gradual crystallization of Islamic orthodoxy, a process completed by the work of al-Ghazzāli in the twelfth century. Mystical thought, however, persisted until modern times, finally developing into a type of pantheism. An outcome of intuition and emotion rather than of reason, it was expressed in the form of brotherhoods professing various types of asceticism. But it, too, eventually lost its philosophical character and vitality as living thought, and turned into something rigid and mechanical.

Islamic thought was at this stage in the thirteenth century, when the high plateau of Asia Minor had come to be dominated by the Turkish Saljūqs of Rūm, the immediate predecessors of the Ottoman Turks and the ancestors of the present inhabitants of Turkey. In the Saljūq schools, or *madrasahs*, the only sciences taught were jurisprudence (*fiqh*) and theology, always in a dogmatic form, always conforming to the precepts of the Koran and to the Traditions of the Prophet. In the second half of the century the great Ṣūfi poet and philosopher, Jalāl-al-Dīn-i-Rūmi, living at Konya, in the very heart of Asia Minor, spoke disdainfully of the ignorance which reigned in philosophical matters. It is evident that neither rational science nor speculative Greek philosophy in its true sense was then apparent in the lands which constitute the Turkey of today.

In the fifteenth century, one hundred and fifty years after the foundation of the Ottoman Empire, Muslim thought was still represented in the *madrasah* by the study only of theology, rhetoric, and jurisprudence; philosophy and rational science, the two pillars of Greek thought re-erected by the Oriental philosophers of the ninth and tenth centuries, were shaken, if not completely demolished. Aside from a few rare exceptions, we can discern no sign of that critical and philosophical spirit which characterized Greek philosophy.

It was at this moment that a young man of twenty-three, Meḥmet the Conqueror, established a closer contact with his European neighbors by penetrating to the last frontiers of Byzantium. In the month of May 1453, he entered Constantinople over the ruins of the last rampart of Western civilization in the East. This young monarch, gifted with a keen intellectual curiosity, developed through his relations with the Muslim heretical Ḥurūfi sect, presently turned his attention to the peripatetic school of philosophy and Greek science which shook the very foundations of medieval scholastic thought in Western Europe. The young sultan's curiosity, extending even to the study of Christian theology, made him at times appear to Western Christendom as an aspirant to the Christian faith. But what Meḥmet really desired was to make a comparative study of the two great religions, as well as of metaphysics, and thus to find out the difference between revelation and reason. Scholastic philosophy and Greek science were both intensively studied during his reign. Symposiums, to which the greatest native and foreign scholars were invited and during which metaphysical and philosophical problems were under discussion, became frequent events, lasting sometimes for days. In brief, this man of the East and West was trying to create a true interaction of Islamic and Western culture and was making a sincere effort to replace dogmatic by critical thought.

But it must be admitted that the efforts of this intelligent and intellectual monarch did not produce lasting results, and that Turkey once more returned to the obscurantism of the Middle Ages which was to continue until the nineteenth, even the twentieth century. During the two and a half centuries that passed between the conquest of Constantinople and the Treaty of Carlowitz (1699), Turkish armies marched on to central Europe, establishing contacts with Western nations; but these military incursions failed to bring about intellectual contact between the two worlds. On the contrary, the critical spirit of modern times, that is of the Renaissance, retreated before the dogmatic spirit which then reigned supreme in the lands of Islam.

Turkey reached the limits of its territorial expansion in the sixteenth century, during the reign of Sulaymān the Magnificent. The cultivation of philosophical and scientific thought did not keep pace, however, with the political and administrative development of this age of splendor and glory. One may once more observe with a recent writer that the golden age of Culture does not necessarily coincide with that of national expansion. For even after these territorial conquests the dogmatic side of Muslim thought held its ground, leaving no opportunity for the development of a renaissance spirit in Turkey. The seventeenth century geographer and polygrapher, Kātib Chelebi (known as Ḥājji Khalifah to Westerners) in his *Mīzān al-Haqq*, an apology for ancient philosophy and science, complains bitterly of the state of mind which had driven these branches of human knowledge from Turkey's institutions of learning. He expresses his disapproval of the mentality in a significant sentence: "Henceforth, people will be looking at the universe with the eyes of oxen." This finds further illustration in the fact that the astronomical system of Copernicus was mentioned for the first time in 1685, in the Turkish translation of Blau's *Atlas Major*, and then only in a few lines.

The date in Ottoman history which marks the beginning of a contact, if not exactly with Western thought at least with Western technique, is perhaps 1716, when there was a tentative reform in the Turkish army. To meet the requirements of this elementary reform, modern mathematics was introduced into the curriculum of the Military Engineering School. In 1728 the great Turkish editor and printer, Ibrāhīm Mutafarriqah, founded the first printing press and began rather timidly to publish works, written or edited by him, dealing with Western science and culture. But even he speaks with reserve of Copernicus' heliocentric system, remarking that he had added an excursus on these new theories in his edition of the *Jihānnuma* of Ḥājji Khalifah with the purpose of furnishing an occasion to Muslim scholars to refute them, and consequently to fortify the basis of the Ptolemaic system, so dear to them all.

It was only with the advent of the French Revolution that a new ideology appeared on the horizon. This politico-intellectual movement of the modern world interested Sultan Selim III and drew his attention to Western culture, although exclusively to the sciences relevant to military art. In the early part of the nineteenth century a modern medical school was opened, emphasizing mostly medical technique, a development which was still insufficient, however, to represent Western thought in its essence.

Finally, there came in 1839 the beginning of a much more essential reform period known as the "Tanẓīmāt," or period of "Organization and Reform." Its influence was felt in all aspects of political life from individual rights to the organization of tribunals; it even penetrated Turkish social customs. Considering that science had now become a part of the teaching in the schools, and that Western thought had at last come in contact with Muslim thought, one might assume that there would be an interaction of the two outlooks in which both would be duly represented. Yet the interaction still did not take place, for the persisting autocratic and theocratic character of the state did not allow a free interchange of opinion between the partisans of the two systems of thought. On the contrary, this period, which was to continue until the Young Turk Revolution of 1908, was marked by a desire to defend the theological precepts of Islam against modern science. This desire was so intense and so characteristic of the age that it may be termed a new era of apology in Islam. Even the "modern" authors, the intelligentsia who had traveled and studied in the West, did not hesitate to defend those very religious ideas which appeared contrary to scientific fact. Considering their Westernized culture, these writers could not have believed in the ideas which they defended in their apologies. Possibly their attitude was a result of official censorship and of the moral pressure which rose to the defense of the old order. The dogmatic side of Islamic thought was immune from attack, for contemporary writers did not dare even to question it. Official pressure against the penetration of Western thought was such that toward the end of 'Abdul Ḥamīd II's reign, just before the Revolution of 1908, the very word *ḥikmah* (philosophy) was taken out of the dictionaries by order of the government.

But it is more than probable that in spite of all these apologies and fervent declarations against free thought, in spite of all the official pressure, Western ideas were being propagated. We might cite the characteristic case of a so-called apologist, Aḥmet Midhat, who translated J. W. Draper's *History of the Conflict between Religion and Science*. In his excursus added to refute Draper's ideas, he deliberately affirms that there is nothing contrary to science in Islam.

Incidents such as this strengthen one in the conclusion that most of the Turkish intellectuals of the Tanzīmāt period retained their Oriental mentality and culture, with all the associated and antiquated beliefs, while adopting the technical side of modern life. Quite a few among them had the courage to attempt a reconciliation between Islamic beliefs and modern science, but unfortunately their syncretism did not succeed. The only institution, though short-lived, which did not attempt anything of this sort but was devoted entirely to Western thought, was the Ottoman Society of Science (1897-1898). It gathered around it Turkish scholars who knew at least one European language, and started the *Majmū-i-Funūn*, the "Review of Science," the first publication in Turkish in which one could read independently written articles on modern philosophy. Since the principal collaborators of the *Majmū'-i-Funūn* had studied in England, most of their essays were inspired by Anglo-Saxon works. They approached a scientific or philosophical question without taking into consideration the religious dogmatism of the official scholars (*'ulemā'-i-rusūm*). Unfortunately, this society did not last long and the review also passed away. But as long as the movement lasted, its supreme characteristic continued to be its independence of the dogmatic thought cultivated in the *madrasah*, and its refusal to fall in with any sort of futile syncretism.

After the disappearance of the *Majmū'-i-Funūn*, the government of Abdul Hamid II suppressed all expression of philosophical ideas, that is to say, of thought itself. Hence in the last days of the period known as the Tanzīmāt, one finds no serious interaction of Oriental and Occidental philosophical thought in Turkey. Nevertheless, in spite of all these obstacles, Western thought was gaining ground in literature, thanks to the literary school called the *Servet-i-Funūn* and the review named after it.

In 1908 the Young Turk Revolution broke out in an exclusively political form. Intellectual activity followed suit when philosophy and the comparative study of religions were admitted to the curriculum of the Faculty of Letters of the University of Istanbul. Political liberty having cleared the way for freedom of investigation, a critical study of religious thought became possible. In the very first year of the new constitutional regime, young writers began to translate the works of the somewhat naïve materialists of the nineteenth century, such as Ludwig Buchner and Ernest Haeckel. Voltaire and Rousseau, as well as the other Encyclopedists of the eighteenth century, also became fashionable, and their works were freely discussed.

Concurrently a religious revival made itself felt in the conservative section of the intellectual circles as well as among the writers of a new school of apologists, and foreshadowed the beginning of a conflict between the already irreconcilable groups. At this time the dogmatic and the critical schools of thought had not yet developed a formalized position toward each other. Though one might say that Western thought had taken an aggressive attitude toward Muslim thought, the conflict was not too apparent, each taking a reserved, or rather an ill-disguised hypocritical point of view toward the other.

In the midst of this incertitude, a Turkish sociologist, Ziyā Gökalp, assumed the role of mediator between the antagonistic groups, attempting in his writings to find some ground of reconciliation between Western scientific thought and the purely religious Muslim thought. A faithful follower of Durckheim, he proposed to make a distinction between civilization and culture. His idea was that Turkey should adopt Western civilization yet retain a national culture, both without alteration. He differed from his predecessors by trying to bring about a synthesis rather than a syncretism. He repeatedly advised his countrymen not to neglect either Islam and Islamic culture or Western civilization.

While Gökalp clearly stated that it was necessary to adopt all of positive science and its technique, he was not at all clear on the subject of philosophy. He went so far as to say that the Turks were to have a national philosophy, but he said nothing on what that philosophy was to be. He himself was saturated with both the sociology of Durckheim and the spiritual philosophy of Bergson, but never attempted to reconcile the two—a task which would have been most difficult indeed.

Ziyā Gökalp's teachings had a profound influence not only upon his own disciples but also upon the members of the Young Turk Central Committee of Union and Progress, most of whom were his political friends. It was owing to him that family law, fashioned in the past by Muslim jurisprudence (*fiqh*), was now modified according to the ancient but more liberal interpretation of the Muslim doctors of law. He did not conceal his intention of undertaking a religious reform, stating on several occasions that even Christianity had not been able to reconcile itself to modern civilization before the Reformation. The movement expressed itself in the *Yeñi Majmū'ah*, a review subsidized by the Committee of Union and Progress in spite of the theocratic character of the state, the head of which was the Caliph uniting in his person both spiritual and temporal power.

Ziyā Gökalp's most unfortunate mistake was the erroneous translation of the word "laic" as "lā-dīni" (irreligious), an error that did much to lead the Muslim clergy, with the Shaykh al-Islām at their head, into a hostile attitude. The reactionary point of view, though hidden in the form of an apology, was expressed in another magazine published at the time, the *Ṣirāt-i-Mustaqīm*, later called the *Sabil al-Reishad*, which rained invective on the heads of the partisans of the liberal movement led by Gökalp. This particular period in Turkish history was dominated by violent and sudden changes of governments and quasi-reactionary uprisings of the opposition, a part of whose political game was to stir the Muslim Turks against the Union and Progress government by castigating the party's modest attempt at modernization as anti-Muslim heresies and atheisms. Persecution of the liberals served only to strengthen their faith and spread their ideas, with the result that during this period a real interaction of Muslim and Western thought was at last under way.

After 1912 the successive wars in Tripoli, the Balkans, and finally all Europe left no leisure to the young liberal group of the *Yeñi Majmū'ah* for intellectual activity. With the armistice an absolute indifference to everything, a sense of being "fed up" coupled with an intellectual opportunism, seems to have taken hold of the reformers. Turks then witnessed the domination of occupation forces of Western Europe. Though the occupation army encouraged the emancipation of women, it came to an understanding with the political and religious reactionaries, and supported the most fanatical precepts of Islam, which were offered as a kind of spiritual nourishment to a people embittered by the misery and the suffering three successive wars had brought.

The puppet Turkish government of those days, established and sustained by the occupying forces, whipped up the religious and fanatic sentiments of the people in order to counteract popular risings in the different provinces of the country, risings which were to turn into a strong, organized movement for liberation and independence. This movement finally developed into the great struggle for liberation which after four desperate years ended in final victory. While engaged in this struggle for life and death, the Turks had no time to argue such cultural questions as the conflict or interaction of Islamic and Western thought; on the contrary the liberation movement took a tolerant, even a soft attitude toward the insolent and at times dangerous clergy in order to enlist their help.

The new Turkish government, once firmly established in Ankara, abolished the Sultanate in 1923, leaving the Caliph in Istanbul without temporal power. Two years later the Caliphate also was abolished, together with the tribunals of the Canon Law and all other religious institutions in the country. The *madrasahs* and the *takīyahs*, the latter a kind of convent for religious brotherhoods, were not spared in this sweeping abolition, and the principle of laicism was established as a special article in the constitution of the Republic. The apologists were not inactive, however. They went on defending Islamic thought and faith, trying at the same time to reconcile them with natural and scientific laws, and emphasizing the true meaning of laicism. This was a praiseworthy effort in a way, for it demanded tolerance from both sides, hitherto antagonistic. But the young Republic had no intention of making any concession whatsoever to Islamic thought, though it tolerated the traditional religious practices of the people. The domination of Western thought, or rather of the positivism of the West, was at that time so intense that one can hardly call it thought. It should be termed rather the "official dogma of irreligion." To paraphrase the imaginative language of Professor H. A. R. Gibb, Turkey became a positivistic mausoleum.

The Republic has never ceased to declare itself the citadel of scientific positivism and of the positivist school of thought. The entire mechanism of the state, by common accord, has been trying to put into its different institutions the positivist formula—the Good, the Beautiful, and the True—as a new doctrine. Within the last twenty years the vast majority of Turkish youth has been brought up without any official religious teaching, Western positivism being imposed on it just as Islamic dogma had been imposed in the past.

At the present moment the New Thought has assumed much the same position as was formerly occupied by the old Islamic dogma. It is thus still impossible to point to any period in the history of ideas in Turkey when a free and critical spirit has stimulated an interaction of Islamic and Western thought for any length of time. There has, indeed, been no true interaction in Turkey, but rather merely an action of Western thought *on* that country.

In December 1946, two deputies to the Turkish National Assembly rose during the budget discussions of the Department of Education and asked a question regarding the fate of religious institutions, and specifically of the teaching of the Muslim catechism by private individuals, in view of the fact that these particular teachings are not favorably regarded by the government, and private individuals do not dispose of the means necessary to procure teachers. The answer of the government to this question was evasive, since it feared the possibility of a religious reaction which might endanger the well-established reforms of the Republic. But a few days later this important and significant discussion was taken up in the Central Committee of the governmental party. This event, which would not be considered as anything out of the way in the West, is of supreme significance in Turkey today, for within the last twenty years or so no such discussion has been possible in political or even in cultural gatherings of any sort.

When a free, critical spirit makes itself felt in Turkey, the interaction of Western and Islamic thought will be accomplished in a more concrete, clear, and lasting form; and it is quite possible that such a sudden interaction may produce a religious and philosophical reform within the lay framework of the Republic. Only when a reform of this kind comes about will Turkey be able to combine the streams of its cultural heritage and evolve an integrated intellectual movement.

INTERACTION OF ISLAMIC
AND WESTERN THOUGHT IN IRAN

BY T. CUYLER YOUNG

TOGETHER WITH THE ARABS AND THE TURKS, Persians shared the heritage of Greek, or Western thought common to all Islam. "The harmonization of Greek philosophy with Islam begun by al-Kindi, an Arab, was continued by al-Fārābi, a Turk, and completed in the East by ibn-Sīna, a Persian . . . who placed the sum total of Greek wisdom codified by his own ingenuity, at the disposal of the educated Muslim world in an intelligible form."[1] Through the great al-Ghazzāli and others, Iran also contributed her share in the development of that dogmatic orthodoxy which became the barrier to any further creative interaction between Islamic and Western thought.

It was, however, in the more fruitful realm of mysticism that Iran made her outstanding contribution to Islamic thought: this found its classical expression in the great poets from Rūmi to Jāmi, who expressed the potential if not the realized interaction of East and West in his famous couplet:

> O Lord, none but Thyself can fathom Thee,
> Yet every mosque and church doth harbor Thee.

It is, of course, amazing to observe the similarities of the Medieval Christian and Islamic expressions of the profound religious mystical experience, but it can scarcely be demonstrated that there was any truly creative interchange between Islam and Christendom during the flourit of this way of life and thought.

Although the mysticism of the ascetic brotherhoods in Iran also—to quote Dr. Adnan—"lost its philosophical character and vitality as living thought, and turned into something rigid and

[1] Philip K. Hitti, *History of the Arabs,* London, 1949, 4th ed., pp. 371f.

mechanical"[2] even as in Islam to the West, significant exceptions to this general rule have, however, persisted here to the East down to recent times. The continuing influence of the Persians' great poetry upon the rank and file of the people, their native intellectual curiosity and speculative turn of mind, and their detachment from Western and Sunnite Islam after 1500 have served to account for the continuing vitality of mysticism as well as of philosophy among groups outside the main stream of Shi'ah orthodoxy. Yet during the entire medieval period there was no true interaction between Islamic and Occidental thought in Iran.

With the establishment of the Ṣafavi Empire, however, a new turn was made in the history of Iran, both in relation to other Islamic peoples and powers and to those of Western Christendom. It was during the sixteenth and seventeenth centuries that Western life and thought began to penetrate modern Iran. This was a period—broadly speaking—of national Iranian revival, characterized by withdrawal from Arabic-speaking society, the designation of Shi'ah Islam as the established Iranian faith, and a subsequent clash between the Ṣafavis and Osmanlis. Yet withdrawal from free and facile intercourse with Islamic society as a whole could not lead to political or cultural isolation, for the expansionism of the Western powers and Iran's own geographic heritage made necessary the determination of the nation's place in an even greater society.

The Ṣafavi rulers, and especially Shah 'Abbās the Great (1589-1629), were hospitable to European contacts of various kinds: political and diplomatic, military and commercial, social and cultural. Envoys were exchanged with several Western European states, including the Vatican, and the superior artillery techniques of Europe were adopted for the common struggle against the Turk; Portuguese, English, and Dutch merchants were welcomed and advantage taken of their rivalries; Augustinian, Carmelite, and Capuchin monks were permitted to settle and establish mission stations; of these the Carmelites were the most important, remaining over a century and a half following their reception by Shah 'Abbās in 1604.

Yet this penetration of Western ways of life and thought, wel-

[2] See preceding chapter.

comed by all on the basis of equality and mutual respect, was not sufficient to effect any creative intellectual interaction between the East and the West. This was in no small measure due to the Ṣafavi patronage and encouragement of Shī'ah theology and practice, which fused Persian patriotism and religion into an increasingly dogmatic, indeed fanatical, amalgam that withstood the corrosive acids of Western modernity. This was the price paid for the new political self-consciousness and power by the usually curious and hospitable Persian mind, which during this period produced only one first-rate, bona fide philosopher, Mulla Sadra of Shīrāz.

During the Ṣafavi period, therefore, Iran continued to be dominated by Shī'ah Islamic thought: its culture was medieval in character and its society essentially feudal in organization. The educational media for the transmission of Islamic influence were the *maktab*, the mosque schools teaching the elements of the Koran and religious literature to a small minority of the community, and the *madrasah*, the mosque theological schools which gave higher education of essentially a religious character to the few who by social position or unusual ability aspired to such learning and distinction. Although Islam offered relatively limited media for a formal education, it must be remembered that there was a host of informal troubadours and storytellers who roamed the Iranian plateau entertaining and educating successive Iranian generations in the ancient lore and literature, so that "the population, though unlettered, is not unlearned, and has a better knowledge of the Persian classics than the average European has of the masterpieces of his race."[3] Even so, the means of enlightenment were woefully meager compared to those developing in the West, which was growing more aggressive with each passing decade.

During the eighteenth century, following the collapse of Ṣafavi rule in 1722, an interregnum of blood-letting and tax-paying conquest under Nādir Shah, succeeded by social confusion and internecine strife before and after the short peaceful interlude under Karīm Khān Zand, coincided with the by-passing of Iran by the expansion of Western European political power and trade, but with the intrusion of Tsarist Russia into the affairs of the northern

[3] Sir Arnold T. Wilson, *Persia,* London, 1932, p. 36.

provinces of Iran. The disparity in power between a weaker Iran and the dynamic, aggressive West reduced disastrously the former's share of true mutuality in the East-West cultural interaction.

This significant shift in the position of Iran marked the rise to power of the Turkish-speaking Qājār dynasty (1796-1926) and put the country on the defensive when, in the Napoleonic era, contacts with Europe were greatly accelerated and Western influence in Iran became of increasing significance. It is no accident that these contacts developed concurrently with the political and economic pressures of the rival imperialisms of Russia and Great Britain. It was especially the Russo-Iranian treaties of *Gulistān* and *Turkomānchāi*, of 1813 and 1828 respectively, which convinced the Iranian government that the adoption of Western military techniques was necessary to maintain national integrity and to resist foreign pressure. It was primarily for this purpose that Nāṣir-al-Dīn Shah's minister, Mīrza Taqi Khān, founded the Dār al-Funūn, or academy of arts and sciences in 1852. This institution was European in organization, staffed by a majority of Europeans, who not only taught Western science, history and culture, but published Persian translations in these fields. Until well into the twentieth century this academy was the center of influence in the dissemination of Western thought, techniques, and science.

Sharing in this educational phase of Iran's modernization were the numerous schools founded by the French, Americans, and British, later augmented somewhat by the Russians and Germans. Beginning as elementary schools, most had reached the secondary level in the twentieth century, and during the reign of Riza Shah Pahlavi (1926-1941) three—two American and one British—had attained college status. Most of these schools were missionary in character—the French largely Roman Catholic and the American and British Protestant. These schools stimulated the Iranians to the founding of both private and governmental institutions of a similar nature.

Strong though both American and British educational programs became, it was the French contributions along these lines which proved most influential up to World War II. The first French school was founded in Tabriz in 1839 by the Lazarite mission which, with Les Filles de la Charité, eventually established seventy-six schools throughout the country. In addition there were foundations of the Alliance Française. It was French culture which proved to be the acceptable channel for the flow of most Western science and thought into Iran. The reasons, no doubt, are to be found chiefly in the prevailing use of French as a diplomatic language; the superior diplomatic representation of France in Iran during parts of the nineteenth century; the absence of French political and economic designs upon the country, combined with French power to resist British pressures; and, probably most important of all, the similarities and affinities between the Gallic and Iranian spirit and temperament. This dominant position of mediating influence enjoyed by the French language and culture was challenged, however, by the English and Americans after World War I, and especially following the more recent conflict.

Of no little significance in the developing interaction of East and West in Iran was the penetration of the country by practical business techniques and enterprises, especially British efforts in the fields of banking and communications, and the rapid increase in the export-import trade. All this stimulated desire for Western material goods and the learning of means for their acquisition. Inevitably this leads to an interest in the intellectual goods of the West, especially when the movement has reached the self-conscious stage of attempting to create in Iran these coveted material goods.

The development of publication by printing accelerated interaction in thought between Iran and the West. A Persian font and printing press had been introduced into Iran by the Carmelites in 1629, but no substantial use of printing was made until after the reintroduction of the printing press in 1816-1817. Throughout most of the nineteenth century its use was largely confined to books and pamphlets, although a beginning was made in the press by the government news sheets (1848 ff.) and scientific periodicals (1863 ff.). No freedom of the press existed until the death of Nāṣir-al-Dīn in 1896 and it was not until the constitution was proclaimed ten years later that the press bourgeoned into prolific activity. Up to this time the most significant channels for the flow of Western thought into Iran were the newspapers *Akhtar* (1875 ff.), published in Constantinople, and *Qānūn* (1890 ff.), published in Calcutta. After 1906, except for the year of Muhammad 'Ali's unchallenged despotism (1908-1909), the papers were filled with news and ideas from the West.

So much for the main channels in which Western ideas reached Iran during the nineteenth century. Of equal importance is an understanding of the intellectual climate and the social situation in Iran itself, and the subsequent reaction of Iranians to these new ideas.

As the nineteenth century progressed it became increasingly evident that there was a new spiritual and intellectual ferment at work in Iran. Exclusive of several significant religious philosophers, or scholars, this country has produced since 1500 but two philosophers of influence and distinction: Mulla Sadra of Shīrāz (d. 1640-1641) and Ḥājji Mulla Hādi of Sabzavār (d. 1878). The former developed the doctrine of the identity of subject and object, which, in the words of Iqbāl, "constitutes the final step which the Persian intellect took toward complete monism";[4] and the latter, building on Sadra's work, freed Persian thought from the emanations of Neo-Platonism and approached the Platonic conception of the Real. Mulla Sadra's influence was also significant in the development of the Shaykhi sect, a liberal movement within Shī'ism, whose founder died in 1827-1828. It was out of this group that Bābism emerged when, in 1844, Mīrza 'Ali Muhammad of Shiraz declared himself to be the Bāb, or Gate, for access to the Twelfth or Hidden Imam. In the next decade, until the Bāb's martyrdom and the exile of his leading disciples, the Bābi movement greatly stirred the Persian people. Mention might also be made of the rebellion of Āgā Khān, the Ismā'īli leader, in 1839-1840, his defeat, and flight to India.

These developments toward the middle of the nineteenth century are noted not for their evidence of the effect of Western thought upon that of Iran, since this is not demonstrable, but rather to indicate the fermentive quality of the Persian intellectual milieu at this particular time when European ideas were beginning to penetrate the country.

In this connection something may be said of Bahā'ism, the successor of Bābism, and its relation to Western thought. With the

---

[4] Sir Muhammed Iqbal, *The Development of Metaphysics in Persia*, London, 1908, p. 175.

exile of the Bābi leaders to the Ottoman Empire, the eclipse of the Bāb's successor, Ṣubḥ-i-Ezel, and the ascendency to leadership of Bahā'ullāh, his usurping half-brother, whose settlement in Acre on the Mediterranean put him on the edge of the Western world, this movement became quite different from the original Shaykhi splinter. Building on Bābism's philosophy of the Real as Will and Love and its insistence upon facing the stern reality of things as they are with a consequent practical emphasis, Bahā'ism found much in the West which was compatible and hospitable to its own teachings which then showed more and more accommodation to the more dynamic West. Although the sect continued to be persecuted in Iran and by its internationalism was out of sympathy with the constitutional movement, nonetheless these Westernizing influences—the concepts of freedom, universal education, equality of the sexes, and the like—mediated back to Iran from Acre, had their indirect effect upon the intellectual climate of Iran and contributed something to the fruitful interaction there between the East and the West. Yet its very cosmopolitan character in a world where nationalism has been God, and its aloofness from the nationalistic struggle of its Holy Homeland have prevented this new religion from striking deep roots either there or in the West, with the result that its early promise as a mediator between East and West has remained unfulfilled; and in Iran today it would appear to be an increasingly negligible factor in the reformation of the country.

It must be recorded, however, that for all this ferment and stirring at the middle of the nineteenth century and the subsequent developments that broadened and diversified the channels for the flow of Western ideas into Iran, the country was comparatively peaceful and tranquil during most of Nāṣir-al-Dīn's reign. Professor E. G. Browne spent the year 1887-1888 in Iran and epitomized the situation he experienced as follows: ". . . the atmosphere was, as I have said, mediaeval: politics and progress were hardly mentioned, and the talk turned mostly on mysticism, metaphysics and religion; the most burning political questions were those connected with the successors of the Prophet Muḥammad in the seventh century of our era; only a languid interest in external affairs was aroused by the occasional appearance of the official journals

Īrān and Iṭṭilā', or the more exciting *Akhtar* published in Constantinople; while at Kirmān one post a week maintained communication with the outer world. How remote does all this seem from the turmoil of 1891, the raging storms of 1905-11, the deadly paralysis of the Russian terror which began on Christmas Day in the year last mentioned, and then the Great War, when Persia became the cockpit of three foreign armies and the field of endless intrigues."[5]

II

These stormy days saw the real beginning of Iran's awakening and the emergence of that pattern of interaction between Eastern and Western thought which, for all its later changing development, obtains to the present day. It is this past half-century or more with which we are now concerned, and for a summary treatment of the period we choose three dominant Western concepts that have had a formative influence on the evolution of modern Iran: imperialism, nationalism, and secularism.

Not that imperialism is peculiarly a Western concept or phenomenon: for imperialism was well known in the ancient and medieval worlds, and Iran had had her own periods of empire. But Western impact upon Iran in the nineteenth century was imperial in character, and imperialism—British and Russian—was the political and economic form in which Western ideas, some of them also spiritually imperial, were embodied and first manifest to Iran. It was this Western challenge which stimulated the Iranian response and determined the dominantly political, economic, and social pattern in which East-West interaction has taken place. Indeed it may be said by way of anticipation that it was this practical nature of the Iranian response to the pressure of the expanding West in a series of successive and increasingly intensive political crises that has prevented the naturally speculative yet equally emotional Iranians from developing a basic rationale for a program of action. So kaleidoscopic have been the events compelling this practical interaction between Iran and the West that even to the present there has been no really profound and creative intel-

[5] *A Year Among the Persians,* Cambridge, 1924, p. 157.

lectual and spiritual interaction between Western and Islamic thought.

And yet, for all this, the interaction between East and West involved primarily in the modernization or Westernization of Iran has not been devoid of significant intellectual character. Although the Iranian contribution to this interaction can scarcely be called truly Islamic, the result is indirectly influenced by Shī'ah Islam, and to understand it we must appraise the present situation and the possibility of future interaction between Western and Islamic thought in Iran. Besides, this whole movement is in itself well worth examination and understanding.

The initiating cause of this rapid modernizing development was the failure of Nāṣir-al-Dīn to withstand the exploitation of the rival British and Russian imperialisms. Although, during the early years of the nineteenth century, the Qājār Shahs encouraged European contacts, by the last third of the century Nāṣir-al-Dīn Shah had become so disillusioned with the exploitive aspects of Western penetration that he expressed the wish "that never a European had set foot on my country's soil: for then we would have been spared all these tribulations. But since the foreigners have unfortunately penetrated into our country, we shall at least make the best possible use of them."[6] But his use of them was opportunistic and short-sighted, being generally to gain funds for his impoverished court and government in exchange for unequal and damaging economic concessions. Against all this, patriotic Iranians protested, expressing their resentment by insisting upon a modification of absolutism through the establishment of a constitutional monarchy whereby a measure of democracy, at least among the educated classes, might provide both a check upon Qājār ineptitude and recklessness and a means for the development of material progress—which, as Miss Lambton points out, was greatly desired by the intellectuals and at that time associated by them with the peoples enjoying Western democratic regimes.

The event which precipitated this astonishing reaction was the Shah's granting of a concessionary tobacco monopoly to an English company. This threatened every man and woman in the country and dramatized the Shah's selfish betrayal of the people.

[6] Quoted in William S. Haas, *Iran*, New York, 1946, p. 35.

The result was a union of all classes—clergy and laity, old and young—to resist this pressure. Wholly successful, the people surprised themselves and for the first time realized their power.

This combination of both negative and positive reaction to the West energized the political evolution at the turn of the century, when a new nationalism brought on the demand for a constitution. In this movement were united the clergy, the conservative and strict Muslims, as well as the younger intellectuals who had been attracted to Western thought and were becoming convinced that only by its adoption could the country be reformed and survive. Muhammad 'Ali Shah took advantage of these internal differences as well as of external Russian support in his attempts to abolish the constitution, but, for all his temporary success, eventually lost his throne in the final triumph of the constitutional party in 1909. These disparate elements remained united until the whole movement was stultified by Russian terrorism and repression from the end of 1911 until the war in 1914.

If the inept, stubborn Qājārs had underestimated the power of the new leaven imported from the West, the Iranian patriots and intellectuals were equally unaware of the organic complexities and the eventual implications of the program of Westernization upon which they had embarked. They were easily disillusioned when political revolution did not bring immediate material progress and the solution of all Iran's problems. Many were soon ready to lay the blame upon Western ideas and institutions, disregarding the inadequacy and cupidity in their own adoption and administration of them. Yet Iranian impatience and myopia were by no means wholly to blame for the meager results of this originally promising revolution. In its very midst came the Anglo-Russian Agreement of 1907, which, necessary though it might have appeared to those powers from the viewpoint of European strategy, was nonetheless a severe limitation upon Iranian independence and a crippling handicap to internal reform. Continued foreign interference in spite of the agreements, highlighted in the prevention of economic and financial reform, cut short the natural growth of any program of Westernization. The general deterioration issuing from the chaos of World War I, when Iran, aspiring to neutrality, became the marginal battlefield of three of the contending powers and the center of intrigue for even more, seemed to snuff out such virility as remained in the pre-war modernist, nationalist movement: indeed, it appeared near to complete paralysis when the post-war political leadership in Iran was ready to surrender national sovereignty to the British in the proposed Anglo-Iranian Agreement of 1919—since sincerely regretted by most Britons themselves. Yet the national spirit rallied to meet this new crisis. Led by Riza Khan, crowned Shāhinshāh and founder of the Pahlavi dynasty in 1926, Iran once more demanded her independence and integrity. Her success in making good these demands was manifest in the abolition of the "Capitulations" in 1927-1928, the liquidation of communist ideological influence in the Caspian provinces shortly thereafter, the insistence on a revised oil agreement with the British in 1933, the signing of the Sa'dabād Pact in 1937, and the increase during the 1930's of a mild but officially encouraged xenophobia.

The "religious nationalism" of the Ṣafavis—if such a term can be used in view of the modern meaning of the word—had withdrawn the Iranian people from the intimate relation with the larger Arabic-speaking Islamic world to the west. Now the Pahlavi nationalism carried this further by culturally emphasizing everything pre-Arab, and thus pre-Islamic, in the Iranian tradition, even to the setting up of an Iranian Academy to purge the language of Arabisms and to replace them with pure Persian, the more ancient the better: with the result that not a little change has occurred in the language in the last two decades. Iranian scholarship "discovered" the ancient glories of Iran, and the faith of Zoroaster became once more honored in the Land of the Lion and the Sun. Adaptations of the ancient Achaemenid style in architecture began to appear along the avenues of Tehran.

Minds that could vault the intervening Islamic centuries were naturally open to more ideas from the contemporary West, and so the nationalists endeavored with a new vigor to emulate the West—particularly by the acquisition of its superior scientific, commercial, and industrial techniques—in order to realize the material progress which the intellectuals desired so passionately and for the realization of which Riza Shah gave them the forceful leadership they needed. Young men were sent to the technical schools and universities of Europe, Britain, and the United States; engineers and teachers were brought from Europe to help build and organize the light industry which would make Iran self-sufficient, and to man the school system which was rapidly expanded to the French pattern. Over 15,000 miles of roads were built, and the Trans-Iranian Railway from the Caspian Sea to the Persian Gulf was built at a cost of $125,000,000, raised by Iran primarily from a high tax on sugar and tea. Modern avenues and parks, shops and theaters, factories and buildings appeared in Tehran and some of the provincial capitals. In the first decade of the reign, Western dress for men became universal in the cities; in 1936 the veil for women was abolished, and an approximate equality of the sexes in society and before the law was promulgated. These are but a few of the outstanding features of the social revolution which gained momentum until the outbreak of World War II.

The nationalist movement in its earlier constitutional phase had managed to unite most classes—old and young, conservative and liberal, clergy and laity—against the threat of internal despotism ready to sell the nation to external imperialism; but this new and more revolutionary Pahlavi nationalism went considerably farther in its accommodation to the West and its way of life. This can be seen most clearly in its acceptance of the principle of secularization. This trend did not clearly emerge, however, until after the coronation of Riza in 1926 and the consolidation of his power. In the years immediately following the coup of 1921 there was much talk of the establishment of a republic with Riza as its first president. But when the new Turkish Republic abolished the Caliphate and separated church and state, the frightened Shī'ah clergy was glad enough to support Riza's predilection for the ancient monarchial forms with the foundation of a new dynasty. Had they perceived the treatment they were to receive subsequently at his hands, they probably would have preferred to take their chances with a more democratic form of government.

Secularization expressed itself in a number of forms. Especially important was the confiscation of clerical *vaqf*, or mortmain, with consequent loss of wealth, power, and independence by the clergy. These endowments were transferred to the reorganized Ministry of Education, and the clerics who were retained in the admin-

141

istration of the *vaqf* became state functionaries. Similar in effect was the reform of the law and juridical system of the country along the lines of the Napoleonic Code. Civil or secular law had long existed in Islamic society, but it had ever remained subordinated to canon law, or the Shari'ah. Now the balance was to be reversed and the competence of the religious law attenuated. The Shi'ah ceremonies in celebration of Moḥarram were so curtailed that the majority lost interest in their enactment. New national holidays were elaborated to take their place. The lunar or religious calendar was allowed to fall into disuse; the solar calendar of ancient Iran was used for all state purposes. So effectively had the Shah demonstrated that the Shi'ah faith had become a matter of personal rather than national concern, that he could arrange to marry his son and heir apparent to a Sunni princess of Egypt's ruling house.

Riza Shah and his regime were not contemptuous of, or hostile to, religion as such; they were indifferent or opposed to it only in so far as the religious leaders blocked modernization and were in a position to compromise the whole movement unless curtailed in power. Indeed, the elements of the Shari'ah continued to be taught in the governmental schools and for a time it appeared as though the government would insist that they be included in the curricula of foreign schools as well. Theological colleges were not closed, though the government began to supervise examinations for, and admissions to, the clerical profession; and the theological school of the Sepāh Sālār Mosque in Tehran was incorporated as a separate faculty in the organization of the University of Tehran in 1935. Muslim holidays generally continued as state holidays. Though pilgrimage to shrines without the country was discouraged and at times forbidden, though prayers and alms and fasts were scarcely encouraged, though the pageantry of Shi'ism was reduced almost to the vanishing point, still most members of the regime would have resented the implication that they were not Shi'ah Muslims and worthy members of the traditional society.

Despite these qualifications, it must be emphasized that the principle of secularism had been firmly established. Religious communities might remain distinct and still be separately represented

in the Majlis, with Ja'fari Shī'ism still acknowledged as the established faith of the state; but both theoretically and practically it
became possible for men—though not women—to change their
faith and name, and their communal registration and affiliation.
For large numbers of the younger generation, openly skeptical if
not cynical toward the orthodox faith of the majority, the new
nationalism became the practical faith by which they lived. Inevitably a gulf widened between this growing group and the
repressed yet considerable number of orthodox believers and their
clerical leaders. The result was a more rapid Westernization of the
former, but a developing suspicion and resistance from the latter,
with consequent failure in significant creative interaction between
Western and Islamic thought at the more profound intellectual
and spiritual levels.

During the second decade of the Pahlavi reforms two new contributions of Europe began to influence Iran: Central European
totalitarianism and Russian communism. It was only natural that
the dictatorial Shah should welcome the expanding totalitarianism
of Europe, especially the German form. The rise of any power
likely to challenge the great traditional foes of modern Iran would
receive favorable attention; and especially would this be true when
that power excelled in the scientific knowledge and the technical
skills which Iran so desired and needed, and when that power
was prepared, as was Germany, to give needed technical aid within
the framework of mutually profitable trade.

Yet this veering of the Westernization movement away from
democracy toward fascism and national socialism, the pyramiding
of power and authority in the hands of a dictator falling more and
more a prey to the lusts attendant on power, and the regimenting
of all classes of society, became more than the thoroughly indi-
vidualistic Iranian could easily accept. Consequently during the
latter years of Riza Shah's police state there was growing unrest
beneath the surface of apparent order and progress. A sense of
spiritual frustration overtook many intellectuals. Not a small portion of the youth was being attracted by the ideology of neighboring communism. This trend was vigorously suppressed and its
leaders thrown into jail, where they at once began a self-disci-
plinary and self-educating regime that was to exert powerful in-

fluence when amnesty and a measure of freedom returned with the "occupation" by the Allies in August 1941.

III

The last decade—of World War II and its aftermath—has continued the pattern of the Riza Shah regime, but with significant shifts and changes. The war years of Allied occupation brought an acceleration of Western penetration and influence on a scale hitherto undreamed. This period also brought a realignment in these influences. The place of Germany as a third major balancing power was soon taken by the United States whose war effort in Iran revealed a technical skill, industrial wealth, and buoyant democratic spirit that made a deep impression on the Iranian people, turning the tide of youth seeking foreign education toward America. If any Iranian had doubted the inevitability that his nation would occupy a strategic place in the world society, it was dissolved by the global war which made Iran "the bridge of victory in Asia" and Tehran the symbol of Big Three collaboration for winning the war and the peace to follow. This period will be discussed subsequently in detail. For our purpose here it is sufficient to note the significant intellectual and spiritual developments, especially as they concern our basic concepts of imperialism, nationalism, and secularism.

The struggle of Iran for independence and integrity against Western imperialism shifted its pattern: the Soviet state returned to Tsarist imperial pressure though now in the guise of a "people's democracy" championing the oppressed masses of Iran in their struggle against the "Western imperialists"; yet it was these powers—socialist Britain, now withdrawn from India, and capitalist America, now taking the lead—who championed Iran's nationalism and were forced thereby into support of the socially conservative ruling class.

Although the chastened and none-too-confident nationalism, with Western support, succeeded in maintaining sufficient unity and drive to weather the crisis of 1945-1947, it was not without adding internal divergences regarding social goals and effective methods in the building of a strong nation. The dynamic force of socialism and/or communism had laid hold of large groups of the educated, especially the impatient youth, who demanded a break with Islamic thought and society and a full acceptance of Western ideas, even as cast by the Russians. Interestingly enough, to this group were attracted the erstwhile fascists and totalitarians. Although this group has tried to mollify the still influential clerics and the believing masses by playing down their and Russia's anti-religious program, only the most naïve and trusting would fail to perceive that they are for a greater secularization of society than was achieved under the Riza Shah regime. It is impossible, how-ever, here to discuss the relation of communism and communists to this dynamic group.[7]

During the war and since, the secularization characteristic of the previous regime has been maintained in official and in most urban circles. Elsewhere, however, the resurgence of the clergy has been evident, symbolized most clearly in the return to the veil of many women. None of the fundamental legal reforms of Riza Shah divesting the clergy of its powers has been repealed, yet there is no question but that the moral influence of the clerics has been enhanced. The bankruptcy of Riza Shah's program, as proved by events; the spiritual dereliction experienced by many devotees of nationalism following August 1941; the superficiality of many of the once heralded reforms; the widespread deteriora-tion of standards of moral conduct under the impact of war and its attendant changes—all these have had a sobering effect upon many and made them cautious about change for its own sake.

The net result of recent developments, then, would seem both to clarify and to complicate the fundamental problem of interaction between Western and Islamic thought in Iran. Clarification comes with a wider realization of the issues involved, the gap that ap-pears to be widening between radicals and conservatives in regard to secularization, and the growing awareness that much of the Westernization thus far effected has been superficial, as regards the bases of both Western and Iranian ways of life. Complication comes from the injection of the East-West power and ideological struggle into the heart of this question, with Iran not knowing whether this is a purely Western dichotomy and struggle, a third

[7] See George Lenczowski, *Russia and the West in Iran, 1918-1948*, Ithaca, 1949, pp. 97-108, 223-234.

philosophy and way of life to be reckoned with, or perhaps one in which she shares something as an Eastern people.

In any case, we may observe that, for all the interaction that forms material for its prolegomena, there has been no real creative interaction of Western and Islamic thought at the deeper levels of faith and philosophy. This is primarily caused by the lack of understanding and cooperation between the intellectual and spiritual leaders in the old Iranian tradition, and the dynamic group, mostly of the younger generation, which is determined upon carrying through an Iranian cultural revolution consonant with Western science and technique. This schism must be healed before Iran can have a fighting chance in solving its problems. The former must learn that isolation in time or space is impossible, and that Iran must continue its process of adjustment to the West so that it may fill its place in world society. The latter must learn that future reforms can be founded only upon a deeper understanding of both Western and Iranian traditions than was the superficially imitative, materialistically motivated program of the Riza Shah regime. Only then can Iran, inspired by its understanding of the West and by its own precious and peculiar genius, create a new culture that is modern yet indigenous.

For all the efforts of the rabidly patriotic and modernizing Iranians to ignore their Islamic heritage, it is difficult for one to believe that the coming new culture of Iran will not be profoundly affected by the Islamic faith still cherished by millions and yet to be integrated intellectually with the present borrowings from the West. It may be her long history of divergence from the Islamic norm and her present ability to accept the intellectual goods of the West comparatively uninhibited by that norm which may fit her, along with the Turks, to achieve a form of Western and Islamic synthesis which will be complementary to the results of Arab experimentation.

In any case, for those who know something of the history of the two millennia and a half of Iranian civilization, of the genius of this people to survive invasion and apparent annihilation with resurgence to new life, of their unusual capacity for assimilation of the alien and the new, and their embodiment of both in better institutions and truer philosophies—for those it may not seem too much to hope that, given the requisite political security and stability, Iran may yet be able to carry this experiment in acculteration to more profound levels and emerge with an answer which may not be only the saving of her own soul but a contribution to the rest of the peoples of Asia searching for some satisfying answer to this baffling problem in inter-cultural relations.

9

THE INTERACTION OF ISLAMIC
AND WESTERN THOUGHT IN
THE ARAB WORLD

BY HABIB AMIN KURANI

THE ARAB WORLD TODAY is in the midst of a crisis. From the Atlantic to Iran and from Turkey to the Indian Ocean, profound changes are taking place which challenge every aspect of Arab life. Some of these changes are readily discernible; others, more subtle, are nevertheless far-reaching in their effect. An old way of life, unchanged for some four hundred years, has felt the impact of a forceful, dynamic civilization which has shaken Arab life to its foundations. Today a fundamental question faces the Arab and Western worlds alike. What adjustments will the Arabs make to the onrushing forces from the West?

The answer to this question is the key to the future of the Arab world. It is equally vital to the Western world. For the Arabs live in a most crucial area, one where progress and contentment are essential for world peace. It is an area where important international interests converge; through which pass vital world communications by land, sea, and air; and where the world's richest oil reserves are situated. The Arab world is the spiritual center of Islam, Christianity, and Judaism. Mecca, Medina, Jerusalem, Nazareth, Bethlehem, Damascus, Cairo, and Karbala are sacred cities to Muslims, Christians, and Jews the world over.

It is in a yet deeper sense that the kind of adjustment the Arab world will make to Western civilization has significance for mankind. At this juncture in human affairs, man's discovery of the laws of the physical universe threatens his existence. The world is faced with a grave moral crisis. A spiritual awakening is sorely needed. In the past the interaction of Near Eastern with Western thought gave the Western world an answer to one of its most pressing problems, namely, the relation of man to his Creator and to his fellow man. Democratic institutions, respect for the sanctity of the individual, and the concepts of individual freedom and responsibility are essentially the products of this interaction of Near Eastern and Western civilizations.

Meanwhile modern science has brought the Arab world much closer to the West. Contacts are increasing rapidly, and their influence is felt by all classes of people. In the past it was assumed that increased contact would lead automatically to better understanding and improved relations among peoples. The tragic events of the last few years prove the unreliability of this assumption. A new vision is needed which science alone cannot give. Will renewed and intensified relations between the Arab-Muslim world and the West yield a solution to the present moral crisis, or will the two cultures drift apart to form two rival worlds of thought and will, each fearful and suspicious of the other, thus adding to man's dangers and jeopardizing his achievements? It is in this deeper, broader sense that interchange of ideas between Arab-Muslim civilization and the West assumes significance and deserves most careful thought.

II

Arab relations with the West are not new. Both in ancient and medieval times, Arabs came in contact with the Western world. The Arab Empire at its height extended from the border of India to the Atlantic. The eastern and southern shores of the Mediterranean and Spain were areas where the Arabs met the West often in conflict and sometimes in peaceful relations.

Numerous attempts have been made to explain the birth and spread of Arab civilization. Some writers emphasize such factors as pressure of population; and social, political, and moral disintegration of surrounding territories. While such explanations are true, they are limited. The political and economic were contributory, not basic causes. The birth of Arab civilization stemmed essentially from a spiritual revival buttressed by the strong and dynamic leadership of Muhammad and his immediate followers.

The initial impact of Islam on the West was that of a crusading, missionary force seeking to convert others and to spread its message through persuasion and, if necessary, by force and military conquest. Islam arose as a revolt against social evils which had permeated Arab society. The core of the message which Muhammad brought was a simple and positive message of affirmation, easily understood by the common man. It proclaimed the unity of God, the Creator and Sustainer of the universe, and the apostleship of his prophets, of whom Muhammad, being the last, was the recipient and proclaimer of the most perfect and ultimate revelation.

"I declare that there is no god but Allah and that Muhammad is his Prophet." This was the battlecry of the Muslims in their whirlwind campaigns both inside and outside of the Arabian Peninsula. This belief in the unity and all-pervasiveness of God inevitably led to a belief in the essential unity of man, at least the unity of the believers. "A Muslim is a brother unto any other Muslim whether he likes it or not" enjoins the Koran.

As a result, the main driving force of the Arabs came to be the *jihād*: a compelling force to unify man under the banner of Islam, *dār-al-Islām*, the abode of Islam and peace, as distinguished from *dār-al-Ḥarb*, the abode of war, where non-believers dwelt. For this reason the missionary aspect of the new Muslim social order was most actively fostered among people of the conquered territories. Particularly at the beginning of its expansion, conversion to Islam became the foundationstone of the new order. The political and economic advantages of conversion—its ease, and the simplicity of the Muslim message—attracted many to the new faith. Conversions were made permanent through the Koran.

The Arabs extended their rule to lands and peoples who were heirs to rich and varied cultures. The sensitive Arab mind was quick to grasp the significance of these cultures and at once proceeded to study and utilize them to preserve his rule and to advance his interests. The universalism of Islam, based on a belief in the unity of God and man, logically led to the acceptance of the unity of truth as a creation of God. These three factors—the resilient Arab mind, the universalism of Islam, and the open-minded attitude toward new truth as a creation of God—paved the way for a great intellectual and cultural awakening in the Arab Empire to which peoples from many lands and cultural backgrounds contributed. From Persia came the arts and poetry; from India philosophy, astronomy, and mathematics; and from Hellenistic civilization philosophy, theology, and science. To these the Arabs added the products of their creative genius. The bond unifying these manifold contributions was the Arabic language—the chief justification for giving them the designation "Arab." It is to the Arabs' eternal credit that they encouraged the study of ancient civilizations far more than military exploits; next to Islam, the Arabs' contribution toward the preservation, enrichment, and transmittal of ancient civilizations accounts for their place in history.

Whereas the first phase of the process of interrelation between the Arabs and the West was characterized by intransigence and conflict, the second phase was characterized, on the intellectual level at least, by tolerance and appreciation which provided the psychological climate for cooperation and intellectual growth. It should be remembered, however, that the benefits arising out of this cooperation at that time were limited to the few—the scholars, rulers, and men of science. They did not go beyond them to touch the lives of the common people. It is here that the effects of interaction during the medieval times differ so markedly from those at present.

To the Arab mind, truth, objective and absolute, emanated from God. It was not subjective or relative depending upon the limitations of human powers and varying accordingly. Truth comes to man by way of revelation or by way of reason, wisdom, or philosophy, and to early Arab thinkers these two ways were fundamentally one—in that they emanated from one source: God. And it is on this concept of the fundamental unity of these two ways that the main tradition of Arabic philosophic and theological thought rested. To reconcile them was its main objective. So long as Islam preserved this universal and unifying outlook toward God, man, and truth, and strove to realize this unity in Muslim society, Islam acted as a generative, constructive force in the life of the individual and of society. Nowhere is the influence of this ideal better disclosed than in the lives and writings of the great Arab mystics.

But like so many other civilizations and peoples before them, the Arabs in time became preoccupied with dogma and doctrines at the expense of reason and spiritual insight. Political dissension and sectarian rivalries broke out. They struck at the very foundations of the Empire. Islam was reduced to a set of doctrines externally imposed on the human mind. The creative synthesizing spirit of Islam which attained considerable heights in its efforts to reconcile reason with revelation was stifled by doctrinal rigidity and narrow sectarianism. This was a turning point in the history of Islamic thought. It marked the beginning of the end of Muslim intellectual and spiritual influence. It marked also the ebb of the Arabs' political power. As the Arab Empire receded back toward Arabia and Western Asia, contacts with Europe narrowed. Intellectually and spiritually the Arabs stagnated for over five centuries, while Europe went forward reaping the benefits bestowed by the Arabs.

III

Arab-Muslim civilization during the seventh century spread westward, conquering, reforming, and converting. Approximately a thousand years later Western civilization was destined to exercise a similar influence upon the Arabs. Through soldiers, diplomats, books, schools, missionaries, and more recently through films, radio, and airplanes, the influence of the West has reached the Arab world. Western penetration was from four important bridgeheads. One was made through Constantinople when the Ottoman government, inspired by Napoleon, attempted to institute military, administrative, and educational reforms throughout the Ottoman Empire. Military academies were opened, Western courts introduced, and the Turkish army reorganized. Schools organized along modern lines were opened in the various Arab provinces. But these attempted reforms, not having their origin in local initiative nor arising as a result of a widely felt need for reform, were short-lived and relatively ineffective in causing any appreciable change in Arab life.

Another contact was by way of Basrah and the Persian Gulf where British traders and other Western commercial interests penetrated Iraq. The trader-consul, the representative of railway and steamship companies or telegraph lines, sought and obtained important trade and navigation concessions. With them they brought many of the ways and things of the West.

A third contact between the Arabs and the West was in Cairo. It came in the wake of Napoleon, who brought with him in his expedition to Egypt in 1799 some of France's ablest scholars and men of science. He installed an Arabic printing press, the first of its kind in the Arab world. Napoleon's successor, the great Muhammad 'Ali, had the vision to employ the talent which Napoleon left behind to modernize and reconstruct Egypt. Many of the French officers were appointed to key government positions. Under their guidance, a military academy and a medical school were founded and numerous other modern schools were opened. Also, promising Egyptian youth were sent to France for training.

The fourth point of contact between the Arab world and the West was the Lebanon, where foreign missionary organizations founded schools, opened hospitals, and established other charitable institutions. Foreign missionary schools played a major role in introducing the youth of Arab lands to every aspect of Western thought. They learned Western science, literature, political and philosophical ideas, as well as Western moral and religious concepts. What is more important, they introduced Arab youth to their past, a step which played an important role in the rise of Arab nationalism.

As more rapid means of travel and communication developed, the contacts between the Arab and the Western worlds grew in number and variety. The flow of goods, ideas, and persons accelerated the influence of the West on the Arabs. This infiltration of Western culture into Arab lands has given rise to three major interrelated movements. The first is political, represented by a growing demand for self-determination, an awakened national consciousness and pride in Arab civilization. The second, economic and social, manifests itself by a rising demand for Western goods and techniques and by the adoption, with or without adaptation, of Western standards for regulating the material and external aspects of Arab life. It is revealed also by a demand for the emancipation of women and the abolition of polygamy and the veil, and in a demand for better conditions for the common man. The third is intellectual and moral.

On the moral side, the movement is manifested by a growing demand on the part of an increasing number of Arabs to adopt understandable means as a basis for regulating behavior and judgment; means forged by the individual's brain and will, not by tradition or arbitrary authority. On the intellectual side, the movement involves a revival of interest in Western thought and science, Arab history and literature. Notable are attempts to modernize Arabic literature by adopting Western standards of literary criticism, in publishing in Arabic some of the more important Western works, and in writing original works in Arabic based on Western standards of scholarship and embodying knowledge obtained through Western education. It is manifest also by an increased application of Western scientific methods to the deeper problems of living.

These three movements are closely interrelated. They began when the Near East felt the impact of Western civilization and awakened from its lethargy. Nevertheless, these movements are not equally strong or rapid nor are they on the same level in every Arab country. But that the flow of Western ideas and all that they imply has penetrated every Arab country—even Saudi Arabia and Yemen—is undeniable.

IV

The main influence of Western civilization on Arab life lies in the rising tide of nationalism and the movement for independence which pervade the entire Arab world today. In the main this movement is a direct contribution of Western education. In Western schools Arab youth discovered their past. They discovered also the "secret of the strength and progress of the West" which they attributed to national sovereignty of the Western powers. These discoveries led to an intense desire to reestablish the past glories of the Arab Empire through creating the ideal of Arab nationalism as its main driving force. In so doing, Arab nationalists substituted the force of nationalism for Islam as the rallying point around which all Arabs should unite. Arab nationalists may be classified in two groups: the Pan-Arab and the state nationalists.

The Pan-Arab nationalists believe that all the Arabs from Casablanca to Iran must ultimately be welded into a single nation which will command the loyalty and allegiance of all Arabs. To the extent that the narrower loyalties to existing smaller units are surrendered in favor of that to the larger Arab nation, to that extent will the aim of the Arab nationalists be realized. Educated Arab nationalists, like their ancestors, believe they have a definite message to give and a contribution to make to modern civilization; but they believe that this message cannot be given nor their contribution made unless they are united, independent, and strong. In the minds of Pan-Arab nationalists, the establishment of the League of Arab States represents a first practical step in realizing the major aim of Arab nationalism. They believe that sooner or later, the League, which is essentially a confederation of independent states, should give way to one unified state exercising control over all the Arabs.

The Arab state nationalists believe in Arab independence, in their cultural heritage, and in their possibilities. They believe, however, that each of the Arab states has its peculiar problems which it must face and solve in its own way; that each state can make a better contribution to the Arab world if it maintains its autonomy; but that it must cooperate closely with the other Arab states on common problems. Their conception of the Arab League is that it represents an association of free, self-governing and sovereign states—a confederation, rather than a federation of Arab states tied together by common cultural bonds and common interests. This concept at present actually governs the organization of the Arab League. It does not have any jurisdiction over the internal affairs of each Arab state, and each state is free to administer its own affairs, subject to certain broad reservations, independently of other Arab states.

The intellectual and moral bases of Arab nationalism have not been given a clear and definite formulation. The work of Dr. Costi Zurayk represents a beginning in this direction. Thus Arab nationalism, lacking a clear formulation of its intellectual and moral bases, is not understood even by the majority of Arab nationalists themselves. It is still a manifestation of the will more than of the mind, and is therefore subject to the dangers of extremism and confusion common to all such undefined movements. A basic question which must be clearly faced and resolved in this connection is "What is the relation of Islam to nationalism and can the basic tenets of and loyalties to Islam be reconciled with those of nationalism?"

The cultural committee of the League is entrusted with the task of fostering cultural unity and cooperation among its member states. Sooner or later, in performing its task, the committee will have to lay down the intellectual and moral foundations of this unity. In September 1947 the cultural committee of the Arab League held a conference in Lebanon on the subject of achieving greater cultural unity among Arab states through unified educational programs, particularly the teaching of history, geography, civics, and Arabic. Although there was agreement on basic objectives and methods of teaching, the problem of reconciling the need for adapting education to local needs with the need for providing Arab youth with broad regional loyalty remains unsolved. The key to the problem does not lie so much in uniform curricula and methods as on the character, ability, and outlook of the teachers.

The idea of Arab nationalism and its achievement does not suffer from confusion and lack of definition only. Its realization is also faced with numerous obstacles emanating from internal and external sources. International rivalries over the area and the lack of a positive, constructive policy toward its ultimate development on the part of the great powers are two major external obstacles facing Arab nationalism. The internal difficulties lie in the conflict of loyalties and dissension among the Arabs, minority apprehensions, dynastic rivalries, social and cultural divergences, and finally the lack of a unifying social idea.

Whether Arab nationalism will move toward cooperation with Western powers or not will depend upon the attitude and policies of Western powers toward Arab problems on the one hand, and on Arab understanding of their interests in so far as these policies affect them. At present the Arabs tend to view Western policies with mixed feelings. There is doubt and suspicion. Doubt arises because of numerous promises made to them by the great Western powers under the stress of war only to be broken in times of peace. Suspicion stems from a general feeling that in determining their policies, Western powers are primarily concerned with their own immediate interests rather than with trying to fit them to a general pattern of world order based on principles of international morality, or the long-range interests of *all* peoples concerned. On the other hand, many nationalists admire Western culture and Western organization and modes of life and desire to see many aspects of Western civilization prevail in their lands. The rise of the Soviet Union and of communism as a world force is causing Arab leaders considerable anxiety. Thus the cultural bond between Arab nationalists and Western democracies and the unknown nature of communism and Soviet policy restrain Arab nationalists from acts too unfriendly to Western democracy. Politically, therefore, the Arab attitude is characterized by tension, confusion, and doubt as to the most helpful orientation toward the West. At no other time in their history have the Arabs been in greater need of wise, determined, and unselfish leadership to guide them through the maze of conflicting interests to their goal of freedom, enlightenment and well-being than today. The tragic aspect of the Palestine question lies in its adverse influence on the future of Arab cooperation with the liberal forces of the West.

V

In their attitude toward the cultural aspects of Western civilization Arabs may be placed on a scale varying between two extremes. On one end of the scale, there are those who advocate following Turkey's example, turning westward, and breaking away completely from Arab traditions and beliefs. Only then, according to this group, can the Arabs prosper and become a modern nation worthy of membership in the family of nations. This group is small and its influence is not great. Its members belong to those Levantines who, though Arab by birth, have been educated in foreign schools. Lacking knowledge of Arab culture, they mix with Europeans and are so steeped in European ways that they have removed themselves from the main currents of Arab civilization. They live on the margin of life around them.

On the opposite end of the scale, there are those who have not reconciled themselves to the superiority of Western culture, who chafe at the greater power of the West and in self-defense reject the West and all that it stands for. They do not believe in the possibility of an Arab nationalism, preferring to go back to Islam, religiously and socially. In their opposition to Western institutions they advocate a return to early Muslim customs and favor the reestablishment of the Caliphate. They advocate the acquisition of Western technology and intellectual discipline only as a weapon by means of which to fight the West and reassert their alleged superiority. The members of this group are drawn mainly from religious and theological circles but include others who have not been exposed to Western cultural influences. They see in the process of modernizing their countries a threat to their influence and prestige. Membership in this group also includes some dissatisfied youth who have been unable to make satisfactory adjustments to the present economic dislocation.

Most educated Arab youth, however, fall midway between the two extreme groups. They believe that Western civilization has possibilities for making significant contributions to the Arabs, but that there are virtues and elements of strength in Arab civilization which are worth preserving. But precisely what elements of Western civilization should be borrowed, or what are the elements of strength in Arab civilization which should be preserved? Is this process of conscious and deliberate cultural selection practical or possible? These are questions which educated Arab nationalists have been able to answer only partially. Before a full answer to these questions can be given, Arab nationalists must make a clear analysis of the intellectual and moral bases on which their nationalism must rest. And these bases must be included in their educational programs.

The tragedy of the present Arab awakening lies in the fact that political and economic questions are pressing so urgently on the Arab mind that the deeper moral and philosophical implications of the process of interrelation with the West have not been given the consideration they deserve. The Arabs need a Socrates, Plato, or Aristotle to help them in tiding over the present critical transitional period of their history, or perhaps an outstanding religious leader to help in revitalizing Islam in order to render it more capable of meeting the demands of the modern mind.

This need is being met by two movements under way in the Arab world. The first is the movement for the separation of church and state. The second is the movement for Islamic religious awakening.

Arab nationalists realize that as long as Islam continues its all-embracing function of both religious doctrine and a way of life, it is impossible for modern nationalism to take root. Hence a movement for the separation of church from state represents an essential feature in the program of Arab nationalists. Only through secularization can the vexing problems of religious minorities be solved and only on a secular basis is it possible to establish a truly national system of education. Islamic law, an excellent institution for its times, should be modernized and rendered more compatible with the progress which is taking place today. These are some of the more cogent arguments which Arab nationalists advance in favor of secularization. Under the stress of international difficulties which the Arabs are experiencing today, however, there is a tendency to link traditional Muslim institutions with aspirations for independence. This fact plays into the hands of the extreme conservatives who are opposed to Western institutions, and prevents the movement of secularization from gaining ground. Thus the position of the liberal Arab nationalists has been weakened by the force of present circumstances, but it is far from hopeless. Secularization has been retarded, not stopped.

The movement for Islamic awakening stems from the need for reinterpreting Islam in such a manner as to render its teachings more consonant with the demands and needs of the modern mind, but which at the same time will retain for Islam its strictly Islamic spirit and principles of judgment. Three attempts at Muslim religious reform are sufficiently significant to deserve special mention: (1) The Pan-Islamic movement begun by Jamāl-al-Dīn al-Afghāni which tries to prove the modern viewpoint of Islam by attempting to show its harmony with the findings of modern science. (2) The Wahhābi movement which is essentially a fundamentalist revival away from the "corrupting" influences of the West back to the purity of original Islam. (3) The Islamic modernist movement led by Shaykh Muhammad 'Abduh which seeks to apply scientific and rational methods of interpretation to Muslim doctrine with a view to rendering Islam more compatible with modern thought. The objectives of this movement are to purify

Islam from alien influences; to reform Muslim higher education, particularly theological education; and to shape Islamic doctrine along modern lines.

The encouraging aspect of these movements is that they have come from within, led by intelligent and sincere Muslims. In spite of their sincerity and positive value, however, the reforms of Muhammad 'Abduh and Jamāl-al-Dīn al-Afghāni are limited and tend toward over-simplification of the issues involved for they are not sustained by a deep knowledge of Greek or Christian philosophy which are the mainsprings of Western civilization. Nor did these reformers have the possession of a deep knowledge of medieval Muslim philosophy or thought. Any Muslim religious reform which aims to bring believers closer to the modern world must take into account the contributions made by classical, Christian, and medieval Muslim philosophy.

It is significant that whereas the study of Muslim philosophy and thought holds an important place in many Western universities, the study of Western philosophy and theology represents one of the weakest elements in the programs of the modern national universities in Arab lands. This deficiency in national higher education renders the interpretation of Muslim thought an exclusive possession of the Western scholars. This is a serious lack, for there can be no abiding Muslim religious reform except through the sincere and enlightened efforts of believers. And these enlightened efforts can come only when Arab higher education provides the opportunity for research in Muslim, Christian, and classical philosophical thought, which European universities have provided for the past twelve hundred years.

VI

In response to the rising demand of nationalism, the national governments have taken two important steps to harness the forces of education for national purposes. The first is to extend the scope and variety of public education and thus increase the level of general enlightenment. In every Arab country new and varied types of schools have been opened. As school enrolment increases and literacy campaigns gain momentum, illiteracy decreases. In Iraq, for example, elementary school enrolment has increased over 500 per cent during the past twenty-five years. In Jordan, considered the least developed of the northern Arab states, before the First World War there were three elementary schools and six private religious schools; now there are approximately seventy-four government schools and eighty private schools. In 1918 Jordan had no health department and only two small private hospitals; now there are two government and five private hospitals, eight government and five private clinics and five epidemic stations. This progress is more than matched in other Arab states. The example of Egypt, where the elements of a modern progressive system of education are found, is particularly noteworthy. But progressive Arab leaders recognize that there is a great deal more to be done in extending educational opportunities.

The second step, which the present governments are taking in response to the rising demand of nationalism, is the integration of the diverse kinds of schools in each of the countries into a national system of education. This involves particularly the coordination of private schools, both native and foreign, with government schools in a common program. It is a difficult task to achieve because of the strongly entrenched tradition of private education and the powerful foreign interests which are prepared to give their schools in Arab lands strong support in an effort to maintain their autonomy. Egypt and Lebanon are at present studying legislation designed to control the operations of private schools. They have borrowed a leaf from the French book and adopted legislation aimed at bringing about uniformity in educational programs for all schools, private and public, controlling the teaching of religion in private schools, and defining the professional qualifications of teachers.

Closely allied with the educational problems growing out of the rising tide of nationalism, which is sweeping the Arab world today, is the psychological problem which finds its most critical manifestation in the invasion of education by highly emotionalized politics. The students in the Arab countries are conscious of themselves as a class and a power. Being vocal, their influence is considerably greater than their numbers indicate. The student problem in the Arab world can be understood only against the background of the fundamental conflict which is going on in the Arab mind and soul. The Arab student is proud of his religion, civilization, and nationality; but his Westernized education has prevented him from being sufficiently rooted in his tradition to acquire an adequate sense of its values or to arrive at an intelligent understanding and appreciation of the spiritual and intellectual meaning of Islam or Arab nationalism. His home does not exercise that restraining influence over him which it once did, probably because he considers himself to be better educated than his parents. Thus the steadying forces of his culture have ceased to exercise a directing influence over his behavior. His environment and the world political developments serve to exaggerate the gap which exists between him and his people, on the one hand, and between him and the foreigner on the other. In his search for a new object of worship the most appealing ideal lies in the political sphere. To the attainment of his country's political ends he gives himself with zeal. Being young and zealous, his actions are often impetuous and emotionally charged. Today the Arab student, believing that he has won the struggle for the country's political independence, is directing his attention to internal problems of social reform which he attacks with the same zeal.

The second type of educational problem coming increasingly into focus as a result of Western influence affects the economic and social life of the Arabs in agriculture, commerce, communications, industry, irrigation, land tenure, settlement of the Bedouin tribes, health conditions, et cetera. The newly born national states awakened to find their markets gone, their industries meager, their fertile lands arid or neglected, old irrigation systems extinct, and the general economic level very low. They found that health conditions were distressing, epidemics not infrequent, causing great damage to the people's life and vitality. Infant mortality was high and the common people were kept down by ignorance, inertia, and a certain fatalism which weakened their fiber and dimmed their desire for improvement.

It is in this area that the greatest challenge to education lies, yet unfortunately it is here that education shows its greatest weakness. Governed by intellectualistic traditions, geared to imitate the aristocratic types of Western education, education in the Arab world today fails to face and solve the great need for social improvement. It is here that the system of centralized education, external examinations, and theoretical programs fails so dismally. In fact, the kind of education which is being offered in the public and most of the private schools tends to draw youth away from the villages and renders them unfit for work on the farms. It is not without significance that when an Arab state needs the assistance of experts in solving some of its basic practical problems, it is obliged to turn to the West.

Egypt has sensed an inadequacy in its educational program and has already embarked on a program of reform whereby elementary education is to be decentralized and adapted to local conditions. The most effective efforts in this direction were made by the British administration in Palestine, where for twenty-five years it carried on a constructive educational program designed to lift the general standard of living, particularly at the lower levels. Emphasis was placed on elementary education as a means for social betterment. Programs were different for rural and urban schools. In the rural schools special emphasis was placed on the improvement of health and agriculture. School gardens formed the core around which the work of the school revolved. Two agricultural training centers trained village school teachers; there were inspectors especially trained and dedicated to give encouragement and help to rural teachers. The main orientation of public education was to raise the standards of the common people in town and village.

Vocational education in the Arab world is inadequate in spite of efforts to strengthen it. The relative expense of properly equipped vocational schools, the dearth of well-trained personnel, and the prevalence of a certain reluctance on the part of youth to take up vocational work or craftsmanship renders efforts at reform and expansion of vocational education very limited. Consequently every Arab country, with the exception of Yemen and Saudi Arabia, suffers from an over-abundance of academically trained youth, unequipped with any practical skill, and a corresponding scarcity of skilled and well-trained artisans. This fact presents a serious social problem as well as an economic one. With the passing of the boom following the war, unemployment with its consequences of social unrest will certainly become acute and education will face a most serious challenge.

The introduction of the necessary educational reforms which are designed to raise the economic level of Arab countries requires skilled teachers and an efficient administrative policy oriented toward this end and possessing a certain degree of continuity. For a number of years now, Arab governments have been sending a number of their promising youth to Europe and America for specialized training. Through this measure these governments hope to obtain an adequate supply of well-trained teachers and specialists for the manifold duties which living in the modern world requires. But the returning student presents some serious problems. In many instances training abroad unfits a man to work under the simple conditions of his homeland. He acquires an exaggerated sense of the value of his training and is therefore unwilling to begin in a modest position. Also, he is liable to meet with opposition from conservative, established elements at home, and this often stifles his initiative and enthusiasm. Often the training abroad has·not been made with reference to any special need at home, resulting in disappointment and maladjustment to a returning student. Finally, many of the students who go abroad are young and the brilliant social life of European or American cities dazzles them. On returning home they find it difficult to adjust to the simpler, less colorful mode of living obtaining in their communities. A wiser course for the Arab governments to follow in selecting their missions for foreign study is to choose men and women who are more mature, who have shown promise in positions which they occupy, and who are sent abroad for training to fit them to fill specific positions.

The intimate connection of education with the changing political scene represents a serious obstacle to long-range planning and educational reform. Ministries change often and with them educational plans and legislation change. Twenty-five years of continuous, painstaking effort were required by the Palestine government to achieve a reasonably effective educational program. This reform can be duplicated in other Arab countries provided a stable educational policy obtains. Furthermore, the attack on the economic and social problems of the region is not the sole responsibility of education. To be productive the attack should be a coordinated one in which the various departments of each government collaborate and in which the Arab League takes an active, intelligent interest.

VII

A more thorough investigation of the effects of Arab-Muslim interaction with Western civilization must face and consider the following problems:

1. Perhaps the most fundamental question is whether the essence of Islam and Christianity, which constitute the spiritual and moral bases of Arab and Western cultures, respectively, have sufficient elements in common to permit of a wide area for harmonious relations and cooperation between the two civilizations. What are the basic similarities and basic differences between Arab-Muslim thought and Western-Christian thought?

2. What elements of the historical process of interaction between Arab-Muslim and Western-Christian thought can be drawn upon to assist in understanding the present process of interaction and in guiding its course along constructive and positive lines?

3. Along what lines should Muslim religious revival proceed in order to render Islam more capable of submitting to the test of free inquiry and of meeting the demands of the modern mind?

4. Are nationalism and secularization compatible with Islam?

5. Specifically, what are some of the most important changes and modifications which must be introduced in the "Westernized" systems of education now prevalent in some countries of the Near East, to make them at once harmonious with Muslim tradition and Western civilization?

6. What are the elements of a positive constructive social program which is desirable in the Near East?

7. During the past decade there has been in evidence a definite reaction in many Arab lands against the West and Western liberal thought. Is this trend a manifestation of a permanent conflict or is it a reflection of some transient phase of Arab-Islamic evolution?

Both Muslim and Christian thinkers must consider these problems dispassionately and, in a spirit of humility, should seek courageously for the truth, which is the only foundation for real co-operation and understanding between East and West.

> "Gazing beyond perishable fears,
> To some diviner goals,
> Beyond the waste of years."

10

THE NATIONAL AND INTERNATIONAL
RELATIONS OF TURKEY

BY LEWIS V. THOMAS

MUSTAFA KEMAL ATATÜRK and his aides made one major, clear-cut gain which, as the years give increased perspective, stands out ever more impressively—namely, they raised *Turkey for the Turks* from a dubious slogan to an established reality. Eloquent testimony to this reality is ready to hand: since the founding of the Turkish Republic (1923) and its subsequent consolidation on up to the present day (1950), no responsible statesman anywhere in the world has ventured far on the assumption that Turkey is *not* for the Turks or that the Turks will not fight to defend their sovereignty if necessary. This worldwide recognition of Turkey's complete sovereignty is doubly impressive when one contrasts it with the late nineteenth and early twentieth century European power politics as they were played in and around the old Ottoman Empire. In those decades it was tacitly assumed not only that the Turks were not a fully sovereign nation but also that they *never* could become one. Atatürk's generation has wholly belied these assumptions.

If the Turks were ever successfully to assert their "rights" to full status as a nation, one essential prior condition was that they should control an area whose population would be predominantly "Turkish" on all social levels—in other words a reasonably homogeneous national state. The Ottoman Empire, last of the traditional multi-lingual, multi-sect, great dynastic states in Near Eastern history, was of course essentially opposed to any such concept of a national state. In consequence, the demise of that Empire was a second prior condition to the assertion of unqualified Turkish national sovereignty. The end of the First World War did entail that Empire's demise, and so presented the Turks with a com-

167

pelling challenge as well as with a most menacing threat. In 1918 if they did not soon attain full nationhood, they risked the loss of practically all.

Prior to the First World War, the ruling groups of the Empire—the Ottoman Turks—had, as proprietors of the greatest vested interest in that non-national state, naturally been obliged to combat nationalism as best they could, wherever it raised its head. Throughout the nineteenth century this had become an increasingly hopeless task. It is true that although each Ottoman territorial loss in Europe enlarged the frontiers of one or another of the newly emerging Balkan national states, it also entailed a more or less important removal into Ottoman territories of Turkish population retreating from the Balkans *pari passu* with Ottoman power. But even though a portion of the Balkan Turks was thus added to what remained of Turkey in Europe (and even to Turkey in Asia), the Ottoman Empire of 1900 or of 1918 still did not include any significant area in which Turks were, on all social levels, sufficiently in a majority to claim to be a reasonably homogeneous national state. The Empire did, however, contain one important area which could form the nucleus around which a modern national state could be assembled: Anatolia.

Anatolia, the heartland of the Ottoman Empire, had a predominantly Turkish population. Even so, Anatolia was still not readily available as the seat of a *Turkey for the Turks* in the modern nation-state sense, for it also contained sizable non-Turkish groups. Chief among these were the Greeks, the Armenians, and the Kurds; and of these peoples the first two were impetuously intent upon erecting national states in Anatolia themselves. In these aspirations, moreover, both Greeks and Armenians could frequently command at least some degree of Western European support, while the Turks immediately after 1918 had almost no powerful well-wishers at all in the West.

The historic development which now had brought Anatolia to be a cockpit of competing peoples had begun about the year A.D. 1071, the date when, after centuries of largely successful resistance, the barriers of Christian Anatolia at last fell before attack from the Muslim world. Most of the Muslims who then began to move into Anatolia were Turkish, and, as they came into the territory, two processes began which continue operative to the present time: the one, basically a linguistic change, was and is the Turkification of individuals, and the second, a religious conversion, is Muslimization. Contrary to the general supposition, these processes ordinarily proceeded in peace and without the use of force. Seen in clear perspective, the spread of the Turkish language and of the religion of Islam in Anatolia, although by no means bloodless conquests, entailed comparatively little extermination of non-Turks or of scimitar-point conversion to Islam. In Anatolia, moreover, thorough linguistic Turkification was not necessarily accompanied by Muslimization: in the nineteenth century the large populations of Armenians who, although remaining Christian, had come to have no language other than Turkish, and also those of Christian but monolingually Turkish-speaking "Greeks" all bore strong testimony to the vitality with which the Turkish language had asserted itself in Anatolia—stronger testimony than the intensely chauvinist Armenian and Greek nationalists of the nineteenth and twentieth centuries cared to admit. In the same way, Muslimization operating in the Ottoman Empire had not everywhere necessarily entailed linguistic Turkification, as witness the one-time Greek-speaking Muslim "Turkish" population of Crete, or the Muslims of Bosnia today. In Anatolia itself, however, with the numerically large but otherwise relatively unimportant exception of the Kurds, the Muslims in 1918 were almost all Turkish-speaking, from the most humble peasant to the most sophisticated urban dweller. Hence the Anatolian Muslim population, on linguistic and religious counts alike, was in fact sufficiently homogeneous to form an adequate nucleus around which a *Turkey for the Turks* might be constructed.

Indeed, in 1918, this region was measurably more homogeneously Muslim Turkish than it had been, say, in 1850, because in the intervening decades the processes of Muslimization and Turkification at work there had been sharply accelerated, not to say embittered, under the direct impact of complex forces from the West, forces which one may sum up under the term "Western European Nationalism." Such nationalism awakened its first tangible response in Ottoman Anatolia among non-Muslim peoples, infecting particularly the Greeks and the Armenians. The larger

Greek people under Ottoman rule, of course, had attained the realization of at least a part of their new, Western-inspired national aspirations relatively early in the nineteenth century with the establishment of an independent Greek state. Thereafter the "great idea" of modern Greek nationalism—a Greek state comprising the lower Balkan peninsula plus as much as possible of Anatolia, the whole to be ruled from Constantinople—became more and more compelling in the minds of those who cherished it, but to the Turks this same "great idea" of course increasingly represented a hostile and new foreign ideology threatening their own very existence. Armenian nationalism had never attained any comparable partial realization of its goals. In consequence, during the latter half of the nineteenth century the Turks came to regard Armenian nationalists primarily as rebels within the Ottoman body politic, albeit rebels who also gladly served as a fifth column working particularly for Russia, while Greek nationalism, although it was also recognized as possessing and manipulating a sizable fifth column in the Ottoman state, was still basically a foreign rather than a domestic foe.

These were among the fundamental reasons which led the Ottoman Turks in the later nineteenth and early twentieth centuries to direct their energies to the problem of excising from their own heartland, Anatolia, large numbers of non-Muslim Armenians, while the Ottoman Greeks in this same region were more usually left unmolested. Put bluntly, the rise of nationalism among the non-Muslim peoples of Anatolia eventually meant that the Ottoman Turks could no longer depend there, as they largely had hitherto, upon the gradual and peaceful processes of Turkification and Muslimization, but were instead obliged to accelerate those processes in Anatolia by force. The earlier consequences, bloody and tragic, were what Western writers have since ordinarily referred to as the "Armenian Massacres." This term is certainly not far-fetched as a phrase to call up an understanding of the unmitigated disaster which Anatolian Armenians suffered. The words do, however, conceal from the Western Christian reader the vital fact that the Armenian "Massacres" truly were also episodes in a slow-burning rebellion on the part of Ottoman subjects who had as their ultimate goal the destruction of the government under which they were living. In the long run the Turks would have had no true alternatives except either to excise the non-Turks from Anatolia or themselves be excised therefrom.

As time went on, moreover, this tragic situation was further complicated by the introduction of yet another explosive factor: the emergence of a self-conscious Turkish nationalism.

We have noted above that of all the peoples of the Ottoman Empire it was the Turks who had the greatest interest in preserving the older, a-national *status quo*, and from this one easily understands why it was that of all the once-Ottoman peoples of the Balkans and Anatolia, it was the Turks to whom nationalism came last. But to account adequately for this "tardy" appearance of nationalism among the Turks, we must also take notice of another, and far more complicated set of facts. Throughout Ottoman times the ultimate essential element which determined a man's status in society was his religion. In theory, all Orthodox Muslims together formed the most privileged group. In fact, of course, the universal brotherhood of Islam was no more universally honored in the observance throughout the Ottoman Empire than it had been in earlier Muslim world-states: instead, accepted practice made a sharp distinction between "non-Ottoman" and "Ottoman" Muslims.

The basic tangible distinction between Ottoman and non-Ottoman Muslim was linguistic, but only *partly* linguistic. The Orthodox Ottoman Muslim was set off from all other Orthodox Muslims of the Empire by the Turkish language which he spoke, but *his* Turkish was not merely the simple Anatolian speech which characterized the Muslim Turkish majority of the Ottomans' heartland. Instead, it was "true Ottoman" speech, an elaborate, highly Persianized and Arabized language, specially and uniquely characteristic of the Ottoman court, high society, and intellectual life of Istanbul, and of high Ottoman life generally throughout the Empire. For full status in the ruling groups of the Empire, i.e. among the true Ottomans, one had not only to be an Ottoman in the religious sense (profess Orthodox Islam) but also in the cultural sense, i.e. speak the high Ottoman form of Turkish and live in accord with the patterns of high Ottoman life. In the Ottomans' own formulation, one "*served* Faith and State" (*dīn ve devlete hizmet*) and also "*knew* the Ottoman 'Way'" (*ādāb-i 'osmāni bilmek*), and it was *only* the combination of all of these *together* which gave one full status in high Ottoman life, free access thereunto always being open to any individual who would establish conformity on all essential points.

The significance of this for us here is that these true Ottomans, who in effect "were" the Ottoman Empire, did not in any sense consider themselves "Turks," this latter being a term which they reserved and used, often in contempt, for the simple peasants of Anatolia, feeling no real sense of identification with these peasants despite the fact that the peasants were also Muslim and although on the folk level of Islam, even "Orthodox" Muslim.

Given this complicated situation—a situation which Western European usage, in ignorance of the facts, has almost hopelessly obscured from us by its use, century after century, of the term "Turkey" at historical periods when the Ottomans not only had no such term or concept but also would have been offended had the concept been suggested to them—one can readily see that the rise of a Turkish nationalism in the second half of the nineteenth century necessarily entailed two things: first, the true Ottomans, the ruling groups of the Empire, would have in some measure consciously to identify themselves with the hitherto contemned "Turks" of Anatolia; and secondly, the Turkish peasants on their part would have to be aroused to some degree of conscious loyalty not only to their own "Turkishness"—a conscious loyalty which they had certainly never previously felt—but also to the idea of a "Turkish" nation which would include themselves *and* the true Ottomans as well.

As research into the origins of Turkish nationalism—as yet a little-studied question—continues, there is no doubt that it will uncover earlier and earlier examples of individual Ottomans who, often through accidental circumstances affecting their own lives, came to have some personal realization that industrializing, nationalizing Western Europe represented for the Muslim World a foe which was becoming powerful not only to a new degree but also in an entirely new sense. Such individuals, moreover, sometimes even attempted to bring these disquieting realities home to Ottoman (i.e. to "true Ottoman") public opinion, and to institute the requisite "reforms," but they did this with little real success until finally Western Europe itself thrust the facts squarely home. This really came only with Napoleon's invasion of Egypt and Syria, and perhaps even more clearly with Muhammad 'Ali's subsequent career as a Westernizer in Egypt and beyond it. Responsible Ottomans who now attempted to respond to the overwhelming new challenges were principally concerned to borrow quickly from Western Europe those particular elements and techniques which, in their exceedingly nebulous and incomplete comprehension of Western European realities, they themselves considered would be most useful in standing off Western European attack. Nationalism, needless to say, was not what made a strong impression upon the Ottoman mind, and the agitation even of any faint idea of Turkish nationalism does not characterize the period in which Turkey, in a halting, piecemeal, and largely unsuccessful fashion, first strove to "face west."

By 1875, however, a few articulate Ottoman intellectuals were already deliberately referring to themselves and to what they, generally speaking, conceived as their "race" (if not their "nation") as "Turkish," and quite soon the idea that Turkishness was something of which one should be proud was a commonplace among numerically small but potentially influential Westernized circles of Ottoman intellectuals. This basically romantic conception of Turkish nationalism was, of course, directly inspired by Western Europe, which is to say almost entirely by France, and for the most part those who entertained and cherished such a concept were as politically ineffective as they were untypical of the majority of Ottoman Turks. The idea of Turkishness was soon, however, popularized more widely and greatly reinforced, but not more sharply defined, by a likewise romantic concept of Pan-Turkishness ("Pan-Turanism") which claimed, and still claims today, that "all the Turks" of history (i.e all peoples who, whatever their culture, geographical location, or historical period, may be regarded as using a language of the Turkish family) form an indissoluble whole whose unbroken history is the key to an understanding of the history of Asia, and even of the entire achievements of historical mankind to date (wherefore all Turks should, of right, be one independent state). The "evidence" on which sweeping theories of this sort were erected was largely borrowed from Western European scholarship. Needless to say, valid evidence upon which such theories rest is scanty, to put the case mildly. As sober research into the intellectual antecedents and origins of Turkish nationalism proceeds, there is no doubt that much of the content of this essentially romantic movement will be proved to be what scholars loftily term "unscientific." But the fact that Turkish nationalism is, in many respects, an imitation—conscious or unconscious—of Western European phenomena should not be construed to mean that this nationalism is therefore "bogus," in any sense, in the minds and hearts of those who profess it. On the contrary, although, like *any* complex of loyalty-patterns and beliefs, like *any* nationalism and *any* warmly embraced ideology, Turkish nationalism in many aspects is a matter of non-logical behavior, this in no way lessens its value in the eyes of its devotees any more than it makes it a less real or less important human force. Instead, the importance of Turkish nationalism is directly proportionate to two sums: the sum of the individuals who profess it, and the sum of the degrees of warmth with which they profess it.

At the start, Turkish nationalism as a potential central loyalty for the life of an individual had not taken on rapidly among any large groups of Turks, high Ottoman or Anatolian. Instead, of the high Ottomans, who alone really concern us here, the majority, even in the later nineteenth century, was still largely circumscribed in its view of life by the confines of traditional Islam. And among those exceptional individual Ottomans who personally experienced the impact of Western ideas of all sorts, and who thereupon adopted and adapted certain of them as concepts which they hoped to further in their own world, Turkish nationalism was not the first to be agitated. Instead, it was a heightened, romantic sort of loosely defined Ottoman patriotism, "Pan-Ottomanism," which found most favor, in part because this concept, in so far as it had coherence at all, promised a method by which all that was still left of the Empire might be held together and eventually "reformed" into a more Western-style state. The goal was usually conceived as a constitutional monarchy in which, under the Sultan, all citizens would enjoy "full rights" irrespective of religion, language, or "race." That such a Pan-Ottoman idea, in the face of the dynamic and mutually exclusive nationalisms which already burned in the breasts of many of the Empire's subject peoples, was quite impossible of realization was demonstrated by the experience of the Young Turks, starting with the revolution of 1908. That revolution began with a short honeymoon period in which it was widely and enthusiastically asserted that "la nationalité Ottomane," now a reality, would automatically usher in the millennium. This "nationalité Ottomane," which, as a most able foreign observer had earlier noted, one simply had to say in French because neither Ottoman Turkish nor modern Greek had the words, or the concept behind the words, to express the French-inspired idea, was itself, moreover, only one of several general romantic concepts which the Young Turks more or less espoused, whether on grounds of intellectual or political conviction, or of expediency. These concepts, in addition to this nebulous Pan-Ottomanism, included Turkism (sometimes conceived as primarily Pan-Turanic and sometimes as a more narrowly Ottoman-Empire or even Anatolian-Turkish nationalism), and even Pan-Islam—each idea, obviously, fundamentally incompatible with all the others. It is certainly not unjust to say that the Young Turk period of Ottoman intellectual life, with all its ever larger circles of westernizing intellectuals, was characterized by fundamental incoherence, ideologically speaking.

Previous to the Young Turks, Sultan 'Abdul Ḥamīd II, resisting all forces which he surmised might further endanger his position, had vigorously combatted nationalism, of whatever complexion, among Turks, just as he resisted each of the other nationalisms which threatened his and his dynasty's state. He had, it is true, attempted to use Pan-Islam—always a movement far divorced from actualities of the modern Muslim world—for his own ends, and eventually paid some lip service also to Pan-Ottomanism. Overt Pan-Turkism, however, even when denatured, was anathema, just as it is scrupulously avoided by the government of the Turkish Republic today, and for the same reason: much of the Turkish-speaking population of the world beyond the frontiers of Turkey is subject to Russia, hence espousal of Pan-Turkism may be construed as a direct and undisguised provocation of

Moscow. Those who know the history of Turkey's entry into World War I will realize that this fact was not an insurmountable deterrent in Young Turk eyes, and will certainly conclude that here both 'Abdul Ḥamīd and the Republic of Turkey display a more realistic appraisal of world realities than did Enver Pasha and his aides. For completeness we should also note that Pan-Turanism is a direct challenge to Iran with its Turkish population, as well, but this is obviously a less important consideration today than forty years ago.

'Abdul Ḥamīd II notoriously strove to insulate his domains from further encroachments of Western ideas, but it is also notorious that Western ideas nonetheless began their serious acceleration among true Ottomans under his own rule. Many intellectuals suffered persecution and banishment and some were even executed. Even so, Western ideas rushed in apace. Probably the most important Ottoman group to be infected, and certainly the group which, if he were to maintain Turkey as an effective military power, 'Abdul Ḥamīd least dared insulate from direct contact with Western Europe, was Turkey's corps of professional army officers.

From the first steps in the effective Westernization of the Ottoman army, from the early nineteenth century, this corps had developed a spirit which has persisted to this day and which has repeatedly helped army leaders to function as a national balance wheel. It is true that the Turkish army has sometimes played politics and that many of its regular officers retained (some of them to the present day) attitudes which a doctrinaire Western liberal would immediately call "reactionary." On the other hand, that same officers' corps has consistently been in direct touch with the basic realities of the entire country, has itself never become in any real sense an hereditary group, but instead recruits from a broad base and largely on the basis of merit. Most important, generally speaking, it has also consistently been able to make available to some of its more able younger members—even under 'Abdul Ḥamīd—perhaps the most balanced and realistically Westernizing education and environment available to any Turks. Many, indeed, of the leaders of modern Turkey were educated there, the elder of them in 'Abdul Ḥamīd's day. From it came Kemal Atatürk and

İsmet Inönü, and from it also not only others of Turkey's political figures but also a share of her intellectuals and professional men. Atatürk himself in 'Abdul Ḥamīd's time, as a fledgling officer, was there exposed to the full available gamut of Western ideas and subrosa Ottoman responses to those ideas as then current and understood in upper Ottoman circles.

When, in 1918, the Turkish Empire lay utterly defeated, its physical equipment seemed to be no more nearly completely worn out and discredited than its ideological equipment. Atatürk, in many respects a typical Westernized, early twentieth-century Ottoman regular officer, at this juncture had a number of advantages. He had certainly subscribed to and shared in most of the Young Turks' ideas and ideals, but he had not attained a responsible political role in the Young Turk party, and so was not now tarred with the brush of their discredit as were most of Turkey's available military leaders. On the military side, his abilities and achievements certainly equaled those which any other Turkish regular officer could display, and, in addition to this, in so far as was humanly possible he could claim to be blameless for the military debacle which Turkey had recently suffered. Beyond this, he had a striking and commanding personality, real intellectual power, and a prime flair alike for command and for incisive analysis of the realities of a situation.

Immediately the Greeks—the Ottoman Empire's despised, erstwhile second-class subjects—set hostile foot in Anatolia (May 15, 1919), one is not surprised that it was Atatürk who made his way thither, rallied to his side the officers' corps and used them as well as part of the Ottoman civilian administration to raise the Turkish peasant population, declaring as his justification what was no more than true, namely, that the Sultan in Allied-occupied Istanbul was but a powerless figurehead and that if Turkey was to be saved— i.e. if her status as a fully sovereign state was to be established— this could be done only by forces working in and from Anatolia, independently of Ottoman Istanbul.

The rallying cry which Atatürk sent forth was, from the start, unconditioned Turkish sovereignty based squarely upon unconditioned Turkish nationalism—a Turkish nationalism which would embrace *all* in the realm whose language was Turkish, peasant or high Ottoman, and whose faith was Islam. By 1923 (July 24, Treaty of Lausanne), Atatürk and his *people* (all the Turks of Turkey) had wrested from "the Powers" unconditional acknowledgment that Turkey was for the Turks, and, as we have seen, since that date no nation has ventured far on the assumption that Turkey is not sovereign and will not defend her sovereignty. In accomplishing this, the Turks virtually eliminated the remaining non-Muslim populations of the country which they were so swiftly transforming into a genuine "Turkey" in the modern nation-state sense. In the end, except for Muslim Kurds and a few unimportant remnants here and there on the frontiers of the country and in its larger cities, Turkey was left truly Muslim Turkish. Today the people are about 98 per cent Muslim in faith and about 90 per cent Turkish in mother tongue. Thus the struggle for national sovereignty so accelerated the now forcible processes of Turkification and Muslimization, so accelerated the excision of non-Muslim Turks, that Anatolia now exhibits a degree of religious and linguistic homogeneity absolutely unparalleled in its entire history.

With a vengeance, Atatürk had got *Turkey for the Turks*, but in many important aspects his Turks were still not "one nation and one people"—not in the sense, say, that the French or the Swedes were. Instead, those Turks in 1923 consisted of a comparatively small, nominally *ex*-Ottoman, predominantly urbanized, literate, and extremely self-conscious upper class who then were, and by and large today remain, the ruling group in the Turkish Republic, plus a second and far larger group of peasant-stratum Turks who (rural *or* urban) were largely illiterate and medieval-minded, and who can best be characterized culturally as representing the folk level of Anatolian Muslim Turkish-speaking life. Obviously such a sharply stratified society, although it contained the possible makings of a modern nation state, was not that state, however heatedly some of its intellectuals might argue that it was. Obviously, too, only a fraction of the people of that state was "modern" in any basic sense, nor were the chances of such a state's ultimate survival particularly bright in the first half of the twentieth century. In other words, to get *Turkey for the Turks* had not been enough. It also remained to get enough truly *new* Turks to ensure that this new Turkey could survive. It was this task which occupied the remainder of Atatürk's career.

II

In their vigorous efforts to develop enough *new* Turks to enable New Turkey to survive in the twentieth century, Atatürk and his aides again achieved a surprising degree of success, but success by no means as unqualified as had been the case with their efforts to get *Turkey for the Turks,* for their second task was of course far more complicated and, in its essential nature, not possible of completion within a short space of time. The most hostile critic of these efforts cannot justly claim more than the following: first, that in his efforts speedily to Westernize the recently Ottoman ruling groups, Atatürk succeeded really for the most part only in altering superficial characteristics, but perforce left many of his upper class compatriots' most fundamental patterns of thought and action quite unchanged; and second, that despite all efforts, the vast peasant majority of the Turkish Republic had not, by the date of Atatürk's death (November 10, 1938), made any significant response to indicate that it was really being aroused from its age-old Anatolian folk-Muslim way of life. As against this, Atatürk's strongest partisans for their part have, at the most, claimed: first, that the literate citizenry, i.e. roughly the total ex-high Ottoman population of Turkey, is now thoroughly Europeanized in way of life and in way of thought; and second, that the Anatolian peasants are visibly and rapidly moving along the path which will make them Westernized too.

The objective observer will naturally expect to find the balance of evidence pointing somewhere toward a middle ground between these two extremes, and when he considers them with specific reference to the current content and nature of Turkish nationalism, he will reach a middle ground. Turkey's venture during the last quarter of a century in attempting to impose, from the top of the social pyramid down, a program of forced-draft, wholesale, compulsory Westernization-plus-nationalization has already so transformed the literate segment of the population that it is only in markedly older age-groups that one finds many individuals who are not today strongly nationalist in outlook. And this is all the more significant because, largely through promoting the spread of literacy and especially by making literacy easier to attain through substituting the relatively easier Latin for the (in Turkish usage) most complicated Arabic alphabet, the Turkish Republic has simultaneously succeeded in increasing the number of literate citizens in the state—in other words, has already visibly broadened the base of the ruling group and thereby somewhat lessened the total percentage of people still living on a largely folk-culture level.

Peasants, of course, are still the large majority of Turkey's total population; although their lot, too, has distinctly bettered and their prospects, compared with what they were at any time in pre-Republican history, are vastly improved, still it is difficult for the objective observer to believe that they are as yet widely infected with much sense of a self-consciously Turkish nationalism in any way comparable to that which non-peasant Turks ordinarily feel. This is not to say, of course, that all Turks, of whatever economic or intellectual level, are not bound together by many strong ties. They obviously are, and chief among such ties may be mentioned strong loyalty to the land (although in the case of the peasant this is rather loyalty to a home-region than to a region with map frontiers), a strong sense of difference from the peoples of all surrounding countries (Muslim or non-Muslim), and a most compelling mistrust and dislike of Russians (primarily as Russians and, in the case of literate Turks, secondarily also as communists, although the peasant may be but little aware of this latter distinction). The reader will note, however, that, generally speaking, such bonds of solidarity among the total Muslim Turkish population of modern Turkey are not, in the first instance, directly attributed to nationalism per se, but rather are in larger measure heritages from the older, a-national Ottoman past—being, of course, all the more firmly-set bonds of cohesion for that very reason. Their existence certainly lends only a most qualified and tenuous support to extreme assertions that "all" the citizens of Turkey today embody a deeply felt, explicitly self-conscious concept of Turkish nationalism, although this very assertion *is* true to a surprising degree when limited to the Turkish Republic's non-peasant Muslim Turkish citizens.

This degree of national feeling attained is doubly surprising when one stops to reflect upon the nature and traditions of the human raw-material which Atatürk originally had at hand.

His Turkish "people" in 1923, aside from those who were so exceptional as to be fairly called a-typical, may in many instances have favored a substantial degree of Westernization, but certainly had not been looking forward to the dethronement of the dynasty, the total excision of Islam—law and state-system—from the government, nor the wholesale jettisoning of most of the impedimenta of the Ottoman Turkish sub-species of Muslim civilization in favor of a swallow-at-one-gulp adoption of Western European ways. But that is exactly what Atatürk's Turkey was to get, and that as swiftly as available human and non-human resources allowed.

In this program of compulsory, forced-draft Westernization, Atatürk made essential use of the entire concept of Turkish nationalism. It, and it alone, was proclaimed the basic point in Turkish patriotism, the central factor around which the personal loyalty of each single individual was ultimately to be rallied. In sphere after sphere of life, nationalism was to replace religion, and has done so. Organized religion was officially regarded as irredeemably reactionary, basically irreconcilable with a modern state, and so was virtually abolished. High Islam, the formal religious institutions of the true Ottomans, are virtually dead in Turkey today, although surviving members of that group, and those of their descendants who wish to, of course may and do preserve a vital *personal faith* as Muslims. Among the peasants, on the other hand, folk-Islam persists, but the consensus of informed opinion holds that this, too, is gradually losing ground. In the case of all levels of Islam which existed or exist in Turkey, it is certainly also fair to assert that to the degree an individual feels himself consciously a Turkish nationalist, to that degree, also, he is unlikely to be deeply concerned about religion.

Here the Turks plainly court the danger of substituting nationalism, concern for the good of the state, in the place of ethical values which religion formerly upheld, and to this degree Turkey has at times been accused of being "totalitarian" in a most basic sense. This danger is recognized by not a few modern Turkish thinkers, their usual response being to attempt the revitalization of Turkish Islam as a personal religion. To date, there is no tangible evidence that such a movement is having appreciable success. Instead, religion is no longer socially esteemed as formerly, and the higher one mounts through the stratifications of Turkish society, the more true this generalization becomes. And by and large, the single greatest force which fills the void left by the fall of religion from its onetime place at the pinnacle of social esteem is nationalism. From one point of view, indeed, one may say that in practice religion now is a negative concept, important only because being born or becoming a Muslim remains one of the two conditions still essential for complete acceptance as a "true Turk" on any level of social life: conforming in language and religion. Non-Muslim minorities are no longer important. Indeed very few Westerners have as yet realized how completely trivial, whether for Turkey's present or Turkey's future, her remaining non-Muslim population is. In law such communities stand on an equal footing with their Muslim-Turkish fellow citizens (provided only that non-Muslims know Turkish, a condition which by no means all of them do, or want to fulfill), but in fact they are discriminated against regularly in almost every sphere of daily and of national life. Many modern Turks, not all of them themselves conspicuously Westernized by any means, feel that this is wrong, and have at times said so with some vehemence, but such individuals are still sufficiently a-typical among the mass of Turkey's Muslim population, regardless of social level, to be disregarded as an indication that on this particular point the fundamental ideas of older times have much altered under Turkey's new regime. Fundamental practices, however, have altered to a real degree, and the life of a non-Muslim holder of a Turkish passport is entirely secure, although his liberties and property may not always be wholly respected. Certainly such individuals are at least as well off in Turkey as are similarly sharply-set off minorities in other countries in Turkey's general area. It is probable that the ultimate solution for Turkey's non-Muslim minorities will have to be emigration or assimilation (linguistically and religiously). No barrier is put before the individual who chooses the latter path, and for him who would emigrate the sole barrier is that he take with him only a small amount of property. Hence, usually it is the less well-to-do who go.

Turkey's important minority, the Kurds (almost 10 per cent of the total population), has a quite different position, for it is a minority only in point of language but not in point of religion. The Kurds, a vigorous, pastoral, mountaineer people, are Muslim. Although it is true that their form of Islam is not strictly orthodox, still like that of the Anatolian peasants, it is best described as folk-Islam; hence the only barrier to assimilation of the Kurds is their non-Turkish language. There is no convincing evidence for a self-conscious Kurdish nationalism on the part of Turkey's Kurds. Despite newspaper accounts of Turkish "wars" against the Kurdish population of the country, of "one hundred and eight separate campaigns in a few years," Turkey's policy toward her Kurds, an admittedly troublesome group for any central authority to deal with, in general deserves the terms "enlightened" and "constructive." The government has used its power to break the Kurdish tribal formations, to relieve the tribesmen of their chiefs (Aghas, it being these latter only who, as a rule, have forcibly been transported to non-Kurdish regions of the country), and to give young Kurdish males equal opportunity in the nation's armed forces with Anatolian Turkish peasant males. In consequence, it is now already rare in large regions of Kurdish Turkey to meet males, except in the distinctly older age groups, who are not bi-lingual, while more and more females are also beginning to learn at least some Turkish. As a result, the language barrier—the one real barrier to the Kurds' assimilation—is dissolving, and the Kurds seem generally moving on the way to complete and unprejudicial assimilation into a society distinctly less primitive than what they have known before. It is not an exaggeration to contend that modern Turkey is here carrying on a successful labor of "civilization." And, of course, in so far as this labor succeeds, its end-product is an ex-Kurd who is not only now a Turk but also, depending largely upon the social level which he ultimately attains, himself a self-conscious Turkish nationalist as well.

It is true that Atatürk, in buttressing Turkish nationalism with an expanded version of the "historical" part of Pan-Turanian theory (the "National Historical Thesis" and the "Sun Language

Theory"—the two roughly maintaining that the Turks are history's original, and mankind's original, people wherefore all human achievement to date is basically Turkish) thereby further injected into Turkism a specific concept of a direct, purposive, evolutionary continuity between the earliest Turks of East-Central Asia and the latest "pure Turkish" achievements of Ankara, a complex of ideas and beliefs which easily leads to "racism." When such theories were first introduced they were scorned by some Turks who perceived the absurdities involved, and such ideas more and more tend to become dead issues among well-informed Turks generally. They do, however, continue to color much of Turkish education, and so to that degree are at least alive. In any event, although there are small groups who today take "racism" and "pure Turkishness" as their war-cries in politics, their leaders know that Ottoman society was for long a most efficient melting pot, and they do not risk the ripostes involved in specific genealogical research in modern Turkey.

So, in so far as nationalism is concerned, modern Turkey's program of compulsory, forced-draft Westernization-plus-nationalism is having extraordinary success. Almost every one of the individual "reforms" which Atatürk introduced and carried forward was of course objected to by many of his fellow-citizens, urban and rural, literate and peasant. Very few of his original collaborators, in actual fact, would have been likely to endorse all which Atatürk and the future had in store for them, had they foreseen the whole of what was ahead. At juncture after juncture Atatürk met opposition and, when necessary, crushed it. But apart from the torpor of the peasant, he seldom had to face strong opposition, in part because even those who most mistrusted and disliked what he was proposing did not, themselves, have any adequate alternative to put forward as a counter-suggestion. Nor could they argue effectively that the old ought to be retained, for the more aware of this century a man was, the more he had to realize—whether he explicitly formulated his ideas or not—that unless Turkey quickly developed enough *new* Turks to enable a New Turkey to survive, the ultimate penalty could well be the end of any sort of Turkey at all.

It should not be inferred that Atatürk and his collaborators were impelled to do what they did solely by desperation. They were also sustained by a vigorous idealism, namely the belief that the Turks could finally be wrought not only into a sovereign nation-state but also into a literate, self-governing parliamentary republic. Of all the goals which Atatürk set, this last obviously was the least capable of being attained in a hurry, and the dispassionate observer today here will pay more heed to concrete gains which the Turks have made and are making as they move toward this still distant goal, rather than reproach them for not yet embodying in fact *all* virtues.

Turkey's Westernization, Turkey's nationalization, and Turkey's democratization are all surprisingly successful to anyone who compares them with the base-line from which the Turks started in, say, 1900. Turkish nationalism has conquered the upper levels of Turks, and now extends its conquest as that group expands into an ever more democratically broad-based literate electorate of linguistically and religiously homogeneous citizens. Turkish nationalism cannot realistically claim yet to have aroused many Turkish peasants, but it can claim to have tried and to be continuing to try. And no one who has traveled widely in Turkey's most backward regions during recent years can doubt that a much fuller impact than any known to date of the West upon the peasant is almost certain to occur, an impact which will inevitably also bring Turkish nationalism more completely to him, provided only that Turkey remains a sovereign state. Those minorities whom nationalism cannot reach because of religious loyalties persisting from the past are practically negligible. The more important minority, that which needs only linguistic assimilation for acceptance into the Turkish nation, is apparently already on that very road. One's conclusion must be that nationalist Turkey's house today is in good—surprisingly good—order and that to date Turkish nationalism under the Republic has been, for all those whom it *can* reach, a preponderantly constructive force.

III

The constructive nature of modern Turkey's efforts toward Westernization-plus-nationalism is nowhere more self-evident than within the specific framework of its effects upon Turkey's international relations. Not only did Turkey assert her unqualified national sovereignty within her own frontiers, she also (with one exception, the Sanjak of Alexandretta, an exception stipulated from the first, and incorporated in Turkey at the first favorable opportunity) asserted that she had no further territorial claims or ambitions, and she has held to that rigid anti-irredentism inflexibly. A harsh critic might term Turkey's nationalism "chauvinist," but never "redentist." This policy, the other side of the coin of Turkey's nationalist sovereignty at home, has been basic in Turkey's consistent record as a comparatively stable, reliable element in international affairs. Turkey's conduct in international relations, both in individual relations with other countries and also in her sober and constructive participation in the League of Nations and in the United Nations, is misconstrued by those who attribute it to New Turkey's "idealism." New Turkey cannot yet afford to be idealistic. Instead, her policy is (1) to survive, and (2) with survival assured, to try to prosper and develop internally. This policy offends only those who prefer not to see her survive, or not to see her develop and prosper domestically. Her course of international dealings during World War II was a model of courageous, skillful, self-controlled, far-sighted, single-minded, enlightened self-interest, and the same characterization holds for her course since the end of hostilities. Her calculations obviously are seldom based on the fact that she is a Muslim nation, but rather on the consideration that she is *the* Turkish Nation. Thus in the Palestine controversy Turkey by no means favored Zionism or encouraged anti-Arab forces, but when matters reached a point involving what Turkey judged to be considerations more truly vital for her own security and future, she at once accepted the situation, and has since not only worked in support of various United Nations undertakings which concern Israel, but also freely trades with Israel. This does not satisfy the Arabs, but Turkey considers them as no vital threat to her security, and the Turks have little fellow-feeling for the Arabs as brother-Muslims. Instead, as recent rulers of, and intimately acquainted with, much of the Muslim world, the Turks frankly consider themselves far more advanced than most other Muslim lands and conduct themselves accordingly.

Relations with Iran, Pakistan, Afghanistan, and the Arab states are correct, and Ankara watches them closely and strives to keep them correct, but they are scarcely cordial in any but a perfunctory diplomatic sense, and certainly not, in Turkey's view, vital. Assertions that Turkey will deliberately take the lead in Islam—politically or otherwise—are without serious foundation. Should Turkey feel it to her *own* advantage, she would certainly head a Muslim bloc, but it is perfectly plain that at present she feels it far more to her advantage to attempt to fill the role of the easternmost bastion of Western democracy. Therein, certainly, lies her best chance of continued existence, and it is a chance which she embraces with unimpugnable courage. That courage, just as is the case in her record of international stability and self-control or her record for vigorous efforts to ensure internal developments which will improve her chances for sovereign existence during the second half of the twentieth century, has vital roots which reach far back into the Ottoman and Muslim past, but its living growth today largely takes the form of self-conscious, twentieth century Turkish Nationalism.

11

THE NATIONAL AND INTERNATIONAL
RELATIONS OF IRAN

BY T. CUYLER YOUNG

"THE RISE OF THE ṢAFAVI DYNASTY IN PERSIA at the beginning of the sixteenth century of the Christian era was an event of the greatest historical importance, not only to Persia herself and her immediate neighbors, but to Europe generally. It marks not only the restoration of the Persian nationality after an eclipse of more than eight centuries and a half, but the entrance of Persia into the comity of nations and the genesis of political relations which still to a considerable extent hold good."[1]

These opening sentences of the fourth volume of *The Literary History of Persia* set forth the considered judgment of the "Master of Persian Studies" concerning the origins of modern Persian nationalism and international relations. Yet critical scrutiny would seem to demand some discriminating qualification in the interpretation of this opinion. Although the turn from Arabic-speaking Islam to membership in world society under the Ṣafavis at the beginning of the sixteenth century marked the true beginning of her modern international relations, so that "political developments in Persia had begun to some extent to coincide independently . . . with tendencies prevailing in the western world,"[2] it is probably going too far to imply that these events were of the greatest importance to Europe. Some would question that "the mighty Ottoman, terror of the Christian world, quaketh of a Sherley fever" and that "the Sherlein arts of war" learned by "the prevailing Persian" really slowed the Ottoman penetration of Europe;[3] and even if true, this probably meant more to Persia than to Europe.

[1] E. G. Browne, *Persian Literature in Modern Times,* Cambridge, 1924, p. 3.
[2] A. K. S. Lambton, "Persia," *Journal of the Royal Central Asian Society,* XXXI, 1944, p. 9. To this penetrating discussion the author gladly acknowledges his debt.
[3] *Purchas's Pilgrims,* quoted by E. G. Browne, *op. cit.,* p. 105f.

Persian commerce with Europe flourished: with the Portuguese in the Persian Gulf, and subsequently there with the Dutch and English when the world-famous mart of Hormuz changed hands in 1622; with the English reaching Persia incidentally from the north in their efforts to open a land route to Cathay across Muskong, although this trade dwindled when the English subsequently consolidated their position in India. Yet all this for the traders of Europe was incidental, merely a development on their way to the farther East where lay their more alluring and rewarding goals, as the comparative commercial isolation of Persia in the eighteenth century indicates. Significant as these developments were for the international relations of Persia, it must be remembered that the personnel involved on both sides was small and that both diplomacy and trade were virtual monopolies of the Persian court, to which most contacts were limited.

Further qualification is to be applied to Professor Browne's remarks on "Persian Nationality"—as he himself goes on to indicate. With a proper understanding of the term its use may be legitimate, but it should be made clear that the usual definitions and connotations of "nationality" and "nationalism" current in the mid-twentieth century do not apply in the Near and Middle East of the nineteenth century, much less the sixteenth. It is true that the Persian people and Persian civilization definitely turned a corner in history with the rise of the Ṣafavi dynasty, which stimulated a new self-consciousness and a real though as yet vaguely defined individuality; but this is not the same territorial state-nationalism which has been the dynamic force of modern Europe and has for nearly half a century dominated the Near and Middle East. Perhaps the situation may best be summarized in the words of Professor Toynbee: "... in modern Shiʻi Iran ... the national religion has become the matrix of a secular or political national consciousness."[4]

The difference between sixteenth-seventeenth century Ṣafavi "nationality" and twentieth century Pahlavi nationalism is best illustrated by their diverse attitudes toward language and religion. The Ṣafavi rulers and the Shahseven, or seven tribes on whose power the dynasty relied, were of Turkoman origin and Turkish-speaking; even after a century of Ṣafavi power and the removal of

<hr>

[4] A. J. Toynbee, *A Study of History*, London, 1934, vol. I, p. 393.

the capital to Iṣfahān the court continued to speak Turkish. Shah Ismā'īl and Sultan Selīm, under whom the rivalry between the Persians and Ottomans was bitter, were poets of considerable talent; yet the Shah wrote in Turkish and the Sultan in Persian, and they hurled abuses at each other in these same languages.

Antipathy and enmity centered around differences in religion, the Ṣafavis championing Shi'ism against the Sunnis not only of the West in the Ottoman Empire but to the East among the Uzbeks and the Afghans. By making Ja'fari Shi'ism the state religion of Persia the Ṣafavis created a new geographical concentration and differentiation of this sect which had a profound effect upon Islam in general and on Persia in particular. Nādir Shah, with his dreams of conquest and extension of Persian borders, tried to reduce this sectarian influence; but so deep-rooted had become the Shi'ah faith in Persia and so ephemeral were Nādir's exploits and plans that no real change was effected.

Quite different is the nationalism of our time with its varying emphasis on the unifying factors of race, language, and territory. As we shall observe subsequently, the sixteenth and twentieth centuries have almost reversed the emphasis on language and religion in relation to national cohesion and integrity. Here it may be observed in passing that to speak of a Persian race has no valid meaning, so mixed is the blood flowing in the veins of the inhabitants of modern Ariana or Iran. The country, however, possesses a definite cultural personality.

An unfortunate deterioration in domestic Persian government and economy, as well as a shift in European power, separated the Ṣafavi and Pahlavi periods. The destruction of the Ṣafavis by the Afghans, their elimination in turn by Nādir Shah whose romantic conquests and ambitions were a drain upon and liability to the Persian people, the subsequent internal struggle for power between the Persian Zands of the south and the Turkoman Qājārs of the north which resulted in the dynastic consolidation of the latter, brought Persia to the threshold of the nineteenth century weakened, if not exhausted.

Meanwhile Russia had emerged as a European power and was marching on Persia's northern borders, ready to take advantage of this weakness. Britain, ousted from much of North America, turned to India and consolidated her position there, and for defense was returning to the Persian Gulf. Yet it was France with her Napoleonic dreams and machinations which served as the catalyst in Persia to precipitate the pattern of British-Russian rivalry which dominated the nineteenth century, almost obliterated Persian independence, and, with recent variations in counterpoint, remains the dominant theme in Persian foreign relations to the present day.

In a treaty with Persia in 1814 the British inaugurated that policy of the defense of Persia against aggression—to make Persia a buffer for India—which obtained for the next century. The year previous, in the Gulistān Treaty of 1813, the Russians had succeeded in establishing themselves south of the Caucasus at Persia's expense. By the Treaty of Turkomānchāi in 1828—following a short war declared by the British to have been provoked by Persia—the Tsar had pushed his trans-Caucasian holdings to the Aras River, approximately to the present boundary; and, what was more important, had secured extra-territorial rights for internal penetration, rights which obtained for a century until abolished by Riza Shah Pahlavi in 1928.

For the next half-century or more Persia was caught in the "Central Asian Question" when Russia was moving to fill the trans-Caspian power vacuum, cautiously countered by British India's championship of the Afghans. It finally required a short war between Britain and Persia to compel the latter to relinquish her ambition to bring the Afghans back under Persian sovereignty as of the Ṣafavi era, for the British feared such extended hegemony would be too easy for the Russians to control, bringing them at one stroke to the borders of India.

II

In the last quarter of the nineteenth century this British-Russian rivalry concentrated on internal economic concessions from and capital loans to the absolutist, inept, and selfish Qājārs, which stimulated in the exasperated Persian people the beginnings of a national revival that continues to this day. Some of the significant events and aspects of this development have already been recorded. It is sufficient here to emphasize that it was this international rivalry which produced modern Persian nationalism. The two have been inextricably intertwined ever since.

In the pattern of mutual interaction between these forces there have been three phases in the last sixty years: the so-called "constitutional phase," continuing to 1911 or 1914 and the outbreak of World War I; the Riza Shah period between the World Wars; and the present period, now a decade old, since the accession of Muhammad Riza in 1941. There is a surprising continuity in the basic pattern that obtains throughout, for all the variations in the separate phases of the development. Each of these has been introduced by a period of confusion, weakness, and foreign intervention giving rise to a new outburst of national feeling and determination which has succeeded in reaffirming the nation's integrity and independence, then pushed on to a new phase in the consolidation of this position. Yet, each time, disruptive and frustrating entanglement in the rivalries and alliances of foreign powers, issuing in two world wars, have cut short this internal development. The major powers have always been Britain and Russia, although each time Germany and the United States have been among the dramatis personae, each playing substantially the same continuous roles, except that for the present Germany has been eliminated and the United States has passed beyond the role of temporary diplomatic champion of Iranian independence and economic adviser in a crisis to that of major power in the West in alliance with Great Britain.

The constitutional phase of modern nationalism was conceived in the response of the united Persian people to a monopolistic British tobacco concession, nourished in embryo by the even more determined and less scrupulous politico-economic exploitation of the Russians, brought to birth in 1905-1906 by the jealous midwifery of British support, but in the Anglo-Russian Convention of 1907 abandoned by the frightened midwife to premature exposure to the more ruthless Russian imperialism. This British-Russian cooperation, disastrous to the new-born movement, was produced by the rising threat of Kaiserine Germany, a threat most effective for British acquiescence in Tsarist leadership in Persia in 1911— year of the Agadir-Moroccan war scare. This defeated the first American financial mission which bid fair to succeed in reorganizing the Persian financial and tax structure, thereby creating a solid foundation for real independence. This the Tsar was not disposed to permit.

Probably only the coming of war in 1914 saved this reborn Persia from dismemberment and death; and the further distraction and disintegration of these years, with the two familiar imperialisms supplemented by the active intervention of German-Austrian intrigues and Turkish armies, no less imperialist and contemptuous of Persia in their designs, appeared to have weakened the nation beyond the hope of recovery.

The soul of the nation, however, was by no means dead, though the constitutional body in which it had found self-expression was too weak to serve it in this crisis; and that is not so surprising considering that the body bore the hallmark "Made in Western Europe." Roused from its stupor by the shock of the Anglo-Persian Agreement of 1919, nationalism gained new vigor by the anti-toxic Soviet offer of friendship and non-aggression, with Riza Shah turning out to be the successful physician administering this and other doses of new medicine that restored the patient to a remarkable degree of health. The forms of constitutionalism were maintained sufficiently to protect the nation from amnesia, but ancient Persian messianism reasserted itself and Riza Shah became the high priest of the new god Nationalism who threatened to undermine Allah and His Prophet.

Britain then had displaced the Russians from Satan's throne in the Persian Hell, though the real Lucifer had but clothed himself in garments of light for a season. General Persian distrust of the British—still a nearly pathological state of mind among the majority of politically conscious Persians—dates from the Anglo-Russian Convention of 1907 when an awakened Persia felt itself abandoned by the century-old British policy of defense against aggression; and became a settled habit of mind following the Anglo-Persian Agreement of 1919. Britain's reputation in Persia is fabulous for ubiquitous and subtle intrigues, the British getting credit for most of history's coincidences and untoward accidents. In a nation so long caught in the vise of rival imperialisms that it cannot forget the two-faced demon of appeasement, it is not too surprising that the majority are bitterly biased and prejudiced. It is part of the price that contemporary Britons have to pay in Asia for the policies—good and bad—pursued by their fathers and grandfathers, as well as for merely being there as a great Western power. Because a strong Iran served, in general, Britain's need for an adequate buffer between Russia and India, Britain in the Riza Shah period followed a policy of watchful waiting and mild co-operation, punctuated by periods of tension, as for example, in Iran's cancellation and later renegotiation of the D'Arcy oil concession in 1933.

From 1917 to 1926 the Soviets followed a policy of friendly benevolence, with special economic consideration for Eastern countries, including Iran; the Soviet-Iranian Treaty of Friendship of 1921 launched this policy. With the triumph of Stalin over Trotsky, the inauguration of the policy of first achieving "socialism in a single state" and of girding the Soviet Union economically toward that end, Iran found itself progressively denied any special treatment, and in 1930 deprived of the last remnants of a favored position. Despite the 1926 Soviet-Iranian non-aggression treaty, the cordial relations dating from 1921 began to deteriorate in 1926. Original Iranian need of Soviet friendship to neutralize an overdose of British influence had been successfully served; hence with the tightening of Soviet commercial policy Persian friendliness to Moscow diminished and Riza Shah in 1929-1930 determinedly cleared the northern provinces of all suspect Soviet revolutionary influences. It was not until 1935 that a three-year Soviet-Iranian trade agreement promised a solid basis for future economic relations; and trade difficulties prevented the renewal of this until 1940. These shifts in Soviet-Iranian relations were closely connected with the Sixth and Seventh Comintern Congress in Moscow in 1928 and 1935.

Throughout this period, however, for all the benevolence of the early 1920's, Iranians continued to regard the Russians with profound fear and suspicion. The Soviets, for all their professions to the contrary, could not convince Iran of their sincerity. Subsequent events proved that they were not only the victims of past policies in trying to change Iranian attitudes, but in reality victims themselves of their own old imperialistic policies.

Riza Shah built his foreign policy on the traditional Persian pattern, playing both ends against the middle—when one could be found. The United States had earlier (1919-1920) advanced its minor role in the drama by officially championing Iranian integrity, which helped not a little in stiffening resistance to the Anglo-Persian Agreement of 1919.[5] But in subsequent isolation it could scarcely play the role of "middle" for Riza Shah, though to it the Shah appealed for unofficial technical financial and administrative assistance which—in the First Millspaugh Mission—furnished the solid foundation on which he built his new state of nationalist reform.

In the 1930's an even better candidate for the role of third power appeared. Nazi Germany's messianic doctrine of the fuehrer and dictatorship, racial myths of Aryanism, European rivalry with both Britain and Russia, and, best of all, a mutually profitable trade program, made it a natural ally and friend of Iran. Riza Shah can scarcely be blamed for not perceiving that once again to stop Germany the Soviet Bear and the British Lion would march together, even in the Land of the Persian Lion and Sun; although after the change in the party line following the Seventh Comintern Congress of 1935 this might have been discerned as a possibility. But it was this very friendship for Germany and the pro-Nazi administration of declared Iranian neutrality which brought on the British-Russian invasion of 1941 and cost the Shah his throne as the price of saving his dynasty.[6] His son, Muhammad Riza, ascended the throne to rule as a democratic sovereign under the restored constitution.

During the decade preceding the war another development in foreign relations produced a pattern quite in contrast to preceding centuries: the Sa'dabād Pact of 1937 of friendship and non-aggression among Turkey, Iraq, Afghanistan, and Iran—all Muslim states, but at varying points of Westernizing reform and still a mixture of Shī'ah and Sunni. Hailed at the time as a new thing in Asia, the catastrophic events of the next few years overshadowed its significance and it has been little heard of since.

[5] The expression of this to the Persian people had to be effected by unconventional methods; cf. Henry Filmer, *The Pageant of Persia,* Indianapolis, 1936, p. 340f.

[6] The same pro-German pattern had emerged at neutral Tehran after the beginning of World War I, except that little significance was attached then to Persia, and there were no disastrous results. Cf. Christopher Sykes, *Wassmus,* esp. pp. 201-206; and Sir Percy Sykes, *History of Persia,* London, 1930, vol. 2, 3rd ed., pp. 442-450.

History in Iran seemed to repeat itself in World War II. The two major powers again cooperated, this time—with sizable United States aid—making of Iran a "Bridge of Victory" in Asia over which went vast war supplies to help turn the Battle of Russia. For all its expression of agreement in the British-Russian-Iranian Tripartite Treaty of 1942 and the Three-Power Iran Declaration of the 1943 Tehran Conference, this coalition fell apart shortly after the shooting stopped, and in 1945-1946 the first major skirmish of the "cold war" centered on the question of Iranian independence and integrity and the implementation of these solemn commitments. Backed by the Western signatories to this treaty and declaration under the vigorous leadership of the United States, Iran was able to secure the withdrawal of Soviet troops in May 1946, to liquidate the Azerbaijan separatist movement by the end of the year, to overcome the internal threat of the Soviet-controlled Tudeh Party, and by the autumn of 1947 to reject in the Majlis the Soviet-Iranian Oil Agreement with the prospect of which Premier Aḥmad Qavām had first effected Soviet troop withdrawal. Subsequently, resolutely resisting Soviet attacks in a prolonged war of nerves, the Iranian government moved into the orbit of the non-Soviet powers, convinced that only so could any hope of real independence be maintained. This remains basically true in mid-1951 despite recent Western ineptitude in Iran, with consequent modification of the quality of Iranian cooperation and faith.

III

From this review of the development of Iranian nationalism some of the principal problems of the present and the immediate future of Iran in the family of nations stand out clearly. Certainly it is abundantly evident that Iranian nationalism is intimately bound up, as always since its inception a little over a half a century ago, with its international relations and is dependent upon the resolution of that polarized opposition of power in the midst of which it stands; except that what was previously a dangerous position between two nineteenth-century European imperialisms sparring in Asia has now been exchanged for an equally perilous position on the frontier of the Western world where it marches in Asia alongside the communist colossus. In few of the smaller nations are survival and integrity so determined by international relations over which the people exercise so little control as in Iran.

This very fact may be a kind of political asset to Iran, but at the same time it is a spiritual liability; one of the greatest weaknesses of Iran is her romanticizing tendency to see this hard reality of foreign interest out of focus, to the dimming of her own responsibility. In the last analysis only Iran can establish and enhance her own independence and integrity; and this effort, though it cannot control, can definitely influence the web of international relations, at least in so far as she herself is concerned: and this influence could be a lasting contribution to world peace. Help Iran surely needs, but it can be effective only as she helps herself to the limit of her own resources, material and spiritual.

To this end unquestionably one of the major problems of Iranian nationalism is the attainment of inner integrity and unity. In this respect she probably stands mid-way between Turkey and the Arab States: much more an entity, politically and spiritually, than the divided Arab States; but not so tightly knit or ideologically unified as "Turkey for the Turks." Iranians would profess the same slogan, but would scarcely be so clearly agreed on the meaning of the terms. As regards the three most important criteria for judging nationalism in Western Asia—a definite territory, homogeneity in religion, the speaking of a single language—Iran faces exceptions which pose real problems of integrity and unity.

Some Iranian nationalists can try to vault the Islamic centuries to pre-Arab greatness, but this does violence to too much Iranian civilization and culture to satisfy most. Indeed, so much of that culture, which is real to most Iranians, is so bound up with the medieval world society of Islam or the subsequent empire of the Ṣafavis that many modern Iranians find the confinement of modern state-nationalism stultifying. Iranian nationalism is not wholly free from grandiose dreams of irrendentism and empire. It is no accident that the present dynasty is called Pahlavi, the ruler "King of Kings," and the realm an empire. At the Paris Peace Conference in 1919, the Iranian delegation was instructed to press for the return of Transcaucasia to Iran. The very name "Iran"—demanded in international usage by Riza Shah—suggests certain territorial ambitions; significantly its use has recently been made optional.

Although by many political sophisticates Baḥrayn irredentism is known to be only a decoy whipping post in the continued rivalry of Britain and Russia and a convenient soap-box for Iranian self-assertive oratory, by the majority it is taken quite seriously. One would not deny a people their dreams—by which the generations live—but these should have some relation to present realities and possibilities. Iranian genius is a powerful mixture of idealism and realism which should not be damaged, but survival and integration in the twentieth century world demand a consistent and effective ideology and a large dose of hard-headed practicality for the attainment of these definite goals. Yet this is minor in importance; for the most part Iran in its nationalism adheres generally to modern standards for judgment and integrity. As already observed, this is certainly different from sixteenth century Ṣafavi Iran as regards religion and language.

In respect to religion, although Iran has not disestablished Shi'ism, it has nonetheless followed the modern secularization movement, albeit of the more limited anti-clerical rather than anti-religious character. Parliamentary representation and the passage rites of the individual, together with personal status in the community, may still be on a religious communal basis; but, almost uniquely among Muslim states of the area, freedom of faith and of change in personal religious communal affiliation are both in law and in practice granted to all citizens. Practically, in social and vocational spheres, it makes considerable difference whether a citizen is a member of the Muslim majority: the communalism of Asia does not disappear that easily. Yet 95 per cent or more of Iranians are Muslim and the vast majority of these adherents of the Shi'ah sect, so that Iran has no serious religious minority problem threatening her integrity.

Iran's real religious problem, for national unity, is the wide gap between her national secularist and Westernizing leaders and those still loyal to traditional Islam and its way of life. The latter includes mainly the folk-Islam of peasants, artisans, and laborers; although the number of those enjoying traditional high Iranian culture who have their serious doubts and reservations about this new nationalism—largely styled by the West—is not inconsiderable. These loyal Muslims have instinctively sensed essential idolatry in their leadership, which has so easily made nationalism and the service of the state the end and goal of its citizens. This excessive patriotism and tendency toward totalitarianism in Riza Shah's regime brought on the semi-paralysis following the defeat of 1941, from which some would question whether the country has yet recovered spiritually. Certainly more balance and therefore perhaps more stability has been achieved between these differing groups with the advent of comparative liberty of speech, press, and assembly. The leaders of folk-Islam, however, decry the growing materialism of the society and the deterioration in moral standards of truth and integrity, generally admitted by most observers, but perhaps more apparent than real because of the terrific economic pressures under which most Iranians have lived for the past decade or so, and not unique in this particular country in this era of social change and ferment.

To counterbalance any undue emphasis on the seriousness or uniqueness of this problem, it may be observed that fundamentally this gap between folk-Islam and the nation's leadership is no new feature of Iranian society, but only aggravated and potentially more threatening in the mid-twentieth century. Heirs to a common, splendid culture in which even the folk participate by means of oral tradition and education, there is a strong bond of Iranian loyalty between the high and the low—a kind of intangible homogeneity which all to a degree share as Iranians rather than as Muslims. Firdawsi and his immortal epic, the great classic poets, the ancient and distinctively Iranian festival of Naw Rūz in which all faiths long have joined—these and similar features have given to all Iranians a sense of oneness which can bear considerable strain and which still gives the nation much of its toughness, especially in a crisis.

Moreover, education should do much to bridge this gap, especially if widely spread to the folk of the land and deepened at the level of cultural leadership; the people as a whole would then become sharing partners in the benefits of the nationalist modernization; and the leaders, especially the clerics, would be able to discriminate in their interpretation of the Iranian heritage. Modern transportation and mass communications, universal military service, and advancing industrialization have contributed to the modification of folk-Islam and will continue to do so. Intensified contact with the West and extension of higher education will certainly improve the leadership available to the group. Vigorous steps, however, will be necessary to exploit these means for the closing of the gap between these religiously divided social strata.

Slightly different complications face Iranian unity in respect to language, which the nation, in keeping with the spirit and pattern of modern nationalism, considers important. Although traditional toleration of minorities allows each to keep its own vernacular, it is only to the distinctive religious minorities such as Armenians that it is permitted in the school curriculum and then only in their communal schools as additional to the prescribed government program. With this exception, Persian is the sole language of the schools and the only medium of official intercourse. No vernacular can be taught, even at the elementary level, among Muslim groups for whom Persian is not a mother tongue—a policy which is neither surprising nor so much of a hardship when it is realized that these languages and dialects have little if any literature.

It is primarily in Azeri-Turkish-speaking Azerbaijan and among certain tribes that language constitutes a problem. Much capital was made of it by the 1945-1946 rebel "democrats," but it was not regarded as vital by most Azerbaijanis, much as they approved of its being taught at the primary level. Among certain tribes, especially the Kurds, the situation is different. Yet even here it is but a minor complicating factor in the larger problem of the integration of the tribes into Persian society and nationalism.

The tribal problem is no new one for any Iranian government aspiring to close central control of the country, as most young nationalisms do. Riza Shah achieved his control by force, which is no permanent solution for unity as proved by the rapid return to autonomy by the tribes when they got arms after the "occupation" of 1941. The extent of Tehran's writ in tribal territory has been largely restored, although it still falls short of Riza Shah's control. That ruler's main mistake in tribal policy—as indeed in general provincial policy—was to expect the tribes, or provinces, to contribute to the state in taxes and military manpower without receiving commensurate services and privileges in the way of education, public health, road building and the like. The result is resentment and resistance, which will continue until the tribes are given their share of the privileges and results of modernization. Only so can true unity be fostered.

The most important of these groups are the Kurds, Qāshqā'i, and Bakhtiyāri, in about that order. Ever since the Bakhtiyāri took a leading part in the constitutional struggle against Muhammad 'Ali and in subsequent government, this tribe has had a friendly disposition toward Tehran, although this loyalty was badly impaired by Riza Shah's sudden turning against, and persecution of, their tribal leaders.

The Qāshqā'i, mostly Turkish-speaking, are very strong in the province of Fars where, off and on for several generations, they have exercised practical autonomy. In both World Wars they were the center of powerful German intrigue and influence, although always eventually kept in line by Allied force or diplomacy. They are always treated with deference by Tehran, and constitute a continuous uncertainty in the drive toward national unity.

The Kurds present Iranian nationalism with its real tribal problem. Half a million Sunni Muslims in the northwestern mountains, they have ethnic and cultural ties with an equal number in Iraq and half again as many in Turkey, not to mention the small groups in Syria and the Soviet Union. They feel least attachment to the Iranian state of any tribe in Iran, and, in a strategic area, are the most open to non-Iranian influences and intrigues. This is shown by the abortive Soviet manipulation of the Kurdish People's Republic in 1946, and by Russia's continual progagandizing of these folk from the Caucasus. The chief figure in this effort is Muṣṭafa Bārzani, an Iraqi Kurdish chieftain who successfully eluded both the Iraqi and Iranian military.

With Ankara successfully integrating the rising generation of these "Mountain Turks" into the New Turkey, and Iraq forced to grant them considerable attention and influence because of their comparative size in that small country, Iran is destined to have trouble until she learns to make them partners in privilege in the modern state and thus, like Turkey, makes progress in integrating the rising generation into Iranian society.

Perhaps the most pressing basic problem of Iranian unity is the economic one. For a generation the Iranian economy has been out of balance. The economic nationalism of Riza Shah almost wholly neglected the basic industry of agriculture, which was forced to pay the price of modernization and industrialization, except for the mitigating oil industry and its royalties. Most conspicuous in this respect was the exorbitant railroad-building tax on tea and sugar. This concentration on industrialization was possible because the oil royalties could carry the burden of foreign exchange and help maintain the top-heavy military establishment. The wealth of the country was drawn toward Tehran and the Shah's pet province of Mazandaran. Unsound economic policies could not withstand the gathering force of world depression and then war, so that when Iran became the channel of a huge war supply effort, inflation reached 1,000 per cent, widened the already yawning gulf between the staggering poverty of the long-suffering masses and the wealth of the privileged few. National unity rose to meet the crisis of Soviet pressure and manipulation for revolution in 1945-1947, but in these days such pressure from Russia cannot long be denied unless the economic foundations of the country are greatly strengthened. This is being attempted in the Seven-Year Plan, one of the boldest and most comprehensively conceived and planned programs of any Near Eastern state. The success of this has yet to be proved at this writing. National survival, not to say unity, depends upon the outcome.

Also of no little importance to Iranian nationalism is the problem of politics. Geography and history have contrived to make this people hypersensitive politically. Their canny shrewdness and clever finesse in the political art often entrap them. Too often too much energy is expended on the politics of a subject or situation, to the detriment of a more fruitful and practical approach. The too-clever manipulator is self-hypnotized, confusing wit and intrigue with hard work and solid achievement.

Moreover, the people are burdened with a cumbersome, ubiquitous, and over-weening bureaucracy, largely the creation of Riza Shah's state socialism. The social and educational system seems to foster white-collar functionaries, too quick to see their security and prestige tied to civil office. Petty peculation by Eastern standards is expected, and salary scales are framed accordingly; but paper work is multiplied unproductively in an effort to prevent this habit from reaching corrupting proportions. Civil service reform is a real need for the nation.

The most pressing political problem is the evolution of a satisfactory and efficient system of government. The political pendulum in two generations has twice swung the arc from absolutism to constitutional parliamentarianism; and there are many who insist on a return to some form of dictatorial control. The forms of democracy seem too much "made in the West" to work effectively; Western political democracy presupposes a broader base in mass literacy than will be possible in Iran for some time, as well as a degree of social solidarity and cooperation, not to mention economic independence, that are not likely soon to emerge. The result is that the Iranian Majlis is truly representative only of the upper privileged classes, and so fractional as to make concerted constructive cooperation with the executive branch of the government difficult. A civilization with a highly developed individualism finds the functioning of representative democracy almost impossible. A fundamental problem of Iran is to work out an effective and satisfying system of self-government that will conserve the rights of all her people, yet satisfy the demands of a modern democratic nation.[7]

IV

By way of conclusion, attention may be drawn to a problem of Iran that is not, however, peculiar to her: that of the nature of national sovereignty and independence. Today there are only two independent nations in the world, and even they are severely limited by each other's power, both facing catastrophe if each does not learn the art of international cooperation and gradual abrogation of sovereignty. How much more must a small country like Iran face the unpalatable but inexorable fact that her independence

[7] Although basically the pattern sketched in this essay remains valid, events subsequent to its writing may call for some qualification and restatement of its analysis, particularly in the estimate of nationalism's achievements toward national unity and integrity. Distance in time may alter the view, but it would appear that the depth, intensity, and social range of national feeling aroused by the movement for the nationalization of the southern oil industry and the attainment of true independence of foreign influence believed to be contingent upon the success of this movement, have served to change the spiritual atmosphere of the country and possibly ushered its people into a definitely new and creative stage in their national development.

is seriously curtailed by the needs of all the other members of the Western nations with whom she has chosen to cooperate, and by the decisions of their leaders. To be sure, these relationships should be on a cooperative basis of relative equality in the United Nations; but realism calls for a cooperation based proportionately on the responsibility shouldered by each.

If this is true in the political sphere, it is equally true in the economic. The pre-war extreme economic nationalism of small and under-developed countries like Iran that manifested itself in a drive for industrial self-sufficiency is mistaken and self-defeating. Only a realistic recognition of the true character of national resources and the interdependence of national economies can effect that progress and prosperity which will bring rising standards of living to all. Some new technique for the fruitful economic cooperation of the strong and the weak, the advanced and the backward, must be developed if Iran and countries like her are to continue as distinct nations and make their unique contribution to human culture.

The future of nationalism in Iran depends upon its ability to find its proper place in a larger internationalism. The same can be said for those other nations, large and small, with whom she stands or falls. Nationalism in Iran and in countries like her depends for its future upon its ability to solve the problems that beset the unity and integrity of the people as a nation; and, perhaps even more, upon the new internationalism's ability to solve the problems of such nationalisms in so far as they threaten the world's unity and integrity. This leads to the heart of the ideological conflict that convulses humanity in the twentieth century—a conflict in the midst of which Iran stands quite squarely. Her most popular poet, Sa'di, stated the fundamental principle of any solution many centuries ago:

"The sons of men are members in a body whole related,
    For of a single essence are they each and all created.
When Fortune persecutes with pain one member sorely, surely
    The other members of the body cannot stand securely.
O you who from another's troubles turn aside your view,
    It is not fitting they bestowe the name of 'Man' on you!"

12

THE NATIONAL AND INTERNATIONAL
RELATIONS OF THE ARAB STATES

BY CONSTANTINE K. ZURAYK

THE RISING TIDE OF ARAB NATIONALISM has strongly influenced the modern history of the Near East. The full story of nationalism in the Arab world has been admirably told by George Antonius in his book, *The Arab Awakening* (London, 1938), but a brief survey of this important movement is essential for a real understanding of the problems that now confront the Arab countries in their relations among themselves and between them and the West.

The Arab world falls naturally into two main parts: the Eastern Arab world consisting of the Nile Valley, the Fertile Crescent and the Arabian peninsula; and the Western Arab world which extends along the North African seaboard from Cyrenaica to Tangier. The Arab countries possess a cultural and spiritual unity that is clear and unmistakable, though popular writers in the West are apt to overemphasize their apparent diversity and to overlook the potent ties that unite them. Indeed, the linguistic, cultural, and historical ties that bind the Arabs give the entire Arab world distinct and special characteristics.

No exact date can be given as marking the commencement of the Arab national movement. Like all similar movements, Arab nationalism was the result of several processes that acted gradually and imperceptibly. The exact inception of the movement is, therefore, most difficult to trace. It can be said, however, that the nineteenth century witnessed a rapid development of national feeling in the Arab world. At the beginning of the century, the idea of nationality was unknown to the inhabitants of the Near East, who looked upon themselves as subjects of the Ottoman Caliph and not as members of a great and all-embracing Arab nation. They were distinguished by the religion to which they belonged and the town or district from which they hailed. Their thoughts and aspirations were limited to the immediate locality in which they lived.

Bonaparte's expedition and Muhammad 'Ali's campaigns taught the inhabitants of the Near East that their Turkish overlords were by no means invincible and that their authority could be effectively challenged. During his nine years of government in Syria and Lebanon, Ibrāhīm Pāsha, Muhammad 'Ali's son, encouraged education and welcomed the establishment of foreign missions. In this he unwittingly and indirectly rendered a great service to Arab nationalism. His plans for setting up an Arab Empire, however, were frustrated by the intervention of the Great Powers, by the absence of national consciousness among the local inhabitants and by the widespread discontent which his financial and military measures aroused among them.

The spread of education in Syria and Lebanon at the hands of foreign missions resulted in the emergence of a nationally-conscious middle class whose members became active in propagating and developing Arab national feeling among the uneducated masses. In this field, there were parallel activities by the French Jesuits and the American Presbyterians. The Jesuits returned to Lebanon in 1831. They established many schools and founded the University of St. Joseph at Beirut in 1875. The Americans came to Beirut in 1820. They installed a printing press and established several schools. The American Protestant College was established in 1866 and served as nucleus for the present American University of Beirut. In addition to the great part played by the American University and its alumni in the revival of Arab culture and in the awakening of national feeling throughout the Arab world, the American Mission at Beirut made a significant contribution to the then incipient Arab aspirations by their encouragement of the use of literary Arabic as a medium of instruction and a vehicle of thought.

With the appearance of a well-educated and politically-minded class, the scene was set for the rise of Arab nationalism, and the second half of the nineteenth century abounded with symptoms of the new spirit. Secret societies were formed, political groups were organized, and plans were drawn up aiming at the realization of Arab national aspirations.

The earliest Arab secret society was founded in 1880. Its members were for the most part young men who had been educated at the Syrian Protestant College. They drew up a national program using a new method for proclaiming their demands by means of revolutionary placards which were displayed in the leading towns of Syria and Lebanon. These demands included the adoption of Arabic as an official language, the freedom of the press, and the grant of self-government to a united Syria. The society continued its activities for a considerable period but in the end its members were forced by the vigilance of the Turkish Secret Police to close down their society, to destroy their records, and to take refuge in Egypt and elsewhere.

The formation of secret societies was followed up by the organizing of political parties. The Turkish Sultan 'Abdul Ḥamīd was trying to stem the growing tide of Arab political thought in his Empire in two ways: on the one hand, he used ruthless repression, and on the other he made assiduous attempts to divert the energies of his Arab subjects from the dangerous path of Arab nationalism to the harmless course of Pan-Islam. The grant of a constitution to the Ottoman Empire in 1908 was at first marked by signs of cooperation and fraternization between Arabs and Turks. The Arabs, however, soon realized that a partnership between the two races on bases of equality was neither practicable nor genuinely desired by the Young Turks. Their belief was strengthened by the ban which the Young Turks placed on all non-Turkish societies. The Arab national movement was driven underground.

Two important secret societies came into being. Both were the product of the growth of Arab national feeling, but each had a different plan of action. The young Arab society of al-Fatāt aimed at achieving complete independence for all Arab countries. Its members were mostly young Arab intellectuals who represented all parts of the Eastern Arab world. The other society, al-'Ahd (The Covenant), was composed of young Arab officers who were serving in the Ottoman Army and aimed at establishing a united Arab-Turkish Kingdom in which the Arab portion might enjoy some measure of autonomy. At first the two societies were not aware of each other's existence but, later on, they united in their support of the Arab revolt.

At the outbreak of the First World War, two courses of action were open to Arab nationalists: one was to support the Turks loyally in their war effort while insisting upon self-government as a reward for their loyalty and cooperation, and the other was to rise in revolt against the Ottoman authorities and to seek independence by allying themselves to the enemies of Turkey after obtaining guarantees in respect to their political future. At first, being highly suspicious of European intentions, they hesitated. Thus the higher committee of al-Fatāt added the following reservation to its resolution in favor of complete independence: "In the event of European designs appearing to materialize, the society is bound to work on the side of Turkey in order to resist foreign penetration of whatever kind or form."[1] The leaders of al-'Ahd took a similar stand and were as anxious as their brethren not to expose the Arab portion of the Empire to European conquest.

In the meantime, the Sharīf Ḥusayn of Mecca was gradually coming to the conclusion that, although there was offered him an excellent chance for securing independence for Arabia, it could not be achieved without foreign help. He was not on good terms with his Ottoman suzerain and began considering the possibility of an Arab revolt which would be backed by all the forces of Arab nationalism. His son Fayṣal made contact with the Syrian nationalists and these informed him that they stipulated as a prerequisite to their participation in an Arab revolt that the Allies should recognize an independent Arab kingdom which should include the whole Arabian peninsula (with the possible exception of Aden) and the Fertile Crescent.

The Turks were aware of the existence of the Arab underground movement. Their governor in Syria, Jamāl Pāsha, spared no effort in suppressing Arab nationalism. Thirty-four nationalists were executed on charges of high treason, and many others were deported. This ruthless policy of repression and deportation drove many wavering Arabs to the side of the Allies. Following the famous Ḥusayn-McMahon correspondence in which the British made definite promises concerning the future independence and

[1] George E. Kirk, *A Short History of the Middle East*, London, 1948, p. 124.

unity of the Fertile Crescent and the Arab peninsula, the Arab revolt was started in June 1916.

Many Western writers try to minimize the importance of the part played by the Arab revolt in facilitating an Allied victory in the Near East and its contribution to General Allenby's brilliant success in Syria. But no less an authority than General Wavell has declared that "the value of the Arab revolt to the British commander was great, since it diverted considerable Turkish reinforcements and supplies to the Ḥijāz, and protected the right flank of the British armies in their advance through Palestine. Further it put an end to German propaganda in Southwestern Arabia and removed any danger of the establishment of a German submarine base in the Red Sea."[2]

The Arab revolt had a profound effect on Arab national sentiment. Its quick tempo and spectacular success touched most deeply the feelings of all Arabs. Even the uneducated masses who hitherto had not participated in any nationalistic activities began to feel the impact of nationalism. They rejoiced in the news of Arab victories in the hinterland and welcomed the advancing British armies as friends and allies of the Arab nation. It is important to note in this regard that the Arabs, in the pursuit of their national aims in this revolt, rose against their fellow Muslims, the Turks, and challenged the authority of the spiritual head of Islam, while allying themselves with Britain and other Christian nations. This is indicative of the degree of development that their national feeling had already achieved.

From then on, nationalism in the Arab world began to gain steadily in intensity and diffusion. Although nationalists in different Arab countries were not in complete agreement as to their political programs, their differences were on points of detail and not on principle. They all wanted independence and unity for the greater part of the Arab world. Claims for special recognition were put forward by minority groups, notably by a large section of the Lebanese Christians, but those claims were strictly local and did not belong to the main movement. The Arab revolt may not have been a military operation of first magnitude, but its stimulating effect on Arab political thought was tremendous. Nationalism

[2] Lord Wavell, *The Palestine Campaigns*, London, 1943, p. 56.

was no longer an attribute of intellectuals but a deep-rooted feeling that swelled in the hearts of most Arabs. It became such a vital force in the Near East that even the Big Powers could not completely ignore it.

Just as in everyday life people's problems become more numerous and more complex as they advance toward maturity and manhood, so it is in the lives of nations and the progress of movements. Following the success of the Arab revolt, Arab nationalism found itself faced with many problems. The most important of these problems were: first, how to achieve and maintain the independence of the Arab countries; second, how to attain a real unification of these countries; third, what attitude should be taken toward the inevitable processes of modernism, Westernization, and social progress; fourth, how to develop a national entity and distinct Arab civilization and what role this civilization should play in a universal scheme of world organization. For over thirty years now, all intellectual and political forces in the Arab world have been busy tackling these problems and trying to arrive at a proper and satisfactory solution for them. This paper will endeavor to examine and analyze each of these fundamental problems. It will attempt to show how far the Arabs have succeeded in moving toward a solution, what duties rest on enlightened and patriotic Arabs in respect to them, and what bearing they have had and will in the future have on the international relations of the Arab world.

II

The peace settlement reached at the end of the First World War was a great blow to Arab national aspirations. Only the Ḥijāz, the most backward of the Arab provinces which had belonged to the Ottoman Empire, was given complete and unconditional independence. The other provinces were placed under European control. Britain was given a mandate over the greater part of the Fertile Crescent, including Iraq, Palestine, and Transjordan, while France was given the mandate for Syria and Lebanon. The French authorities expelled Fayṣal from Damascus and subdivided the territories under their influence into four states with all the show of autonomy but none of its real attributes. Lebanon was enlarged and created into a separate state which had a bare majority of Christians. Two other minority groups were given separate governments, the Druzes at Jabal al-Durūz and the 'Alawites in the district round Latakia. What was left of geographical Syria was constituted into a Syrian state. In the south, the British subdivided their zone into Palestine, which was placed under direct British administration, and Transjordan which was made into an autonomous dependency under al-Amīr 'Abdullāh, the brother of King Fayṣal and the son of Ḥusayn. Iraq was at first placed under military administration, but after the revolt of 1920 it was created a kingdom under Fayṣal, who had been expelled by the French from Syria.

The peace settlement was an arrangement which satisfied the Western powers but fell short of what the Arab nationalists had hoped for. The mandate system was a fake. In 1920 Lord Curzon, the British Foreign Secretary, told the House of Lords, "It is quite a mistake to suppose that under the Covenant of the League or any other instrument the gift of a mandate rests with the League of Nations. It rests with the powers who have conquered the territories, which it then falls to them to distribute."[3] The peace settlement, in fact, meant a virtual annexation by Britain and France of the whole area of the Fertile Crescent. Some form of independence was given to parts of the annexed territories, but the Arab movement aimed at real independence. It wanted equality with the other nations and an opportunity to develop a great Arab nation which could take its rightful place in the sun. The Arab nationalists were embittered by the whole arrangement and began their struggle to throw off European domination. This struggle for independence and unity still continues and we shall try to follow its course in all the countries of the Eastern Arab world.

The main national movement in the Fertile Crescent and Arabia coincided with the development of a parallel movement in Egypt. At the outset of the First World War, Egypt was declared a British protectorate and Ottoman nominal suzerainty was repudiated. At the Peace Conference, Egyptian nationalists were not given a hearing. The Wafd Party under Sa'd Zaghlūl led the opposition to the British. After three years of struggle, Egyptian independence was

[3] Kirk, *op. cit.*, p. 130.

recognized by the British government in 1922. Four points, however, were reserved to the discretion of the British government. These included the defense of Egypt, imperial communications, the protection of the minorities, and the Sudan question. Egypt was not admitted to the League of Nations; and, with all the above reservations, its independence amounted to much less than dominion status. The Egyptian nationalists were fully aware of this. They demanded the negotiation of a treaty with Great Britain that would recognize Egyptian independence and would end British military occupation of the country. In 1936, an Anglo-Egyptian treaty was signed by virtue of which Egypt was to enter the League of Nations and British military occupation was to end. During the Second World War, the Egyptians faithfully fulfilled their obligations under the 1936 treaty, and rightly expected that at the end of hostilities the treaty should be radically revised. Negotiations to this end carried on by successive Egyptian governments finally broke down; and in July 1947 Egypt submitted its case against Britain to the Security Council of the United Nations. Her complaint consisted of two main grievances, the presence of British troops in Egypt and the status of the Sudan. The Security Council could not resolve the dispute, and the unsettled relations of the two countries remain one of the major problems of the Arab world.

To conciliate nationalistic feeling in Iraq, the British proposed the appointment of Prince Fayṣal as king. This was done in 1920, but the country continued under British Mandate until 1932. In 1930, an Anglo-Iraqi treaty of alliance was signed which provided for the termination of the British Mandate. Two years later the independence of the country was officially proclaimed, whereupon Iraq became a member of the League of Nations. The termination of the British Mandate and the death of great King Fayṣal, which took place shortly after, were followed by a period of instability, during which the army became such a dominating force in Iraq that no government could remain in power without its support. The claims of Arab nationalism were difficult to reconcile with the special position which Great Britain was determined to maintain in the country. Moreover, the policy pursued by the British government in Palestine incurred the displeasure of the nationalistic elements in Iraq. The mounting anti-British feeling led to a definite rupture in Anglo-Iraqi relations during the critical period of 1941. Rashīd 'Ali al-Gaylāni, having seized power after a successful *coup d'état* by the army, drove the pro-British regent out of the country and came into open conflict with Great Britain. The British, however, succeeded in suppressing the Gaylāni government and restored the regent to power. In 1947 the Iraqi prime minister, Ṣāliḥ Jabr, asked for a revision of the Anglo-Iraqi treaty of 1930; but when the terms of the newly negotiated treaty of Portsmouth became known, Iraqi public opinion forced the ministry to resign and the Iraqi regent had to broadcast a promise that the new treaty would not be ratified. Thus, in Iraq as in Egypt, relations with Britain have not been finally settled.

In Syria all nationalistic elements refused to recognize the French mandate which was imposed upon them; and they were dissatisfied with the division of geographical Syria into a number of states. With unflinching determination they continued for twenty-five years their struggle for independence. During this period many disturbances took place, the most serious of which was the Syrian revolt of 1925. In 1936 the French government negotiated a Franco-Syrian treaty and a Franco-Lebanese treaty on the lines of the Anglo-Iraqi treaty of 1930. Neither of these treaties, however, was ratified by the French Chamber of Deputies. This, as well as the cession by France to Turkey of the Syrian Sanjaq of Alexandretta, strained Franco-Syrian relations to the limit. The collapse of France in 1941 and the subsequent occupation of Syria and Lebanon by the Allied forces gave these two countries their chance of achieving real independence. After four years of friction with the French authorities resulting in such serious incidents as the bombardment of Damascus in 1945, matters between the Syrians and the French came to a head. The Syrian nationalists were supported by the newly formed Arab League while the French, under pressure from Britain and the United States, were forced to accede to their demands. In this way, and after the intervention of the United Nations, Syria and Lebanon became independent sovereign states. All foreign troops were withdrawn from their soil.

Under the Turks, Transjordan was not a separate political entity. It was part of the Vilāyet of Damascus. From 1918 to 1920, the Transjordan territory was administered by the Arab government at that city. On the collapse of this government, Transjordan was placed under British mandate together with Palestine. In 1920, Britain obtained the consent of the Council of the League of Nations to the exemption of Transjordan from all the clauses of the mandate concerned with the establishment of a Jewish National Home; and in the following year, it recognized Transjordan as an independent government under the rule of al-Amīr 'Abdullāh, Fayṣal's elder brother. In 1946 Transjordan became a kingdom and concluded a treaty of alliance with Great Britain. This treaty provided for the termination of the mandate but preserved for Britain its special position.

Transjordan has been a member of the Arab League but, unlike other member states, not a member of the United Nations. The backward state of the country's population as well as its natural poverty have limited the development of national feeling among the rank and file of the inhabitants. But the conflict that was taking place between the forces of Arab nationalism and those of aggressive Zionism to the west of the Jordan was bound to affect the life and feelings of the people of Transjordan who could not remain indifferent to the fate of their Arab brethren.

The Palestine war that followed upon the termination of the British mandate influenced Transjordan more than any other Arab country. The smaller and poorer part of Palestine that was not conquered by Israel was united with it to form "The Hashemite Kingdom of Jordan," and the influx of Palestinian Arab refugees into it more than doubled its original population and is bound to produce far-reaching effects on its political, economic, and social structure. The daily increasing Jewish threat and the accession to the Kingdom of more than half a million embittered Palestinian Arabs has contributed to the strengthening of national consciousness among its people.

In no other part of the Arab world did Arab nationalism have to struggle against such great odds as in Palestine. After the First World War, Palestine was not merely placed under British mandate, but the British government was further committed by the Balfour Declaration of 1917 to the establishment of a Jewish National Home in Palestine. The avowed intention of Zionism has always been the establishment of a Jewish state in the whole of

Palestine, or even in Palestine and Transjordan. The Jews were backed in their efforts by the mandatory power as well as by the financial resources of world Jewry. Arab opposition to their plans was early, determined, and unwavering. The Arabs of Palestine, representing not only the Arabs who conquered the country in the sixth century of our era but those conquered inhabitants who soon became Arabicized, saw no reason why they should now be ousted in favor of an alien people, and why they should pay, in terms of their national patrimony, for the persecutions which the Christian West has for centuries inflicted upon the Jews. They saw in the Zionist program a clear threat to their very existence. Again, owing to the presence of an ever-increasing Jewish element in their midst, the Arabs in Palestine found themselves not only unable to achieve complete independence but also deprived of all forms of autonomy and self-government. More galling to them was the fact that the realization of the Jewish program would cut them off from the rest of the Arab world and would prevent them from fulfilling their desire for the incorporation of their country into a greater Arab nation.

As early as 1919, a Syrian congress held at Damascus expressed the view that Palestine was included in the promise of independence given by Great Britain to the Arabs in the McMahon-Ḥusayn Correspondence. It rejected both the mandate and the Balfour Declaration and constituted an Arab Executive to direct the Arab national movement in Palestine. This body, reconstituted several times, continued to be the only official group representing the Arabs of Palestine and controlling their political activities.

The struggle between Zionism and Arab nationalism has been going on for over thirty years. At first Arab hostility was directed mainly toward the Jews but, later on, they realized that the real force behind the Zionists was the British administrative authorities who were protecting them and who worked in close coopera-tion with the Jewish Agency. Thereupon, Arab resistance began to be directed to the British mandate and the Jewish National Home equally. As the Jewish community grew, this resistance be-came stronger and more desperate. It was manifested in a series of disturbances, the most serious of which took place in 1920, 1929, and 1936. In 1939 the British government published a White Paper containing its proposals for a solution of the Palestine question. These proposals fell short of Arab demands, but they limited Jewish immigration and placed some restrictions on land purchased by the Jews.

The White Paper proposals continued in force during the whole period of the Second World War. At the end of the War, the Jews, backed by the United States, began to demand the abrogation of the White Paper. Jewish terrorism became an alarming feature of the conflict. The Arab-Jewish dispute in Palestine ceased to be a local problem. The Arab states declared their intention to protect the rights of the Arabs of Palestine, while American Jews secured United States support for the establishment of a Jewish state in Palestine. The Palestine question was finally taken to the United Nations. Under American pressure a plan for the partition of the country was approved by the General Assembly in November 1947. Neither the Arabs of Palestine nor the Arab states could accept a plan which gave the Jews the best part of the country. Feeling ran high, and it was evident that at the termination of the British mandate in the following May, war was inevitable. All efforts to avert an armed conflict failed, and on May 15, 1948, the Jews announced their state of Israel which was immediately given de facto recognition by the United States. On the other side, the armies of the Arab states crossed the Palestine frontiers.

As a result of the Palestine war, Arab prestige has suffered greatly. The Arab states did not make sufficient preparation for the conflict, and the Jews were strongly supported by the Big Powers. The result was disastrous and humiliating for the Arabs. It may now be too early to try to estimate the effect of the Palestine war on the Arab nationalist movement. There can be no doubt, however, that it was the most prominent event in the history of Arab nationalism since the Arab revolt of 1916.

The Arabian peninsula contains two independent states: Saudi Arabia in the north and Yemen in the south. In 1934 a war took place between the two countries and the generous terms granted by ibn-Sa'ud to his opponent were a sign of Arab national solidarity. The great oil resources of Saudi Arabia have drawn it into the realm of international rivalry and conflict. They have become a vital factor affecting the life not only of the Arab world, but of the whole Middle East.

Aden is a crown colony directly administered by Great Britain. The principalities in the Persian Gulf are under British influence, but their direct administration is in the hands of local chiefs. The oil concessions granted to Anglo-American companies in Kuait and Bahrein have recently caused the rest of the Arab world to show greater interest in their political future.

Our attention in this chapter has been directed right through to that part of the Arab world which lies within the "Middle East." It should not be overlooked, however, that the Arab world also includes the North African coast, otherwise known as the Western Arab world. This consists of Tripoli, Tunisia, Algeria, and Morocco. The main Arab national movement has never excluded these countries from its possible scope of action. Indeed, the recent events in Palestine were sharply echoed in both Tripoli and Morocco, and the recent measures of the French to suppress nationalist feelings in Morocco have evoked widespread denunciation and protest throughout the whole Arab world. Moreover, the Arab League has shown special interest in defending Arab rights in all this region.

To sum up, the problem of achieving and maintaining the independence of the Arab countries is still the main concern of the Arab national movement. The Arabs, having suffered a long period of foreign domination, are anxious to preserve their national existence and to consolidate the independence which they have won by hard struggle. They note with alarm that imperialism has not yet disappeared from the world. They are now facing what they must view as one of the most potent forms of this imperialism and one that is replete with the most serious dangers to their very existence—namely Zionist aggression. Being convinced that this aggression, together with the conflicting interests of the Big Powers, constitute the chief obstacle to their unity and free development, they find themselves forced to concentrate their effort on developing their military resources in order to be able to defend themselves and to safeguard their integrity.

They find themselves also unable, in the present widespread struggle between East and West, to align themselves fully with either side. On the one hand, they are embittered by Western—and particularly United States—policy regarding Palestine, and, on the other, they are afraid of the dangers of communism to their new and rising nationalism. But since the Zionist danger is uppermost in their mind, and everything else seems secondary in comparison with it, they will increasingly deviate from the West and turn to the East, unless a dramatic reversal is effected in Western policy with regard to the Arab-Zionist conflict.

III

Pan-Arabism has always been one of the main tenets of Arab nationalism, and the creation of one great Arab nation is constantly at the back of the minds of all patriotic Arabs. The Arabs, inspired by the glorious memories of their past and realizing their cultural and historical ties as well as their common interests and dangers, are now anxious to strengthen the bonds of unity among themselves and to translate the cultural unity of the Arab world into some form of federation or political union.

As has already been stated, Arab nationalists were disappointed with the settlement imposed on them by the Western powers after the First World War. Instead of a great kingdom that would comprise the Fertile Crescent and the Arabian peninsula for which they had hoped, they were forced to accept an arrangement which divided the newly liberated Arab provinces among the Great Powers. But this did not change their belief in the indivisibility of the Arab lands and the unity of the Arab nation.

The first practical move toward the political unity of the Arab countries was a series of treaties of "Brotherhood and Alliance" which were concluded between Saudi Arabia and the three Arab kingdoms of Iraq, Yemen, and Egypt between 1934 and 1936. The struggle of the Palestine Arabs against Jewish aggression, which in 1936 took the form of an open revolt against the British mandatory power, stirred the feelings of all Arabs and served as a rallying point of unity for the surrounding Arab countries which could not fail to be interested in this vital problem.

In 1943, the Arab states, encouraged by the British government, began to seek some form of union. The working out of a satisfactory scheme which would be acceptable to all the Arab states concerned took more than two years to accomplish. In 1945, however, negotiations for the formation of an Arab League were completed, and the League itself finally came into being. Every independent Arab state was given the right to join the League and to be represented on its General Council on an equal footing with the other states. Seven Arab states—Egypt, Iraq, Syria, Lebanon, Saudi Arabia, Transjordan, and the Yemen—became members of the League and signed its charter.

According to the Alexandria Protocol which paved the way for the formation of the Arab League, its mission was "to execute agreements reached by member states; to organize periodical meetings to reaffirm their relations and coordinate their political programmes, with a view to effecting cooperation between them, so as to safeguard their independence and sovereignty against aggression; and to concern itself with the general interests of the Arab countries." The League planned to assist non-member Arab countries in their struggle for independence and to encourage the economic, cultural and social cooperation of the Arab world by such projects as the simplifying of passport regulations, the unification of laws, and the development of closer relations in the fields of public health and education.

The League started off well. At San Francisco, the Arab delegates forgot their petty differences and worked together as one team. During the Syrian crisis, a meeting of the League was held in Cairo and a resolution was passed asking for the evacuation of foreign troops from the Levant. The League backed the Syrian and Lebanese demands at the Security Council of the United Nations; and in 1946, all foreign troops were withdrawn from the two states. Then came the Palestine question. In facing this problem the League was put to a severe test. At first the Arab states showed unity and determination in dealing with it; but later their weakness and disunity became apparent. Facing the combined forces of Zionism and of the Big Powers and their satellites, the Arabs were defeated, a Jewish state was established, and about a million Arabs were driven from their homes in Palestine to seek refuge in the neighboring Arab states. This was a catastrophe which the League was unable to stand. The states of the League began to quarrel openly with one another. Each was trying to saddle the others with the responsibility for the disaster. Serious accusations were made by each of the two rival blocs within the League against the other. The League's complete collapse was prevented only by the pressure of Arab nationalist opinion which favors Arab solidarity.

The Arab League has been an experiment, though not a successful one, in developing some form of unity among the Arab countries. Many reasons contributed to its weakness, among which may be counted the unprogressive leanings of its leaders and the fact that many Arab countries and states are still under varying degrees of foreign influence. But the weakness of the Arab League, divided so far by dynastic and regional loyalties, should not blind one to the rising urge for unity among the intellectuals and the masses. The way to a real Arab unity may be long and thorny, but the Arabs have already started on it. Arab unity is no longer the dream of unpractical idealists, but a goal that is not beyond the reach of Arab national endeavour.

IV

Independence and unity are essential for the advancement of the Arab world. More important than both, however, is economic and social progress. In the evolution of a great nation political independence is the beginning and not the end. Today the Arabs are facing the problem of building up their internal organization and life by economic development, social progress, and the spread of education.

After four hundred years of dormancy, the Arab world began in the last century to awaken under the impact of Western civilization. The change in Arab life caused by contact with the West varies in the different Arab regions. Big towns have been more fully Westernized than the countryside. In Egypt and the Fertile Crescent, the coastal parts around the Mediterranean Sea are more advanced than the hinterland; and as for the Arabian peninsula, it has hardly been touched by the influence of the West. This influence of the West, however, has not been deep and penetrating. Arab society as a whole is still medieval and feudal in character. The peasants in most Arab countries are backward and ignorant. Their income is far from satisfactory. They suffer from the effects of ignorance, poverty and disease.

If Arab society is to survive and to serve as basis for a new Arab revival, it must adapt itself to the modern conditions of the world. Greater attention must be paid by Arabs to social and economic reform. The standard of living among peasants and workers must be raised. New methods must be used in developing industry and agriculture. In short, a new progressive society must be built upon the old. To do this, four essential changes are necessary:

First: The machine must be more extensively used in developing the natural resources of the Arab world. More intensive industrialization must be introduced. Cooperative societies and Trade Unions must be encouraged.

Second: Arab governments must become completely secular. In a truly advanced community there is no place for sectarianism or theocratic principles.

Third: In the field of education greater attention must be paid to the applied sciences. The scientific training of the mind and the scientific approach to things is a mainstay of modern civilization.

Fourth: The Arabs must try to assimilate what is best in Western civilization. This they can do only if they arrive at a better and less superficial understanding of the West. So far they have seen the mechanistic and materialistic side of Western civilization. This should be supplemented by a proper appreciation of the true and abiding values of Western tradition. They should learn the secret of Western dynamism and adopt the positive contributions of Western culture.

The necessity of these economic, social, and educational reforms is being increasingly realized in the Arab world. In the face of popular demand, the Arab governments are exerting great efforts in the fields of economic development, social legislation, education, public health, et cetera. These efforts, however, are being limited by the troubled state of the world, by the restricted financial resources of the Arab countries, and by their urgent need to build up their military defenses to face the Zionist danger.

V

The fourth fundamental problem which the Arabs are facing today is how to define their distinct national entity. They have now reached a crisis in their spiritual evolution and are wondering what is to be their particular contribution to modern civilization: whether they are destined by reason of geographic position, racial endowments, historical traditions, and other factors to represent something individual and positive in the modern world, or whether they will lose their essential identity and be completely assimilated by the West.

But, it may be asked, is such a phenomenon as Arab civilization possible in the world of today? The answer is *yes*, but the possibility is inextricably linked to the possibility of civilization as a whole. The development of technique has bound the various regions and peoples of the world in one common destiny. From now on, it is either one world or none, it is either Civilization with a capital "C" or nothing. It may be asked further whether there can be a place for an Arab or any particular culture in a truly universal civilization. The answer is again in the affirmative, for a civilization which is truly universal is open and all-embracing. It encourages the development of particular achievements, and takes pride in embodying and harmonizing them. Conversely, any particular civilization would not be worthy of the name unless it embodied universal values. It is only under these conditions that both an Arab and a world civilization can exist—if the universal embraces the particular, and the particular manifests the universal.

Today the Arabs, as other peoples attempting to organize a new life under the impact of Western civilization, find themselves before a dilemma. On the one hand, they are afraid of certain aggressive features of Western civilization; on the other, they cannot achieve progress and contribute their share unless they assimilate that civilization. In general their attitude is taking the form of nationalistic doctrines and endeavors of different degrees of breadth or narrowness. This nationalism, in its various forms, is partly a reaction against the dangers from outside, partly a basis for internal unification, for revival of past achievements, and for preparation for contribution to world culture. Whether this nationalism becomes broad or narrow, tolerant or exclusive, progressive or reactionary—whether, in other words, it becomes the outward expression of an inner civilization or contracts upon itself and dies of suffocation—will depend upon the Arabs themselves, but also, and even more, upon the attitudes and policies of other peoples, and upon the course of modern civilization in general.

In facing the difficulties that now stand in the way of their national progress, and to be able to tackle the serious problems that are confronting them, the Arabs are in need of two things: enlightened and capable leadership and a radical change in their attitude toward life. From them the new attitude requires searching self-examination; merciless rejection of all weakening and reactionary factors in their national life; objective appreciation and cultivation of universal values in their culture; readiness to assimilate Western technique and, above all, the positive intellectual and spiritual tradition of the West. It also requires conviction of the need for radical inner transformation; and the willingness and ability to achieve this transformation with vision and courage. Furthermore, the leaders of the revived Arab nation must be capable and progressive. They must have a real understanding of the political and social conditions of the modern world, and must be able to adjust themselves to the requirements of those conditions.

It must be emphasized, however, that for a successful revival of the Arab nation and for the establishment of a spirit of mutual and fruitful cooperation between the Arab countries and the West, it is not enough that the Arabs should adjust themselves to the requirements of modern life. The West much change its attitude to them. Indeed, a new attitude by the West will help them in solving their pressing and urgent problems and will encourage the more enlightened Arabs in their struggle against the retrogressive influence of the reactionaries. This new attitude must be based on principle and justice rather than interest and power politics. If adopted, it will promote a feeling of friendship and good will between Arabs and other peoples, and will bring peace and prosperity to the Near East. On the other hand, there is no limit to the harm which an opposite attitude may produce. In fact, nothing can hinder more the orderly development of the Arab world and endanger the peace and tranquility of the Near East than the feeling of bitterness which an aggressive policy by the West will produce among the Arab people. Such an unsympathetic attitude as the one taken by the Big Powers in the Palestine question can cause irreparable harm to Western-Arab relations.

But why, it may be asked, should the West be interested in Arab cooperation? Because the peace and welfare of the world is one and indivisible. A unified, strong, and progressive Arab nation can effectively contribute to the stability of the Near East and can cooperate in the construction of a more peaceful and more prosperous world. It is this which makes the Arab problem a challenge not only to the Arabs but to the world as a whole.

CONCLUSION

13

NEAR EAST PERSPECTIVE:
THE PRESENT AND THE FUTURE

BY H. A. R. GIBB

WHERE AND ON WHAT COMMON GROUND can the Muslim East and the modern West meet together on terms of mutual understanding? Scientists in their laboratories, technicians of all kinds in industry and agriculture, physicians in clinics and hospitals, can and do cooperate in their common tasks without distinction of race or religion. Individuals of different nations can and do form close personal ties, undisturbed by differences of social heritage or conflicts of opinion on many matters. Representatives of diverse states sit round the same table in conferences or commissions. Yet neither all this intercourse, whether on the scientific and technical, or the individual and personal, or on the international and political level, nor association in the United Nations and lip-service to the ideals which should constitute the moral force behind the United Nations, has sufficed to bridge over the suspicions and antagonisms which continue to divide people from people. Understanding is based upon an appreciation of values, and that in turn upon a genuine discipline of thought, a discipline that embraces both subject and object. Without this, all relations are superficial and all ideals merely sentimental; and sentimentalism falls an easy victim to the emotional catchwords which the skillful propagandist exploits to advance some sectional interest at the expense of the common cause. So the lines of decision harden, and even when some joint enterprise or common peril temporarily brings together nations of different traditions, the tensions persist below the surface, ready to be goaded into active or passive hostility.

East and West are in contact with one another today on four fronts. Two are external: the political and economic policies followed by the leaders of the Western nations in their relations with the Eastern nations, and those followed by the leaders of the Eastern nations in their relations with the Western nations. These are two fronts, not one; although they intersect, their operations are frequently carried out on different levels and with different means. Underlying these external relations are two more fundamental planes of contact: the attitudes adopted in the West to Eastern culture and cultural traditions, and those adopted in the East to Western culture and cultural traditions. The two latter are quite independent of the external contacts; in some cases they existed before any political relations had been formed, and they would continue to exist if political relations were cut off; but both sets of relations exert an influence, and often a powerful influence, on each other.

Both types of contacts have existed between the West and the Muslim East for many centuries, but outside a few rare instances and occasions they have not produced understanding. Approaches have been made at times on one side toward an appreciation of the other's values, even if only on the part of limited groups. These have laid, and should continue to lay, the foundations for understanding, but they cannot do more until they are met by a responding approach from the other side. Bridges, to be secure, must be anchored on both banks, and without the element of mutuality no relations can lead to a true meeting of minds or of policies.

In attempting to assess the efforts made in the past toward achieving a community of understanding, the factors which are working in that direction at the present day, and the obstacles which stand in the way of their success, it would be superfluous at this point to enter into any full analysis of them. Most of the relevant topics and arguments have been lucidly set out and expanded in detail in the preceding chapters. In spite of many differences between the precise situations and reactions in Turkey, Iran, Egypt, and Arab Asia, the fundamental problems are common to all, and it may not be without value to combine them in a single perspective. The overall picture today is full of deep shadows, and fills many a close observer with despair. Only by standing a little farther back can we perceive and try to estimate the significance of the lighter strokes that relieve the general somberness of tone.

If we look back at the situation as it was little more than a century ago, we should find then no common ground whatsoever between the West and the Muslim East. The attitude of Western political circles toward the Ottoman and Persian governments was critical and aloof; that of the Turks and Persians toward the West was suspicious and uncooperative. Western Orientalism was still in its childhood and more strongly tinged by romantic interest in the antique, the "medieval," or the outlandish, than by a positive desire to understand Muslim ways of life and thought; while the great body of Christians still knew no more of Islam than the scrappy, crude, and perverted notions inherited from the Middle Ages, supplemented by the fictional extravagances of the *Arabian Nights*. On their side, the Muslims knew nothing whatsoever of Western thought, literature, and science, and were content to be ignorant of them.

How greatly the situation has been transformed in one short century! Although it can be said, with truth, that the change has been more profound on the planes of cultural contact, it has affected also political and economic relations, in spite of present tensions. Indeed, it began in the political field, and our first inquiry may well be directed to a study of the reasons why the incipient movements toward understanding failed to achieve mutuality.

II

The first approaches were made in the time of Muhammad ʿAli, the open-minded Pāsha of Egypt, ambitious to consolidate his power and to expand the material resources of his province. Not only did he introduce (prematurely, as it turned out) Western industrial techniques and medical science into Egypt, but he also placed political relations between Egypt and the Western powers on a new footing. His program was taken up and developed still further by his grandson, the Khedive Ismāʿīl, and at the same time a roughly parallel development was taking place in Turkey. The cumulative results of the contacts thus established was to raise up in the next generations a new élite of political thinkers, trained in Western schools and animated by a passionate faith in the ideals held up before them by Western education. These men spread among their fellow-countrymen the gospel of Western liberalism and democracy, sometimes at great personal danger and sacrifice.

Aiming, to begin with, at reorganizing their national and social life on Western principles, they accepted the humanitarian and perfectionist assumptions of the current Western political philosophy, and looked forward to a time when the Eastern nations, free, reinvigorated, and governed by enlightened patriots, would cooperate on an equal footing with the Western nations; and these ambitions were shared and encouraged by their Western mentors.

Suddenly, in the first quarter of this century, the current began to turn. As the nationalist movements grew to maturity, opposition to the West increasingly replaced the old ideal of cooperation. That this rift was due in the first place to the policies and attitudes of the Western governments cannot be denied. Western political and economic controls in the Near and Middle East, and the disregard of Western political leaders for human and social interests, forced the nationalist leaders to devote all their energies to the struggle against Western domination. The necessities of this conflict forced a reorientation of their aims; the reorganization of their political and social systems on Western lines now became not so much the foundations for future cooperation with the West as a means by which to gain the strength to stand up against the West on their own feet. At the same time, they utilized and intensified the feelings of resentment caused by economic stresses and Western encroachments to build up a following amongst their own peoples.

Familiar and true as all of this is, it is not the whole truth, and an exclusive concentration upon it leads to the dangerous illusion that with the removal of Western controls the Eastern nations would be ready to cooperate harmoniously with the Western nations. In reality, the reaction was a complex movement, deriving from a great variety of factors and causes which can scarcely be disentangled, and which have differed in their relative strength and influence from region to region.

The nationalist movements were originally led, in most countries, by a small group of Westernized intellectuals. As these movements grew into nation-wide organizations, the leaders were far outnumbered by the mass of their followers. These followers were not Westernized in the same degree, or at all; they accepted, externally, the political aims and objectives of the leaders, but interpreted them in terms of their own traditional concepts of the state and society, and of their own private grievances. The wider a nationalist movement became, the greater grew the proportion of its non-Western constituents, and the more the leaders were compelled to adjust their public aims and policies to the traditional attitudes of their peoples. Only in Turkey, thanks to the prestige acquired by a successful revolution and defense of the nation's territory, did the leadership retain the power to carry through its program, and achieve the conditions in which a real relation of mutuality with the West could be founded.

Elsewhere, the general trend has been in the opposite direction. Leadership in the national movements, the more they expand, tends to pass into less Westernized hands. Some leaders still profess the original faith in liberal democratic ideals, but show in practice little understanding of the principles on which they are based. Others, more strongly attached to the principles of their own social traditions, consciously aim at combining in some way its values with a Western political and economic organization. Finally, in some countries, a new generation of leaders has already arisen who reject outright the Westernized outlook of their predecessors and who have substituted objectives and methods derived from their own historic cultures, in more or less open opposition to the West. The outstanding example of this later development is offered by the leadership of Gandhi in India. To regard Gandhi's denunciation of the "satanic civilization" of the West as if it were a mere foible or parenthesis or journalistic exaggeration is a typical piece of Western self-satisfaction and protective delusion. It is the most solemn warning that has yet come out of Asia, and the most significant pointer to the strength of this second and deeper factor in the Eastern reaction to the West.

Such a judgment sweeps aside all consideration of external attitudes and achievements, to condemn the inner motive forces of Western civilization and to repudiate its values. But it owes its violence to the deception which overtook the enthusiasm of the earlier nationalist reformers. The element in Western thought to which they were sincerely attracted was its humanistic idealism. It was under its influence that they accepted also the practical institutions of the West and its social and political norms as vehicles and expressions of that idealism. At the same time, sharing the infectious optimism of their guides, they accepted the facile Western assumption that, if the right kinds of political and legal machinery were introduced into their countries, they would of themselves produce a political system and social institutions in keeping with the ideals of Western liberals and democrats.

We are beginning to realize how precarious were the foundations of this idealism. Extreme Western man, swung out of his biological environment by the almost unlimited freedom and power of change offered by the age of colonial expansion and the opening up of virgin lands, induced by his scientific discoveries into the belief that in his own hands lay the mastery of nature and the remaking of himself, fascinated by the rewards of economic power and encouraged to strive for them by the assurance that the survival of the fittest was the natural law by which were furthered whatever ends the universe might contain or serve, has ultimately, in the industrialized and politically powerful sectors of the Western world, come near to losing almost all connection and concern with the biological roots of the community life of man and all sense of its primary social needs.

Among the Eastern peoples, whose own ages of colonial expansion lay far back in the past, the physical basis for development along most of these lines did not exist. Not only so, but the social attitudes which they had produced in the West stood in direct opposition to the lessons derived from their own experience. No one who studies the constitution of Oriental societies can fail to observe how consistently, over many ages, the preoccupation of their lawgivers has been directed to the basic task of maintaining a society in being, in face of natural calamities and human destroyers. From long habit, familiarity with external perils and internal eruptions, and need to overcome them, the peoples of these societies have, like the remaining peasant populations in our Western world, acquired a kind of biological sense, an unconscious but tenacious grasp of the means and organisms by which the community preserves its continuity and its cohesion.

Down to 1914, the contradiction between the external forms and ideals and the inner forces of Western civilization was no more clear to the leaders of the Eastern reform movements than it was to the Western peoples themselves. Nor, with a few exceptions, did they realize its divorce from the imperatives of Eastern socio-logical thought and structure. Their eyes, like those of Western observers, were fixed on the technological backwardness of their peoples, and in their impatience with the social institutions which seemed to stand in the way of achieving a "free" society like that of the West, they more often seemed ready to sweep them away than to try to harness the vital forces behind them to the necessary tasks of reconstruction.

But when we ourselves stand appalled at the moral regression and the cancerous spread of barbarism among the most "advanced" Western nations, we cannot be surprised that the revelation has reinforced the trend toward reassertion of the native cultures of the East. There is no Eastern nation today that does not denounce, with justified if self-righteous horror, the inhumanity and "geno-cide" not only of Germans and Russians but also of Britons and Americans, even if under the stress of war. Some of this denuncia-tion may be mere verbiage, but for the Arab peoples repulsion has been made more intense and personal by the rape of Palestine. At every level, the contrast between the humanitarian ideals pro-claimed by the West and its disregard of humanitarian values in action has produced a profound disbelief in the whole system of Western public and private morality.

III

The utter failure to achieve a truly mutual relationship on the political fronts, except on a temporary and contingent basis, has its roots, therefore, if the preceding argument be true, more pro-foundly in cultural than in political antagonism. This situation clearly threatens also the progress made in the last century toward mutuality in cultural relations, and poses before both West and East the problem of achieving it on new foundations and in new conditions.

In its self-confident past, the West assumed that mutual under-standing would be attained through the adoption of its culture and thought by the leaders of the Eastern nations, and the earlier national and reformist leaders sincerely accepted this assumption and attempted to realize it in practice. The events and circum-stances of more recent years have shown that a true meeting between East and West is not to be accomplished in such summary fashion. It can be brought about, if at all, only as the end-product of a long and difficult process of thought and self-discipline on the part of both Eastern and Western leaders. On the Western side there are needed both a cleansing and readjustment of its thought and modes of action in order to bring the moral and technical elements of Western civilization into better balance, and an openness of mind toward the Eastern civilizations, based upon a genuine knowledge of their essential characteristics and qualities. Likewise, on the Eastern side, there are needed both a reformation of the content and institutions of the traditional national culture to accommodate the expansion of scientific knowledge and technology and their consequences, and an openness of mind toward the profounder formative elements in Western thought.

When the issues are phrased in these terms, it can be realized how far, in spite of the failures in political understanding, both East and West have progressed within a single century toward a cultural understanding. The first part of this book, with its surveys of the growth and inner development of Orientalist research in the fields of art, religion, science, and literature, has brought out clearly the evolution of Western attitudes to and interest in Muslim culture during this short period of time. In every field hasty judgments and generalizations, based upon romantic enthusiasm or a scanty range of materials, externally and imperfectly understood, have given place to a sober evaluation of the immense complexity of the tasks still to be undertaken. Even with all the achievements of the past century to assist him, the Orientalist is keenly aware of the long process of time and effort which will be required before a genuine comprehension can be reached of the relevant aspects of Muslim civilization. Yet one aspect of Orientalist studies deserves particular mention in this connection. This is the increasing cooperation between Muslim and Western scholars in these tasks; and even if cooperation may sometimes take the form of rivalry and competition, it is one of the advantages of scholarship that rivalry between genuine scholars always subserves the progress of knowledge and conduces to clarification of the issues.

It would certainly be premature, however, to make any sweeping claims for Orientalist scholarship in bridging the gap or easing the strains between East and West. On the one hand, in view of the small number of scholars who engage in Oriental studies in all the Western countries, their progress seems slow and hesitating when it is compared with the immensity of the tasks; on the other hand, the average educated Muslim, apt to overvalue the achievements of medieval Islam and ignorant of the technical methods of modern scholarship, misunderstands its spirit of critical enquiry, and suspects Orientalism of being a tool of subversive Western imperialism—a suspicion which some nationalist politicians are quick to exploit for political ends.

But the primary task of Orientalism is not to bridge the gap between Muslim and Eastern scholars; it is to bridge the gap of ignorance of Muslim culture among the Western peoples. This task it is performing, slow though its progress may seem to be. It is not to be expected that the literature of the Muslim peoples will ever become as widely known in the West as the literatures of Greece and Rome, or that it will be as fully appreciated, except perhaps for a few works of more universal significance, such as the mystical poetry of Persia. Yet the increasing volume of translations from the Muslim classics at least places within reach of the educated public a means of appreciation of Muslim culture, and the growing collections of Muslim art testify to an expanding interest in it and provide for ever wider ranges of non-specialists a channel of aesthetic appreciation which may prove to be no less valuable as a means to the same end. That these will continue to exert an influence on the Western attitude toward Muslim civilization can be confidently anticipated from the part already played by Orientalism in inducing a general reassessment of Islam as a religion, and a clearer understanding of the values that it stands for. It is no longer possible for any scholarly or conscientious writer to repeat the old misrepresentations of Islam derived from former ages, and even on the part of popular writers such ignorance has become inexcusable and disgraceful. Certainly to this extent the labors of Orientalist scholars may justly claim to have opened the minds of the educated Western public toward Muslim civilization.

The progress of Orientalism in laying a foundation for future mutuality is not, however, limited exclusively to a study of the past, whether of the Muslim classical tradition, or of the elements of Muslim ancestry in the Western tradition. It is relevant also to the study of the present, by interpreting to the West the cultural achievements of the Arabs, Persians, and Turks. It is assisting to create within the Western nations a body of informed opinion, able to observe the movement of ideas in the Muslim world, if not yet with full understanding, at least with fewer preconceptions and greater awareness of the social and psychological experiences underlying their forms of expression. In the future this may even become its most important social function, as the genius of the Muslim peoples rises into full power of aesthetic creation and internal reconstruction, and they set out to reformulate and rebuild their national cultures on their own distinctive lines.

To use the term "rebuild" may seem to beg the question: yet it is the only word which describes the task that lies before the leaders of the Muslim peoples. There are two factors in their situation, if not three, which exclude any alternative process. In the first place, the earlier phase of Westernization has left its deposit, in every Muslim country outside Arabia, of Western institutions in government and administration, codes of law, medicine and technical services, Western professions, and a press emulating that of the Western countries. If, in an excess of hostility to every element in public life inspired by the West, all these were swept away, it would still be necessary to construct something to put in their places.

Dismissing this as an improbable hypothesis, rebuilding is still imperatively demanded in almost all Near Eastern countries by the social dislocation, amounting in some cases to disintegration, which has followed on the impact of the West. Among all classes the old social structures have been weakened or destroyed, and with them the old social loyalties and obligations. The new institutions are unstable; they have no roots as yet, and are devoid of any authority in themselves which can compel loyalty, except in Turkey, where they enjoy an authority derived from the revolution. Elsewhere, the only stable element, and the only institution which still possesses authority, is Islam.

It is this fact which explains the attraction of movements like the Muslim Brotherhood among those sections of the population which have been the hardest hit, economically and emotionally, by the Western impact and the intensification of social strains. But it explains also the phenomenon briefly mentioned in the first section of this chapter, the emergence of a new generation of Muslim intellectual leaders who aim at combining in some way the values of the Muslim social tradition with a Western political and economic organization. They foresee danger in both extremes, whether of uncontrolled reaction against all Western influences or of uncontrolled self-abandonment to a flood-tide of Westernization. They reject the Western doctrine that religion is a matter only of private conscience, and realize that Islam in the full and operative sense cannot be dissociated from questions of social order or from intellectual and moral values. The conviction by which their thinking and their public actions are governed is that the future of the Muslim peoples depends upon the integration of these Islamic elements with the newer forces and obligations arising from the spread of Western material culture and public institutions, as well as of Western intellectual and scientific techniques and the processes of thought behind them.

The task which this imposes on the new leadership is thus far greater than the task before Orientalist scholarship in the West, and calls for a sustained effort of will and comprehension not to be attained in one or two generations. As yet, their central conviction is still only emotionally or intuitively grasped, and the issues have not been clearly formulated in relation to the categories of Muslim thought. It is difficult to believe, however, that any clarification can be adequate until the Muslim leaders acquire a profounder knowledge of Western thought and abandon some of the reticences which continue to hamper their understanding of it.

We have seen that the earlier generations of Muslim leaders studied Western literatures and embraced with enthusiasm Western political principles and theories. Although disillusionment led to a reaction against Western culture that has sometimes gone very deep, the reading of Western literature has continued to spread among ever-widening sections of Muslim society, and there can be no doubt that the ordinary educated Muslim knows far more of the West and its thought than the educated Westerner knows of Eastern culture. Valuable as this foundation has been and is, however, for intercourse between the Muslim and Western peoples, it still falls far short of the essential condition of openness of mind toward Western thought in its deeper formative or creative aspects. It is not difficult to be open-minded toward psychologically neutral studies, like physical science, medicine, or geography. The difficulties arise in those studies which involve deep-seated beliefs and emotions by disturbing familiar modes of thought, established religions, historical mythologies, or the presuppositions of accepted social attitudes, like philosophy, history, psychology, and sociology. The effort which it costs to examine and weigh the evidence impartially and to face the conclusions in these fields is by no means peculiar to Muslims; but because of the Muslim's evasion of these difficulties hitherto, his knowledge of Western thought—even if he possesses a textbook acquaintance with the history of Western philosophy, psychology, or sociology—is still superficial.

It is in this respect that the third of the three factors referred to above may prove to be of special significance. This is the speed of technological advance both in the West and in the East. Up to the present time the impact of modern technological developments on the Muslim countries has been patchy and uneven, and their effects have been on the whole limited and localized. As technological skills become more firmly and widely established and are expanded by indigenous effort, they will inevitably influence social usages and attitudes; and who knows what technological developments may occur in the next few years and decades, and how they may affect the ideals and institutions of all human societies?

In order to meet the challenge of this new factor in the situation, the intellectual leaders of the Muslim countries may well be forced to come to closer grips with Western thought. The problems which it sets have their origin there, and are of longer standing and have gone deeper in the Western countries. Western thinkers, faced with the same challenge, have set themselves to grapple seriously with the task of integrating technological advances with their national cultures. Different though social needs and traditions may be, involving different formulations of social patterns, the underlying realities are the same, and in a context where speed is of the essence of successful action, the most direct route by which Muslim thinkers may reach an understanding and eventual solution of their problem lies through the close study of Western analyses.

The effort of penetration which this involves must of itself break down most of the barriers to Muslim comprehension of Western modes of thinking. And when we recall how much has been achieved in the past three generations, it is surely permissible to believe that, unless political antagonisms set up another barrier, the alert Muslim minds of the next three generations will, in pursuit of their own problems, go far toward achieving that truer appreciation of the thought and culture of the West which we have called openness of mind. Perhaps, too, apart from any question of relations with the West, this is the only way in which they can recapture that flexibility of mind which enabled Muslim thinkers of the early creative centuries to solve the social problems of their day in accordance with Islamic principles.

Yet, for all that Muslim thinkers and Western scholars may do to lay new foundations for the bridge across which East and West may meet, the bridge itself cannot be built unless the Western nations resolutely and effectively solve their own problem. This is not the place in which to expound, or even to outline, the question which ever more urgently engrosses the ablest minds on both sides of the Atlantic Ocean. Enough has been said above on the effect of the cleavage between the moral and the technical culture of the West in alienating the East. In spite of our scientific and technical achievements, the repulsion of the Muslim world from Western civilization can only be reinforced the more that the Western nations display their powerlessness to control the demonic forces within them.

INDEX

241

INDEX

Nallino, M., 54
Namrūni, al-, 95
Napoleon Bonaparte, 24-5, 35, 133, 142, 152, 153, 173, 206
Nāṣir-al-Dīn, 133, 134, 136, 138
nastaʻlīq writing, 71
National Historical Thesis, 183-4
nationalism, 140, 141, 143, 144-5, 153-7, 157-8, 160-1, 165, 167-81, 183-4, 184, 185, 189, 190, 191-2, 193, 196-223
Naw Rūz festival, 199
Nazareth, 148
neo-humanism, 48, 54-5, 56
Neo-Platonism, 108, 120, 135, 151
Neubauer, Adolph, 96n
New Turkey, 179, 184, 186
Nicholson, R. A., 51, 77
Niebuhr, Carsten, 22
Nile River, 3, 205
Nīshāpūr, 34, 38
Niẓāmī, 61, 71, 72, 72-3
Nöldeke, Theodor, 49n, 50, 77
North Africa, 217
numismatics, 21-2, 42
Nykl, A. R., 52, 56n, 109

oil, 140, 148, 194, 196, 203n, 217
Olearius, Adam, 68
O'Leary, DeLacy, 110
oriental rugs, 19, 27, 33-4, 40
Orthodox Church, 90, 101
Osmanlis, the, 131
Ottoman Empire, 93, 120, 121, 136, 152, 167-73, 174-7, 190, 205, 207, 208, 210, 211
Ottoman Society of Science, 124-5
Oude, King of, 78
Ouseley, Sir Gore, 72, 74
Oxford University, 68

Pacha, Yacoub Artin, 30
Pahlavi period, 11, 141, 147, 189, 190, 197
Pakistan, 44, 187
paleography, 22, 29, 97
Palestine, 35, 44, 163, 186, 209, 210, 211, 214, 214-15, 216, 219, 223, 233
Palmer, E. H., 76
Pan-Arabism, 154-5, 218
Pan-Islamic movement, 159, 175, 207
Pan Ottomanism, 174-5
Pan-Turanism, 173-4, 175, 175-6, 183-4
papyrology, 26, 29
Paris Peace Conference of 1919, 197
Parthians, 5

peasants, 180, 181, 183, 184, 185
Pentateuch, the, 67
Pérès, H., 55
Persia, 4, 25, 86, 87-8, 100, 151, 188
Persian language, 140, 200
Persian literature, 66-82
Pertsch catalogue, 73
Pertsch, W., 52
Peter the Venerable, 103
philology, 97
Philoponos, Joannes, 90
philosophy, 88, 124, 126, 130, 132, 135, 151, 158, 160
Pidal, R. Menéndez, 52
pilgrimages, 85
Piper, F. M., 24n
Pizza, 77
Plato, 120, 158
Platonism, 61-2, 135
Platts, J. T., 73
Plutarch, 103
poetry, Arabic, 108-9
politics, 161, 164-5, 202
Polo, Marco, 91
Pope, A. U., 31
Portsmouth, treaty of, 213
Prangey, Girault de, 23
Presbyterian Church, 206
Price, 72
Princeton University, 95, 96, 113
printing, 71-2, 79, 80-81, 123, 234-5, 153, 206
propaganda, 102-3, 104, 106, 111-12, 209, 227
prosody, 52-3, 59-60, 61, 74-5
Protestantism, 114, 133
Provençal poetry, 52
Ptolemaic system, 123

Qājār dynasty, 133, 138, 139, 190, 191
Qalʻat Bani Ḥammād, 37
Qānūn, 134
Qāshqāʼi, 201
Qaṣr al-Ḥayr al-Gharbi, 34, 38
Qavām, Aḥmad, Primier, 196
Qazvīni, Mīrza Muḥammad, 77
Qazwīni, al-, 59
Qutaybah, ibn-, 56

racism, 184, 195
Ranking, H., 73
Raqqah, al-, 38
Rashīd al-Dīn, 89
Ravoisié, Amable, 25

INDEX

Umayyad Khirbat al-Munyah, 38
Unitarians, 85
United Nations, 186, 204, 212, 213, 214, 216, 219, 227
United States, 133, 144, 192-3, 195, 196, 213, 216, 218, 233
Upjohn's press, 71
Upton, J. M., 33
Uri, Jaonnes, 95 and n
Uzbeks, 190

Vatican, the, 131
Vever, H., 33
Vida, Giorgio Levi della, 29, 95n
Vienna, 5, 40
Vienna Academy, 27
Vienna, University of, 41
Vilāyet of Damascus, 213
Voltaire, 125
Vullers, 72, 73

Wafā' abu-al-, 97
Wafd Party, 211
Wahhābi movement, 159
Wallis, H., 33
Walters, Henry, 39
Walzer, R., 110
Warner, Levinus, 67
Wavell, General, 209
Weit, Gaston, 28, 29, 36
Wellhausen, J., 49n
Whinfield, E. H., 76

White, 72
White Paper of 1939, 215-16
Wilber, D. N., 33
Wilkins, Charles, 71
Wilkinson, C. K., 33
Wilkinson, J. U. S., 33, 38
women, emancipation of, 127, 141, 143, 145, 153
Wright, Walter L., Jr., 29, 105

Xavier, Francis, 67

Yarmūk, 100
Yathrib, 99
Yazdāni, Ghulām, 29
Yemen, 154, 163, 216-17, 218, 219
Yeñi Majmū'ah, 126, 127
Young, T. Cuyler, 110
Young Turk Central Committee of Union and Progress, 126
Young Turk Party, 177, 207
Young Turk Revolution of 1908, 9, 123, 125, 175

Zaghlūl, Sa'd, 211
Ẓāhir, li-I'zāz-dīn-Allāh al-, Sultan, 18
Zaki, Ṣāliḥ, 93n
Zand, Karīm Khān, 132
Zhukovsky, 76
Zionism, 186, 214-15, 217, 218, 219
Zoroastrianism, 77, 140
Zurayk, Dr. Costi, 11, 12, 155, 156